KING DAVID: YOU ARE THE MAN!

A Story of the Heart and Life of David Highlighting Events in I Chronicles

By D. Owen Kaiser

Cover Credits: The Dog Ear Graphics Team ably
implemented the author's cover concept on both the front
and back covers. Jeff Flynn then added or enhanced the
details on the front cover to produce its final look.

First published by Dog Ear Publishing
4010 W. 86th Street, Ste H
Indianapolis, IN 46268
www.dogearpublishing.net

ISBN: 978-145750-471-6

This book is printed on acid-free paper.

The narration of the events of David's life, which are included
in this book, draws heavily on the Bible at all times. The only
Bible version used in writing *King David: You Are the Man* is
the Authorized King James Version of the Bible (KJV) first
published in 1611. When Bible language is used, it is often
adjusted to fit smoothly into the flow of the narration.
Whether the Bible is quoted or not, extreme care has been
taken to make every sentence of this book entirely accurate to
the meaning and the spirit of the KJV Bible texts and
contexts.

Printed in the United States of America

With great love and gratitude, this book is dedicated to
my parents, John and Mary.

I have depended upon their gracious, encouraging support – this book would not
have been written without that. In numerous ways, they freely help and encourage many who need extra support. I am honored to be their son and to be able
to experience and draw upon their godly example.

CONTENTS

Preface

This book tells a story of the life of David, King of ancient Israel, in sequence from shepherd boy to king to his death. The reader observes David as he lives and grows through the episodes that are familiar to so many and through others that are not as familiar. In order to present these events in the light of David's developing life, the narrative weaves them into a single story.

Yet, this is not a simple biography describing everything that happened in his life; rather, most of the narrative deals with the events surrounding two astounding revelations God gave to David. This book examines these two revelations taking note of their historical contexts and future fulfillments. They are considered from both David's and God's perspectives.

David's life here is not a fictionalized drama; the events, the history, and the background all come from the Bible, read literally. Much biblical information is brought together in a way that should bless the reader and possibly aid him or her in discovering more of the wealth of the Old Testament.

After David becomes king in Jerusalem, this book focuses on the account of David's life in I Chronicles. I Chronicles has many lists of names and is often skimmed or skipped. However, only I Chronicles records the second revelation and some of the great works David accomplished following that revelation.

Some will read this book casually, as they would any biography, while others will often pause to consider the events as they are recorded in the Bible. Those who search the Scriptures to obtain further information or to confirm the accuracy of what they have read are welcomed and assisted.

The narrative does not address the reader and suggests no specific application for the reader. Even so, there are indications that God's Spirit often applies these experiences of David to the prayerful reader's life and world.

Foreword

In his yearning to live a life filled with purpose and an abiding connection to God, D. Owen Kaiser has devoted himself to the Holy Scripture by reading and meditating on its truths. As one of the friends with whom Kaiser has shared his ideas, I applaud his passionate and meticulous attention to precise detail and his unyielding determination to find truths within the biblical text.

Working largely from I Chronicles, a book rich in content yet often overlooked, Kaiser leads us through a concise account of the life and times of King David, making tangible in the process David's heart and God's grace. Kaiser moves us beyond the common themes gleaned from David's life and into the realm of new discovery and renewed awe.

The biblical accounts of key moments in David's life are plentiful and well known, but they can be truly appreciated only when examined in totality and in the context of all that transpired before, during, and after David's life. Writing in a style that is accessible, engaging, informative, and true to Scripture, Kaiser weaves together a tapestry of David's life that moves the reader beyond fragmented knowledge and toward comprehensive understanding, with numerous "aha" moments sprinkled throughout.

As you prepare to read *King David: You Are the Man*, I leave you with a few of the "aha" moments that I took from the book. In no way does what I represent here capture the depth presented in the book, but hopefully my comments will whet your appetite for what you can expect.

- Although David was clearly devout, even as a child, his life took on exponential purpose and significance only after the LORD commanded Samuel to anoint him, with the result being that "*the Spirit of the LORD came upon David from that day forward.*" (I Samuel 16:12-13).

- As you read the pages that follow, I encourage you to register this truth deeply while contemplating its significance. David was extraordinary, not because of physical or intellectual makeup, but because God's Spirit came upon him in power. All the good that David did flowed naturally from what God had done in him and through him! Amazingly, for all who have placed their faith in

Jesus Christ as Lord and Savior, the same Spirit of the LORD is given so that they too may live a life set apart for God's purposes.

- David had a *genuine* relationship with God that defined his life. For David, God was not abstract, distant or aloof, but rather, concrete, proximate, and engaged. Through *King David: You Are the Man,* Kaiser provides a window into a set-apart relationship between a man and his Creator, and through that window the reader is challenged to consider his own relationship with the LORD.

- Kaiser traces how David's life was filled with challenge, but God showered him with abundant grace throughout. Having studied the Scriptures concerning David numerous times, and having read a variety of books and commentaries about David over the years, I have understood that God was graceful to David. But Kaiser's presentation of the whole of David's life illuminated this truth for me as never before. John Calvin wrote that "David is like a mirror, in which God sets before us the continued course of his grace." As you read the pages that follow, be sure to look into the mirror that is David while considering the depth of God's grace to David – and to yourself.

I trust that you will enjoy this special gift offered by D. Owen Kaiser and will be blessed by your reading of *King David: You Are the Man.*

Michael Gafa
Executive Director of Ministries – Beechwood Church, Holland, MI
Author of *Alphabet Soup: A Recipe for Spiritual Fulfillment in Christ*

Introduction

On two extraordinary occasions, God showed parts of His vast eternal purposes to David. The first of these revelations came when his heart grew increasingly absorbed with love and respect for the presence of God. In contrast, the second occurred when his heart was broken with his sin and its consequences. When he was humble before God, repenting of his sin and demonstrating his gratitude for God's mercy, God amazed David with another astounding revelation.

He acted confidently in the light of each revelation, knowing that he was working in harmony with what God was doing. As a result, David accomplished significant works toward the fulfillment of God's purposes.

Some of his accomplishments profoundly affected Israel's worship of God. The nation of Israel had changed since Moses received laws regarding worship. At that time, the Israelites were a nomadic group of ex-slaves having a strong patriarchal heritage, but no national identity. Several hundred years later, the people of Israel were securely settled in a land with borders. They boasted a strategic capital city in Jerusalem, a strong King David, and a national history with God. Key aspects of the worship and structure of a nomadic Israel were not applicable to a stable monarchy. This book develops how David, Israel's second king, wholeheartedly embraced God and His purposes to become the right person in the right place at the right time to make appropriate changes in Israel's worship and government.

About This Book

Brief Overview. The first three chapters of this book review the early years of David's life until he is king in Jerusalem. It is an informative, event-filled narration, introducing David to the reader. Chapters 4 and 5 expand on David's love for the presence of God, which was, in Israel, associated with the Ark of the Covenant. After God dramatically brings David to a proper respect for His holy presence, He makes His first revelation to David. Chapter 6 slows to reflect upon that event at some depth. Chapter 7 begins with King David acting on a part of that revelation. As a transition chapter, it also contains details about his administration and offers a timeline of his life. Chapters 8 – 12 dwell on the events leading up to and following God's second revelation to David. Many of these are hidden treasures found only in I Chronicles. The initial reason for writing this book was to draw attention to these lesser-known events, which happened near the end of David's reign.

Structure/Format. Each chapter of this book contains several sections. Most section headings include a Bible passage, which is a source for the narration in that section. The paragraphs of each section are numbered so that an exact paragraph reference can be made to the specific Bible texts used. The listing of these specific textual references is at the back of the book, along with a name pronunciation guide and an index. Narration that is inset and italicized identifies character dialogue that is also spoken in the biblical record. Other quoted biblical passages are inset but not italicized.

Reference Listing. All biblical references have been ordered by paragraph at the back of the book for three reasons. (1) The story is easier to read without numerous textual references encumbering the narration. (2) Those who choose to study the Bible while they read can use the reference listing, as well as the passages in the section headings, to assist them. (3) A key objective for this book is to be verifiably accurate to the biblical texts and contexts.

Background Information. This section at the back of the book includes a summary of the biblical history of the nation of Israel prior to the anointing of Saul as its first king, biblical details about the writing of I Chronicles, a table that lists the corresponding passages in Samuel and Chronicles describing the history of David, and some background nuggets found among the genealogies and lists of names that fill the first nine chapters of I Chronicles. Some readers may want to examine this background material before continuing, but for the rest, on to *King David: You Are the Man*.

Part One

David's Early Years

Chapter 1

David: King in Waiting

1-1 Saul is Israel's first king; David is prepared (I Samuel 7 – 14)

Anoint a son of Jesse?
God's instruction stunned the prophet Samuel.
Saul is still King! If he hears of this, he will kill me!
Samuel had reason to fear for his life because he had just confronted King Saul with the fact that God had rejected him as king. Although Samuel's explanation and God's firm judgment against him deeply troubled Saul, the king did not see that he had shown himself unworthy to lead God's people. Samuel dreaded the possibility that those who participated in a new anointing could face the wrath of the proud, unrepentant king.

2   At the same time, Samuel was greatly disappointed by King Saul's demise. Many years earlier, he had anointed an impressive looking Saul with great hope for the nation and for Saul. God Himself had chosen Saul to be Israel's first king and had given Saul His Spirit and a new heart. With these divine gifts, Saul possessed all of the resources he needed to fulfill his responsibilities as king over God's people, the descendants of Israel.

3   (The revered patriarchal heritage of the family of Israel included Abraham and Noah's son Shem, who was born 97 years before the great flood and who died just ten years before the birth of Abraham's grandson, Israel himself. Yet, when God chose this family to be His people, the Israelites were an insignificant collection of lowly slaves. God made them a nation when He freed them from slavery in Egypt. This nation of Israel was organized into family units, called tribes, descended from the twelve sons of Israel. Throughout the early centuries of Israel's existence as a nation, God called upon prophets, a prophetess, priests, and military men to lead His people. Beginning with Moses, then Joshua, then various judges up through their current leader Samuel, the nation of Israel had never had an actual king to rule over them.)

4   The public presentation of their first king was the fulfillment of a dream for most of the Israelites. They had, in fact, demanded that Samuel give them a king like other nations. When he introduced King Saul to the people, Samuel announced,

Look at this man whom the LORD has chosen!

Is there anyone else like him among all the people?

The people responded by shouting,

God save the king!

5   An imposing figure, Saul was taller than any other man in Israel. He was the husband of one wife with whom he had four honorable sons and two daughters; he also fathered two sons with a concubine. The family of Saul was a part of the tribal family of Benjamin, whose land was centrally located in the land of Israel, extending from Jerusalem north and east to the Jordan River.

6   As the new king of Israel, Saul began his reign humbly, not feeling as though he deserved the position. After his anointing, he actually returned to his home in Gibeah and ruled Israel from there. Saul also continued his domestic labors as a responsible, hard worker on the family ranchlands. Saul's authority as king became evident to all in Israel after he organized and led an army to liberate Jabesh, an Israelite city located east of the Jordan River. Until Saul came to their rescue, the citizens of Jabesh were on the verge of being enslaved by a ruthless Nahash, king of the neighboring nation of Ammon.

David: a young shepherd

7   Saul's army included the three eldest sons of Jesse. Their service gave David, their youngest brother, special reason to rejoice in the initial success of King Saul and to anticipate a battlefield report on how his brothers had fought valiantly. A good-looking young man, David was responsible to care for his father's sheep. Jesse's family belonged to the large tribe of Judah, located in the vast southern section of the land of Israel.

8   While David worked faithfully at his daily duties, he prepared his body and his heart. Not only did he develop the physical abilities necessary for the rugged work of a shepherd, David also disciplined his heart to trust God for help while he did his job. As a result, when a bear and a lion attacked his father's sheep, David did not run away or send for help; he faced these threats. God kept David from harm while he chased the attackers, rescued the sheep, and killed both the lion and the bear. Though he was an ordinary family servant, he began to understand that Israel's Almighty God cared for him and helped him. This realization became more than a religious belief; David experienced that God did in fact help him when he was in his proper place, faithfully doing the work he was given to do. For him, it was a place of peace and power, enabling him to live without fear.

9   David took time to learn and develop many skills which helped him in serving God and his family. For example, he mastered the slingshot, which he could use to defend the sheep. David also became a highly accomplished musician, ably playing various instruments, especially the harp, and even crafting instruments that Israel would use in its worship for many centuries. A gifted songwriter, his psalms continue to be sung and used for meditation to this day. These songs show how he learned to express his heart's concern, his prayers, and his

faith. Many people recognized that David excelled in broad musical abilities, abilities which would help to qualify him to play the harp in the presence of King Saul. Certainly, God also knew of David's musical talents and their value in advancing His purposes. God guided him, and David's growth in becoming God's obedient servant would facilitate his participation in many of God plans and activities on the earth.

King Saul's coronation

10   As far as David and the people of Israel could see, crowning Saul as king was good for their nation. After the victory over the Ammonites, the Israelites were full of joyful anticipation as they assembled to renew the kingdom at a coronation ceremony for King Saul. They enjoyed a jubilant celebration until an aging Samuel justified his own actions and confronted God's people with weighty exhortations. Before officially crowning Saul as king, Samuel compelled the crowd to acknowledge three facts:

(1) That Samuel himself had led them with transparent honesty and integrity. (Samuel did not mention that his two sons took bribes and perverted judgment – it was a reason the people demanded a king.)

(2) That the LORD their God had always treated them well. Samuel recounted historical examples of the LORD's helping His people when they trusted and called upon Him but not helping them – even opposing them – when they neglected and rejected Him.

(3) That Samuel had previously objected to the people's desire for a king to lead them against the Ammonites.

11   Samuel reminded those gathered for the coronation how they had insisted on having a king despite his disapproval:

But you said to me, "Nay: a king will reign over us," even though the
LORD your God was your king.

At that time, Samuel prayed about their request, and God permitted them to have a king. God explained to Samuel,

They have not rejected you; they have rejected Me from ruling over them
– as they have done many times since I brought them out of Egypt.
Protest solemnly and explain what a king will do, but give them the king
for which they ask.

12   It was against the backdrop of these sobering facts and with little fanfare that Samuel set King Saul before the people. Samuel took no responsibility when he proclaimed,

Behold the king whom you have chosen, whom you have desired!
Behold, the LORD has set a king over you.

Next, instead of leading the people to rejoice in their new king, Samuel compelled the Israelites to consider what was at stake and declared,

If you fear the LORD and obey His voice and do not rebel against His commandment, then both you and your king will continue following the LORD.

On the other hand, if you do not obey the voice of the LORD but rebel against His commandment, then the LORD will be against you as He was against your ancestors who rebelled.

13   However, Samuel was not certain if God's people recognized that, even with a king, their highest priority and urgent need was to serve God. Since words could not properly impress upon the Israelites their wickedness in rejecting God's rule and asking for a king, Samuel announced,

Stand up and watch the LORD do a great thing before your eyes. This is the season to harvest wheat, but I will call unto the LORD and He will send thunder and rain.

In response to Samuel's call, the LORD sent a sudden thunderstorm, which alarmed the people. This thunderstorm stirred up vivid memories of an earlier battle against the Philistines, their militant neighbors living along the Mediterranean Sea to the west. At that time, God had answered Samuel's request for assistance by sending a violent thunderstorm to confuse and help defeat the Philistine army. Now, God was sending a storm on them, and they cried out to Samuel,

Pray to the LORD your God that we not die for adding to our sins by asking for a king.

14   The dramatic storm amplified Samuel's next exhortation to these trembling Israelites:

Fear not: you have done wickedly but do not turn from following the LORD. Serve the LORD with all your heart. Do not turn aside and go after vain things, which can neither profit nor deliver.

He continued by assuring the people,

The LORD will not forsake His people for His great name's sake because it pleased the LORD to make you His people. As for me, I vow to pray for you always, and I will teach you the good and the right way ....

Samuel ended with the ominous warning:

Only fear the LORD and serve Him in truth with all your heart: consider the great things He has done for you. But, if you do wickedly, you will be consumed, both you and your king.

15   On what became a somber day, Saul was confirmed as Israel's first king, and the people were made to understand the importance of serving God. Samuel's words were clear, and God's weather demonstration stamped this event in their memories. The Israelites knew that Samuel was God's prophet, and now they were even more convinced that God was behind every word Samuel spoke. King Saul himself desired the direction, blessing, and word from God that Samuel possessed.

16   Alas, even after the deep impression made by the God-sent thunderstorm, King Saul, ruler of Israel, began to act on some of his own good ideas, without regard for the word communicated by Samuel. Early in his reign, while attempting to stand against a large Philistine army, Saul was losing control of his small force and was distressed about his deteriorating situation. Samuel had promised to join Saul at the battle camp, but he seemed late in coming. The desperate king decided that he could not wait for Samuel any longer and took it upon himself to offer sacrifices. Samuel arrived to witness the king finishing a sacrifice, and asked,

What have you done?

Saul defended himself, saying,

The troops are restless and you are late. The Philistines are ready to attack, and I had not made supplication unto the LORD: I forced myself therefore, and offered a burnt offering.

But Samuel rebuked him:

You have acted foolishly in not doing exactly what the LORD your God told you. He would have established your kingdom in Israel forever, but now it will not continue. The LORD is looking for a man after His own heart to rule His people.

Samuel told Saul bluntly that his kingdom was at risk and that he was the cause. God sees the heart, but this rebuke from His prophet appeared overly harsh. King Saul must have wondered what was so bad about offering a sacrifice to ask for God's help in the battle that was looming. Samuel seemed to ignore his current dilemma.

17   Nevertheless, in this perilous circumstance, King Saul did not honor Samuel's word. Although he may have had good intentions, he did not do exactly as God had said, and instead, foolishly chose to act on his own. Even more tragically, when he did not respond to Samuel's reprimand, Saul acted as though he had little, if any, concern for the condition of his heart. After Samuel rebuked him, Saul did not humble himself, confess his sin, seek forgiveness, or resolve to be that man after God's heart. In his eyes, the Philistines, not his heart, threatened the strength and security of his kingdom. He may have reasoned that as long as Samuel was with him and he practiced a few religious ceremonies, God would be with him to bless Israel. Even that may have been enough if only King Saul had had a heart humble enough to obey Samuel's instructions to him, faithfully and completely.

18   The battle that day actually turned out well for Israel. Because of the faith and courage of Jonathan, Saul's son, God gave Israel's army a stunning victory over the Philistines. Jonathan had caused these hostilities by wiping out a Philistine guard unit. When the Philistines gathered soldiers to retaliate, many Israelites chose to fight for the Philistines, who were stronger and better armed. The Philistines were in such control of parts of Israel that they prevented the

Israelites from forging swords. At the prospect of a conflict with these mighty Philistines, Saul's meager and ill-equipped troops hid in fear.

¹⁹   In stark contrast to his father, Jonathan trusted God and privately said to his armor-bearer,

> Come, let us go to the Philistines: it may be that the LORD will work for us. The LORD is able to save by many or by few.

At God's direction, Jonathan and his armor-bearer engaged the enemy and killed about twenty soldiers at the edge of the Philistine army. This small success created confusion in the ranks of the Philistine army and emboldened the Israelites among them to turn against the Philistines and fight instead for King Saul.

²⁰   The ensuing victory gave Israel the confidence to stand against the surrounding nations. They fought Moab and Ammon to the east, Edom and Amalek to the south, and Zobah to the north. Mainly, though, Saul and Israel's improving army pestered the Philistines. King Saul appointed his cousin Abner to command Israel's army and drafted every valiant Israelite he found.

1-2 David vs. Goliath (I Samuel 17)

During one encounter with the Philistines, Saul and the Israelite army faced an unusual contest for which David alone was prepared. As far as David knew, he was running a quick errand for his father, delivering food to his brothers and their captain in Israel's army.

²   David arrived to hear Israel's soldiers shout their battle cry as they took their positions against the Philistine army. He then heard the Philistine champion Goliath defy the armies of Israel. Goliath was magnificent in every way. A giant in physical size and strength, Goliath wore impregnable armor and wielded deadly weaponry.

³   King Saul and his troops were primed to wage war, army against army. Instead, Goliath emerged from the Philistine army, challenging any Israelite soldier to a fight, one-against-one. Goliath set the terms for this battle proposing,

> Choose a man to fight with me. If he kills me, then we will be your servants, but if I kill him, you will serve us.

The strength of either army did not matter; the winner of the duel would win the entire battle for the army he represented. The soldier who accepted the challenge would jeopardize far more than his own life.

⁴   Every day for forty days, Israel's army rallied to face the Philistine army, but they never fought. Every day for forty days, Goliath came out with his challenge. Goliath confronted the army of God's people as a superior warrior with intimidating physical power. Every day for forty days, King Saul and Israel's army fled in fear. Even though many of the fierce Israelite soldiers would risk their lives to face daunting foes, losing this fight had unacceptable consequences and not even one of them was certain that he could defeat Goliath. With the Philistine army apparently unwilling to engage Israel's army in battle, and with no one in Israel willing to fight Goliath, the forces were at a stalemate.

5   But Goliath did more than challenge an Israelite warrior to a contest; he faced the army of Israel in an attitude of total defiance and taunted them saying,

I defy the armies of Israel; find a man to fight me.

It was one thing to kill a soldier or defeat Israel's army in battle, but it was quite another thing to disgrace Israel. Goliath belittled the army of God's people, and, at the same time, he belittled the God of Israel's army. In fact, Goliath issued a second dare on each of the forty evenings, possibly during the ritual of Israel's evening sacrifice, brazenly insulting the God of Israel.

6   More was at stake than the outcome of a battle, or even soldiers' lives: Goliath was tarnishing the glory of God in Israel, yet no one in Israel stood for God. Did anyone in Israel's army hear Goliath's challenge to God's glory? Of course God heard it, but He did not just destroy Goliath while the king and Israel's army cowered in fear and unbelief. God did not validate their destructive behavior by miraculously rescuing them, but neither did He let Goliath continue his defiance. A shepherd who knew and worshipped God had come to camp. David heard what God heard.

7   David was disturbed that Goliath's slander mocked Israel's God and wondered how anyone in Israel could allow this to happen. After yet another retreat in fear, the soldiers informed David of the great rewards King Saul had promised to give the one who killed Goliath. Although he was a shepherd, not a soldier, David was dauntless. He responded with a question that judged the promised rewards to be worthless when compared to honoring God properly in Israel.

What shall be done for the man who kills Goliath and takes this reproach from Israel?

He knew Israel's great God and this situation bothered him. He asked the soldiers,

Who is this uncircumcised Philistine that he should defy the armies of the living God?

What a question! It placed the focus on another conflict – a conflict higher than a mere warrior-to-warrior challenge. The soldiers did not see themselves in God's army and neither did they see God as their commander. Intimidated by Goliath's words and appearance, they saw him to be the mightiest warrior on the battlefield. They did not see that Goliath had no right to defy God's armies or anyone representing God's army. Attempting to inspire a soldier to halt Goliath's defiance, David continued asking his rousing questions. While the soldiers respected David's attitude, no one would fight Goliath with so much at stake. David could not accept their timid response and did not back down. When King Saul heard of his persistent questioning, he had the young shepherd brought to him.

8   David saw that God's glory actually had two enemies: Goliath's defiance and Israel's unbelief. Passion for God's glory consumed David. That passion burned in spite of his eldest brother Eliab's contempt and condemnation:

*Why have you left those few sheep? I know your pride and your evil
heart, having come to see the battle.*

That passion burned in spite of the unbelief of those who saw only physical
strength, armor, and weaponry. As King Saul stated,

*You are not able to fight this Philistine. You are but a youth, and he a
man of war from his youth.*

David's passion was not a proud or immature fanaticism eager for a moment of
significance in the spotlight, nor was it an out-of-control rage. David's passion
did not come out of a religious teaching, and his purpose was not to promote a
religious ideology. His passion grew as his knowledge of God grew during his
times of quiet service with those few sheep. His passion burned because he heard
what God heard and saw what God saw. From this perspective, he saw in Goliath
nothing more than the bear or lion he had killed in carrying out his responsibility to protect the sheep. The objective of David's passion was to defend God's
honor at this pivotal moment when two enemies of His glory were staining His
reputation in the world.

⁹   Now in the presence of King Saul, David understood what he must do: he
knew that he must silence Goliath's blatant mockery of God. Acting in harmony
with God, David volunteered to be the one to fight Goliath and pledged to the
king,

*Your servant slew the lion and the bear: and this uncircumcised Philis-
tine shall be as one of them because he has defied the armies of the living God. The LORD delivered me out of the paw of the lion and the
bear, and He will deliver me out of the hand of this Philistine.*

King Saul would not oppose such resolve. He blessed David to the task, saying,

Go, and the LORD be with you.

The king was sending a young shepherd to fight a physically superior, highly
experienced man of war. "The LORD be with you." Indeed!

¹⁰ Significantly, David called Goliath an "uncircumcised Philistine." Historically,
the act of circumcision signified that God had accepted Abraham's faith; circumcision was Abraham's part in God's never-ending covenant-promise to multiply and
bless him and his descendants. Abraham, demonstrating his faith that God would
keep His promise, circumcised all the males under his roof. Centuries later, after
freeing them from slavery in Egypt, God also made a special, detailed covenant with
the family-nation made up of the descendants of Israel, who was Abraham's grandson. In David's time, circumcision set the nation of Israel apart from other nations
and was a sign that the Israelites were included in the covenant-promises that God
had made with Abraham and his seed. David, unlike Israel's army, knew that his
place in God's covenants gave him the decisive advantage over the uncircumcised
Goliath. Although Goliath possessed great natural, physical, and visible power, he
was not in a covenant with the Almighty God.

¹¹   Assured of his superior position, David moved forward to accept Goliath's challenge. When Goliath saw him approaching, he cursed David by his gods and then taunted,

Come to me and I will feed you to the animals.

David countered by verbalizing his faith. He declared,

You come to me with a sword and a shield, but I come to you in the name of the LORD of hosts, the God of the armies of Israel, whom you have defied. Today the LORD will deliver you into my hand, and I will defeat you so that all the earth will know there is a God in Israel.

Though he was but a simple, young shepherd, these confident words showed no fear. He was certain that God would give him the victory, silence Goliath's blasphemy, and cause the whole world to know of Israel's God. David continued his declaration:

And all this assembly will know that the LORD saves.

He was certain, too, that his victory over Goliath would assure these soldiers that their God saves, giving their faith a desperately needed practical boost. Israel's army would see Goliath defeated on his own terms of battle, but not with a sword and spear like those he wielded, and not with a divine blast from heaven to rescue the fearful, unprepared army of God's people. David finished his declaration to Goliath:

This battle is the LORD's, and He wins His battles.   I SAM 17:47

This was no mere man-to-man duel. Because he knew that this was the LORD's battle, David was the man to defeat both enemies of God's glory.

¹²   David ran to face his foe. He did not need any special armor or weaponry; he used a weapon he was skilled to use. The victor was decided quickly as David killed the uncircumcised Goliath with one well-placed, smooth stone launched from his slingshot. Seeing their champion dead, the Philistine soldiers fled to their land with Israel's army chasing.

¹³   This was an amazing victory, but David's primary concern was to uphold God's honor. Even though silencing Goliath's defiance was significant, it was but a start. David had appealed for Israel's soldiers to show a zeal for God's glory, but not one of them would risk losing to Goliath. Certainly, many soldiers prayed for the God of Israel to show Himself victorious, and of course, their Almighty God could defeat Goliath. Yet, these warriors neither understood the nature of this contest nor recognized their unbelief in this circumstance. They did not know their God well enough to see what He saw – no soldier was personally prepared to stand with God for His glory. Goliath defied God and ridiculed His people, yet every Israelite soldier ran. Why? Whether the result is victory or defeat, whether the events happen quickly or drag on exhaustingly, whether the aftermath is glorious or degrading, no risk is too great and no consequence is too brutal for a servant of God to trust God and stand with Him. In fact, God's servants

often engage the enemies of God's glory in their hearts and spirits; they humbly express their obedient and victorious faith without using any physical weaponry. It was a shame upon Israel that a young shepherd distinguished himself – that he alone was prepared to win the day for God and His glory. In the decades to come, David would be the man to exalt God and build up Israel's faith in Him.

1-3 King Saul disobeys and God rejects his kingdom (I Samuel 15)

Before the contest, King Saul met a resolute David and allowed him to face Goliath. Then, as David went to fight, Saul turned to Abner, the commander of Israel's army, and inquired,

> *Whose son is this youth?*

Because he did not know the answer, Abner brought the victorious David back into the presence of the king, and Saul asked him,

> *Whose son are you, young man?*

David answered,

> *I am the son of your servant Jesse the Bethlehemite.*

Unfortunately, Saul did not honor David's passion for God's glory, and Saul did not display a resolve to become the man after God's heart that God was seeking to lead His people. Without such a heart, a very needy King Saul would again require David's help.

2 Yet, neither the all-wise God nor a constantly hopeful Samuel undermined Saul's ability to serve God properly as Israel's king. Samuel had previously delivered a stern warning after Saul had acted on his own to make a sacrifice. Now, God graciously provided Saul another opportunity to show himself worthy of his position as King of Israel. God had an important task for the king, and He sent Samuel to make the mission clear. To help Saul understand that it was imperative for him to do exactly as he was told, God reminded King Saul of two key events. First, Samuel said,

> *The Lord sent me to anoint you king over His people: now then, hear*
> *and obey the voice of the Lord.*

Saul was to remember that God had chosen him to be king; he was directly responsible to God. Samuel made sure King Saul knew that he must receive his instructions from God and that he must carry them out precisely as God instructed.

3 Secondly, Samuel told King Saul,

> *Thus saith the Lord of Hosts, "I remember what Amalek did to Israel,*
> *how they set a trap for My people."*

Saul heard God's point of view. God remembered how the Amalekites had attacked the weakest of the Israelites soon after their deliverance from slavery in Egypt. At that point in its journey to the land of Canaan, Israel was extremely vulnerable; the new nation did not have an army and had never fought a battle.

On that occasion, God helped His people defeat the opportunistic Amalekites and then pronounced Amalek's doom. Forty years after this battle, when Israel prepared to enter Canaan, Moses reminded the people about Amalek's attack and directed them to remember God's judgment:

When God gives you rest in the land He promised to give you, do not forget to blot out the memory of Amalek from under heaven.

Now, several centuries later, the ruthless attack and unfulfilled curse remained on God's mind, and He sent Samuel to make His concern clear to King Saul. God allowed King Saul to consider His curse upon Amalek and to share His burden. Saul, on this occasion, was not asked for blind obedience; God gave him clear reasons to obey.

4   With this preparation, King Saul should have expected the first part of Samuel's instruction:

Go and defeat Amalek.

Under King Saul, Israel now had a military force strong enough to carry out God's judgment against Amalek. Samuel's instruction continued,

Utterly destroy everyone and everything that they have. Do not spare them.

This directive may have been unexpected, and Saul may have questioned why it was necessary; victorious armies typically kept the spoils of war. Yet, God's curse upon Amalek made this battle quite different. Samuel specifically told Saul that he must not spare any Amalekite person or animal. The command was clear. Saul did not need to make any decisions or use any kingly wisdom; he must defeat the Amalekites and destroy everything. There were no exceptions. Saul heard the instructions and he knew his duty.

5   After Samuel's words, the king should have understood that God was sending him on a historically significant mission. Even more, God Himself was entrusting King Saul with an opportunity to demonstrate that he could act in a manner worthy of his calling and humbly do what he was told. Since Samuel would not be there for the battle, it was up to King Saul to carry out the orders on his own.

6   Saul and Israel's army routed the Amalekites. After the battle, Saul and the victorious soldiers killed all the people, *except the Amalekite king*, whom they took prisoner. Saul and his army also destroyed all of the useless booty, *but they did not destroy any valuable Amalekite animal or possession.* During the entire day of victory, Israel's army did not finish its job. Though King Saul himself may have communicated exactly what God had wanted done, and though the king may have objected to soldiers' keeping the useful items they had plundered, they did not obey God's direct command to destroy everything.

7   God, of course, knew of Saul's disobedience. Even though King Saul had successfully led Israel's army to an overwhelming victory over a God-cursed enemy, God was not pleased. God told Samuel,

I regret setting up Saul as king because he has turned back from follow-
ing Me and has not performed My commandments.

Samuel grieved for Saul and prayed to the LORD all night. When Samuel came
to Saul the next morning, Saul was ready with his excuses and outright lies. He
greeted Samuel, announcing,

The LORD bless you: I have performed the commandment of the LORD.

Saul was not ignorant; he knew that obedience was the main concern of both
God and Samuel. With his first words, the king boldly stated that he had done
what he was told. Knowing that he had disobeyed a part of God's command,
Saul may have wanted Samuel to accept his own royal assessment of his kingly
actions. Or, possibly, Saul had so deceived himself that he believed his lie and
thought his actions were within the scope of God's instructions.

8   But Samuel already knew that Saul had disobeyed. Samuel could also hear
the animals that they had kept alive and asked Saul,

Why do I hear sheep and oxen?

Saul assured Samuel that there was no cause for concern when he replied,

The people kept the best of the sheep and oxen to sacrifice to the LORD
your God; we have completely destroyed everything else.

Even if Saul's words had been true, God's instructions gave no one an option to
keep anything alive. But, again, King Saul did not speak the truth; he and his soldiers retained more than just animals to sacrifice. Not only did they disobey
God, but they also manifested the attitude that there was no reason to destroy any
of the valuable or useful spoils of war. It was a serious error. King Saul was
responsible before God to make sure everything was destroyed. God had given
King Saul His spirit and all the authority he needed to fulfill his responsibilities
to rule God's people properly. The soldiers would have obeyed their king's orders,
but King Saul did not direct them in the way God had commanded. King Saul
did not do his job.

9   Saul had changed. Samuel reminded Saul,

The LORD anointed you king when you were small in your sight.

At that time, Saul did what God had wanted done. But now, Saul no longer followed God's instructions exactly as Samuel communicated them, and Samuel
asked,

Why have you disobeyed the voice of the LORD to take the spoils of war
and do evil in the sight of the LORD?

Samuel gave the king a chance to humble himself before God and repent, but, once
again, Saul argued that he did obey. King Saul knew that God had honored him
with an important task, and he was proud that he had so easily defeated the cursed
Amalekites just as God had told him. He could not admit any error in his actions.
To Saul, if anything were wrong, the people were to blame. He answered Samuel,

I have obeyed the voice of the LORD. I went where the LORD sent me and
utterly destroyed the Amalekites, but the people saved the best to sacrifice
to the LORD your God.

Saul told Samuel that even if the people disobeyed, they had a good reason for
their actions. Saul did not consider the fact that the animals to be sacrificed
should not now be alive. Sacrificing them would do nothing to make up for dis-
regarding God and His authority. This desire to appease God with a gift
impressed neither God nor Samuel.

10   Samuel dismissed Saul's excuse and denounced him with the stinging rebuke:

Obedience is better than sacrifice …

rebellion is as the sin of witchcraft …

because you rejected the word of the LORD, He has rejected you from
being king.

Rejected! Saul did not like that. Finally, after hearing this verdict and realizing
the consequences of his disobedience, Saul confessed his sin and asked for pardon. There was no humility; there was no submission; and there would be no
pardon. Saul had rejected God's word, and now God had rejected Saul as king.
Samuel pronounced God's final decision concerning King Saul when he declared,

The LORD has torn the kingdom of Israel from you and has given it to a
neighbor better than you.

Still not broken, Saul pleaded with Samuel to honor him before Israel. Samuel
agreed and returned to worship the LORD with Saul one last time.

1-4 David's anointing (I Samuel 16)

God's rejection of King Saul was a great disappointment to Samuel. Samuel
was old and now had lost any hope of seeing a king lead the nation of Israel to
trust and glorify God. He had often prayed and passionately pleaded for the
Israelites, especially King Saul, to serve and obey their God, yet the situation
seemed to worsen. Although the tearing of the kingdom from Saul was a great
disappointment, Samuel did not lose his faith in God or in God's mercy or in
God's purposes for Israel. In fact, he continued to pray and mourn for Saul.

2   But God interrupted, telling Samuel,

Take anointing oil and go to Jesse of Bethlehem, for I have chosen one of
his sons to be king.

Samuel resisted,

How can I go? King Saul will hear of it and kill me!

God instructed Samuel,

Take a heifer with you and hold a sacrifice there. Call Jesse and his sons
to the sacrifice. Anoint the one I name.

He obeyed and called Jesse's family to the sacrifice. When Samuel saw Jesse's sons, he was almost certain that God's choice would be Jesse's firstborn, the tall and vigorous-looking Eliab. But God cautioned Samuel,

Do not be impressed by his appearance because I have refused him.
Unlike men, the LORD sees the heart.

Furthermore, God did not choose any of the sons whom Jesse had brought to the sacrifice. Therefore, Samuel asked Jesse,

Do you have any other sons?

Jesse replied,

The youngest is not here; he is watching the sheep.

Samuel told Jesse,

Send for him. We will not continue until he comes.

So David was called. When he arrived, God declared to Samuel,

This is the one. Get up and anoint him.

Samuel anointed David among his brothers, and the Spirit of the LORD came upon David.

3   To God and Samuel, this was the anointing of Israel's new king, but there is no record that Samuel gave any instructions or reasons for what he had just done. To Jesse's family and those present, this was a surprise anointing. Maybe his family thought it was a special occasion to set David apart or to honor him. Regardless of whether they understood or fully supported him, David's family did not show any ill feelings or jealousy. Although Samuel had just anointed Israel's next king, the Bible does not again mention this private event. Life continued as before for Jesse's family, and David returned to his family responsibilities as shepherd. His life, however, was about to change quite dramatically. His preparation and God's providence unlocked yet another amazing opportunity.

4   Significantly, the Spirit of the LORD left King Saul and came upon the newly anointed David. At the time He had chosen Saul to be king, God not only honored Saul, but God also trusted him with the authority, with His Spirit, and with all of the resources necessary to rule God's people in God's way. Now, since King Saul ignored God's Spirit and chose to rule God's people in his own way, God chose another king for His people. Here, at David's anointing, many years before he was to become king, God's Spirit moved from King Saul and came upon David to enable him to mature as God's servant while he learned what his anointing meant.

5   This transfer left Saul without God's Spirit, but God did not simply leave him the same as he had been before he became king. God now sent an evil spirit to trouble King Saul, causing him to suffer serious personal consequences for his failure to act with humility and in a manner worthy of his calling to lead God's people. The evil spirit, along with Samuel's earlier denouncement of Saul and his kingdom, agitated King Saul and caused him to lose his inner peace.

⁶ Because the change in their king was obvious to those around him, Saul's advisors suggested that a musician be found to play for him. King Saul agreed, and one advisor immediately recommended David in glowing terms:

One of Jesse's sons is a skillful musician, a strong, valiant man of war,
wise in his activities, a handsome man, and the LORD is with him.

This assessment indicated that some in Saul's court had investigated David after his victory over Goliath. With a resumé perfect for the job, David was chosen to play the harp and calm the king when he was troubled. The music had exactly the desired effect; Saul was refreshed, and the evil spirit left.

⁷ Additionally, David's personality and wise service were such a blessing to Saul that he grew to love David greatly and made him his armor-bearer. As God's servant, David had now become a special servant to the king of Israel; he relished this opportunity and served competently in this distinguished position. When Saul's son Jonathan also grew to love David, King Saul kept him at the palace and made a gracious, formal request of Jesse for David's full-time service.

⁸ Jonathan and David became close friends whose hearts were knit together. Jonathan even took his own royal vestments and weapons and gave them to David. These were highly significant gifts; at the very least, Jonathan assured David that he belonged in the palace of the king.

⁹ David discharged his duties with such excellence and wisdom that King Saul made him his battlefield general in charge of directing Israel's military campaigns and troop deployment. Because he handled this powerful new position with confidence and led Israel's army to many victories, all of the people accepted him, including the soldiers and officers who were directly affected by his decisions. Since serving his king and his nation was a high honor, David may have thought that Samuel had anointed him for this assignment.

1-5 King Saul is threatened by David's success (I Samuel 18 – 20)

David's valuable service helped Saul experience a good life. Saul, his kingdom, and the people of Israel were all being blessed, possibly leading Saul to believe that despite God's rejection of him as king, he maintained a solid hold on his kingdom. But, he had a delicate inner peace and could not sustain such good hopes. A breaking point came when David's military successes were honored in public. King Saul was infuriated when he heard women singing that

Saul has slain his thousands and David his ten thousands.

Such praise of David stirred up Samuel's haunting condemnations and ominous words that his kingdom had been given to someone better. Saul felt threatened and reacted with intense anger, saying,

They proclaim greater exploits for David: what more can he have but
the Kingdom?

² Saul eyed David suspiciously from then on; never again would he see any good in David or in his excellent service. It did not matter that David took pleasure in

serving the king; he was content and did not ambitiously seek authority or fame. It did not matter to King Saul that principled military geniuses strengthen a nation and its king. Neither did it matter that David loved Israel and the king's royal family. Saul remembered that God had ripped the kingdom from him, and he began to realize that God planned to give it to David. Saul opposed that possibility with a fierce passion. Although David would have been delighted to continue his service under King Jonathan, Saul's madness would make that impossible.

3   When an insecure King Saul felt his hold on the kingdom slipping away – slipping to David – he did not seek the truth or obtain objective counsel from others to verify his jealous suspicions. Instead, he became consumed with anger against David. The next day the evil spirit from God came upon Saul and he again needed David's harp-playing. But Saul no longer relaxed and waited for the relief of the evil spirit's departure; instead, the music therapy sessions became opportunities for the king to eliminate the one who threatened his kingdom. During the next session, Saul threw a spear at David in an attempt to kill him. Although Saul's first attack surprised his faithful and trustworthy servant, David escaped harm. Saul attacked again, but when he escaped a second time, Saul perceived that the presence of God was with David. Saul himself had previously enjoyed that same presence when he was anointed as Israel's first king. Seeing that God was with David, Saul also became aware that God's Spirit had left him. When he realized this, the king became afraid of David.

4   Therefore, King Saul changed David's military responsibilities, reassigning him to a field command over a company of 1000 soldiers. David took these incidents in stride and continued to behave wisely as Saul's servant. But the better David served, the more dangerous he appeared to Saul. All Israel saw David's good service and loved him – all except the king, who saw his wisdom and feared him even more. Though Saul kept his opposition to David private, his inner turmoil increased.

5   The king did not know what to do. To oppose him was to oppose God because God was with David. Then Saul had an idea:

Instead of me, let the Philistines kill David.

Saul offered David the honor of marrying his oldest daughter Merab if he were valiant against the Philistines, but after David satisfied the requirement, Saul gave her to a man named Adriel. Later, Saul offered David his younger daughter Michal in marriage if he brought Saul proof of 100 Philistine kills. After David safely exceeded this bridal price, the king allowed him to marry Michal.

6   Saul saw that God was protecting David, and he became still more afraid of him. In contrast, the people of Israel noticed David's continued excellent service and exalted the wisdom of the king's young servant. Such praise intensified Saul's preoccupation with David, and he could no longer keep his opposition private; he told his son and his servants to kill David. Jonathan, who cared for David,

absolutely opposed this order. After telling David to hide, Jonathan went to his father and implored him,

> *Let not the king sin against his servant David. He has not sinned against you and has served you in an exemplary manner. You remember when he risked his life to kill Goliath – you were thrilled. Why then sin against innocent blood to kill David for no reason?*

King Saul heard his son and rescinded his order to kill David. He pledged to Jonathan,

> *As the LORD lives, he shall not be slain.*

7   This reprieve was short-lived. Saul's motivation to kill David was rekindled after David led a successful battle against the Philistines. Once again, while David played the harp for the troubled king, Saul tried to kill him with a spear. When that attempt failed, Saul sent men to watch him at his home and kill him when he came out. To Saul's dismay, Michal warned her husband and helped David escape through a window. David then fled to Samuel to discuss what King Saul had been doing to him. He was becoming increasingly frustrated that he served Israel and the king to the best of his ability, yet Saul persecuted him. Learning of David's location, Saul sent men to arrest him, but God delivered David from harm.

8   He then went to Jonathan and expressed his consternation:

> *What have I done? What is my sin? How have I failed your father that he seeks to kill me?*

Jonathan did not answer the cry of David's heart. He thought the rescinding of his father's earlier order remained in effect and told David,

> *There is no way you will die. My father tells me everything he does. Why should he hide this from me? You are entirely wrong about this.*

David countered,

> *Your father knows that you want the best for me. Your father has hidden his intentions to kill me because he does not want to upset you, but I assure you that I am barely staying alive.*

Jonathan yielded and offered,

> *Let me know what you want me to do and I will do it.*

9   David told Jonathan his plan to cause Saul to show his true intentions. The next day was the first day of the month, one of Israel's holy days. The monthly celebration included a safe worship time when the king's family and special servants customarily shared two evening meals together at the king's table. The plan was for David to be absent from the celebration and for Jonathan to observe his father's reaction; they expected Saul to manifest his inner thoughts toward David. Regardless of how his father reacted, Jonathan promised to support and protect David.

10   As planned, David was not in his place. During the second evening meal, King Saul asked about David's absence, and Jonathan told his father that he had given David permission to celebrate with his own family. King Saul exploded. In a fit of rage, he denounced his son for safeguarding David, and he even tried to kill Jonathan with the spear meant for David. Saul exposed his deep-seated purpose to kill David; Jonathan could no longer reason with his father. It became obvious that there was no hope for David to reconcile with King Saul. David and Jonathan bound themselves together with a strong, permanent covenant and parted with great emotion. David could never return to the palace.

11   After this violent outburst and King Saul's earlier order to kill David, more people in Israel had no doubt that Saul wanted him dead. Saul's motive became especially clear to those at the meal when he roared at Jonathan,

> *As long as the son of Jesse lives, neither you nor your kingdom will be established. So, send and bring him to me now, for he shall surely die.*

With these ferocious words, Saul became the first person to publicize that David might be Israel's next king. Saul knew that God planned to give his kingdom to a neighbor and resisted it. Tragically, King Saul no longer feared God or submitted to His purposes; instead, he thrust himself into an unrelenting pursuit of David with no regard for the consequences. He hated the prospect of David's becoming king and did everything possible to prevent it. Saul's intense preoccupation with killing David began to weaken Israel, as well as Saul himself. Not only was the king greatly distracted in his duty to lead the nation, but David's beneficial service to Israel was now lost.

1-6   David runs from King Saul (I Samuel 21 – 23; I Chronicles 12:8-18)

Even though he was widely respected in Israel, David's future looked grim; the reality that the king wanted him dead turned his life upside down.

- His music had blessed the king in upsetting times, but now the very thought of David upset Saul.
- David had been thrilled to serve Israel and the king, but now he was a fugitive, fending for himself in the wild.
- His best friend was the king's son, but now they were separated.
- David was honored to become the king's son-in-law, but now he was shut out of the palace and his family there.
- He had directed the king's soldiers in battle, but now they hunted him as the state's number one enemy.
- David had been surrounded by people who loved and respected him; he had all of the support and fulfillment a young man could ever hope for, but now, that too was gone and he was alone.
- He had faithfully served God and God had always helped and blessed him, but now David was anything but blessed.

2   Such an unfamiliar situation left David confounded with many perplexing questions.

- He could never serve King Saul again. Could he still serve Israel?
- Had he already used up his anointing?
- How aggressively would Saul chase him?
- Where was he to go? Did he have a place in Israel?
- Should he plead his case and fight for his rights?
- Would his fellow Israelites still respect him, take him in, or protect him from the king if necessary?
- Where was God when his life became difficult? Why did He allow King Saul's injustice toward him to succeed? Was God actually good? Was He trustworthy?

His future – whatever future he had left – was in God's hands. God's guidance and protection were now a critical necessity, regardless of how difficult it was to trust Him.

3   Being alone and needing support, David quickly enlisted a few friends to run with him. Needing direction and supplies, he took his little group to a place of worship in the city of Nob to request the help of Ahimelech, a priest. Ahimelech was afraid at this surprise visit and asked,

> *Why are you alone? Why are there no soldiers or government officials with you?*

David's response was a lie:

> *The king has commanded me to do a job, and he told me not to tell anyone what I am doing or where I am going.*

At David's urgent request, Ahimelech gave him the priest's holy bread for food and Goliath's sword for a weapon. Unfortunately, Doeg, a servant of Saul and an Edomite foreigner, witnessed David's visit.

4   Although King Saul could command the army and the citizens of Israel to help expose, capture, or kill his enemy, David himself had only a few friends and no place of safety or rest. Being vulnerable and afraid of King Saul, he made a frantic, ill-conceived attempt to flee and seek asylum from a Philistine ruler at Gath. But, since David was famous as a highly successful Israelite warrior, he was in imminent danger among Israel's enemies and became even more fearful. When he barely escaped the Philistines by acting insane, he found refuge much closer to home in the cave Adullam.

5   Many Israelites supported David, even at the risk of facing Saul's wrath. First, his family came to him in the cave. Apparently, they held no resentment that Samuel had anointed him in their presence. In addition, about 400 motley men came to be with him, and he became their captain. Some of these men were fugitives themselves, while others were in debt or among society's outcasts. Having lived hard lives, they not only had nothing to lose in running with David, but they were also prepared to scrape out a living in the shadows. Still others were

not content with their situation in Israel or simply preferred being with David. At this time, David took his parents to the King of Moab to keep them safe from King Saul. Heeding the counsel of a prophet named Gad, David left the cave Adullam and found hiding places in forests belonging to the tribe of Judah.

6 Meanwhile, Saul found out that Jonathan had allied with David to help him escape. The king berated his servants, and complained,

> No one told me that my son made a league with the son of Jesse – have you all conspired against me?

Adamant that everyone must treat David as an enemy and assist in capturing or killing him, Saul dangled his power to grant rewards and promotions as an incentive for them to help bring David in. This policy weakened Saul and his kingdom even more. The more King Saul opposed David and God, the more troubled he became. The more time and resources that Saul squandered in pursuit of David, the less that were available to bless Israel.

7 Saul's tirade prompted Doeg to disclose that the priest Ahimelech had helped David. Saul then sent for Ahimelech, along with all the priests at Nob, and confronted them with their inexcusable support of David. The king accepted no explanation and commanded his troops to kill the 85 priests who had come. But none of his soldiers would follow the king's general order to kill Israel's priests. Tragically, Doeg obeyed King Saul's direct order and brazenly murdered these priests; he also went to Nob and killed their families, flocks, and herds. These priests served as an example to the Israelites that anyone who assisted David in any way would die.

8 Abiathar, Ahimelech's son, escaped the slaughter of the priests. He came to David in the forest and told him that 85 priests had been executed and that the city of Nob had been decimated. David grieved and acknowledged his responsibility, saying,

> I have caused the death of everyone in your father's house.

Although his heart was sensitive and he regretted his actions, this distressing tragedy showed that David did not trust himself completely to God in his new and desperate circumstances. The consequences of his reckless lie and Abiathar's continued presence with him as a fellow fugitive were a constant reminder that God required integrity, regardless of the difficulties.

9 Providing a heartening endorsement, a group of well-trained men from the tribe of Gad joined his band. Additional men came from David's tribe of Judah and from Saul's tribe of Benjamin. However, since his powerful enemy Saul, also from the tribe of Benjamin, would stop at nothing to have him killed, David feared betrayal and was wary. He asserted,

> If you are truly coming to help me, my heart will be joined to you. Since I have done nothing wrong, God will see any betrayal and will rebuke it Himself.

Since he wanted and needed help, and since he had done no wrong before God or before King Saul, David committed himself and these new volunteers to God's all-seeing eye.

10   These men had observed that God helped David and vowed,

> *We are yours, David, and on your side. Peace to you and your support-ers because your God helps you.*

With this pledge, David received them and made them captains. These reinforcements increased to 600, the number of men willing to leave the relative safety and security of their former lives for a life with a precarious future as enemies of the king. Some may have anticipated that God would help David become king and that they would be rewarded for their support. If so, they could not have predicted the difficulty of the long days ahead. David was growing as God's servant and learning to trust Him in hard circumstances; he would not solve the problems that confronted them in the easy or expected manner. But during their arduous years together on the run, these men would bond and develop into the core of the mightiest army of that time.

11   Merely staying alive was a challenge for this band of fugitives; they were in grave danger several times. On one occasion, when David heard that some Philistines were raiding Israelite harvests in the city of Keilah, he asked the LORD,

> *Shall I stop these Philistines?*

For David to ask God about the plight of others and further risk his own life to help them demonstrated that, even as an enemy of the king, he maintained a selfless desire to serve God's people. The LORD answered him,

> *Go. Kill the Philistine raiders and save Keilah.*

But David's men objected to this mission:

> *We are not safe in Judah and you want to anger the armies of the Philistines?*

Once again, David asked the LORD for direction. This time He answered with a firm command and a favorable promise:

> *Get up and go to Keilah, for I will give you the victory over the Philistines.*

Although many of those with him had serious doubts that God's way was a wise way, David obeyed God. At the word of the LORD, he and his men went to Keilah and routed the Philistines who were oppressing the Israelites.

12   Since this public rescue exposed their location, David called for the priest Abiathar to support him as he asked God about their own precarious situation. David inquired,

> *O LORD God of Israel, Saul has learned that I am here, and I have heard that he will attack Keilah. Is this true?*

The LORD answered,

> *Yes, Saul will come to Keilah.*

Because of this threat, David asked God,

Will those living in Keilah give us up to Saul?

Although his courageous action had blessed the people of Keilah, David did not assume they would, or could, repay him by providing asylum or protection from Saul. The LORD answered,

Yes, they will hand you over to Saul.

With this word, David and his men left Keilah, but Saul continued to chase them.

13   The fugitives found hiding places in the hills and forests of Ziph, a wilderness area in Judah, and, with God's help, were able to avoid King Saul's daily pursuit. Jonathan, however, managed to visit David there. Jonathan encouraged David to be confident in God, saying,

Fear not: my father Saul will not find you. You will be the next king over Israel, and I will be next to you. My father knows this too.

Jonathan's perspective was refreshing – very different from that of his father. The knowledge that David would be king did not threaten Jonathan; he came to realize and to support God's plan. His father, however, wasted personal and national resources resisting what he knew God wanted to do.

14   After this, some men living in Ziph informed King Saul of David's preferred haunts. The Ziphites even knew David's current hiding place and led the king and his soldiers there. In an intense chase, King Saul had the fugitives surrounded but was forced to break off pursuit in order to repel a Philistine invasion.

15   These were extremely perilous circumstances, and it was hard for David to maintain good courage. Since the king resolutely sought his life, David did not know if he would remain alive another day. Jonathan had challenged David's doubts when he asserted not only that David would live, but also that God wanted him to be Israel's next king. Jonathan's words raised additional questions for David. If that really was God's plan, how would it happen? One tempting possibility used in that era would be to kill King Saul in a coup to take over the kingdom (McKenzie 86). In doing so, David would demonstrate his power to rule and reduce the threat of a revolt. Such an action would also deliver him from his persecutor and would likely be supported by the populace in Israel.

16   David knew how to worship and call upon God, but his life had never been this difficult.

- He poured out his heart and mind to God: "O LORD, I am constantly in danger! Saul is sparing nothing to kill me! Hear me and deliver me that I may praise You." David was learning to commit his present hardships and obscure future to God. He must know that his God is good and does right, not only in times of blessing, but also in exceedingly vulnerable times when he was but a step from death.

- David desperately needed God's wisdom and direction: "Where am I to go and what am I to do? How am I supposed to treat King Saul, my father-in-law and my best friend's father, who wants me dead?" To this question, David must have an answer. It was critical that he know what God wanted him to do when he encountered the king.

[Note: David's pleas here were not set apart like other dialogue because Samuel's history of these events does not contain these prayers. Some are similar to expressions in the Psalms and are included in this story to underscore David's struggles at this point in his life. See, for example, Psalm 54, when the Ziphites exposed his location, and Psalms 57 and 142, when he hid in the cave.]

1-7 David encounters Saul twice (I Samuel 24 – 26)

David fled southeast to a defensible stronghold near the town of Engedi by the Dead Sea. When King Saul learned that David was in Engedi, he brought 3000 elite soldiers to find him.

2   During this pursuit, Saul needed personal relief and went into the very cave where David's group was hiding. This opportunity excited David's men, who told him,

> *This is the day the LORD spoke about, saying, "I will deliver your enemy*
> *into your hand for you to do what you think is right."*

David was not sure what was right, but he personally approached Saul's location and secretly cut off a corner of the king's robe. After performing this small, harmless act, David's heart convicted him. He then restrained his men from any further action against Saul; no one would be allowed to harm the man whom the LORD had chosen to be king.

3   This was a pivotal moment; God clearly answered David's essential question concerning how he must treat King Saul (Steussy 56). He, with all of his men, must respect King Saul's life; they must not harm their anointed king. Without wavering, David declared,

> *God forbid that I should do anything to my master, God's anointed.*

Having this answer resolved one dilemma, but respecting King Saul would be a struggle for David. He had many good reasons to hate or hurt Saul, and his men still wanted to kill Saul. In addition, David was frustrated by the continual need to run for his life and regularly found himself in extremely perplexing, even dangerous, circumstances. This made it especially hard to wait while God worked out His purposes. Yet, instead of taking control of his life and situation, David humbled himself to obey God's clear instruction. He was experiencing the slow, painstaking process of trusting God to be in charge of Saul, the anointed King of Israel, and, at the same time, trusting God to be in charge of the seemingly incompatible fact of his own anointing. He took another step toward becoming the man who could lead God's people in God's way.

4   Eventually, David would realize that setting this high standard of treating God's anointed rulers with respect would be good for him if he were to become

king; it would also be good for the entire nation of Israel and all of its future kings. But David gave no hint that he wanted to be king. If God wanted him to be king, then God would be the One to make him king. While Saul remained king, David did not allow anyone to harm him, even though King Saul was a grave threat to David's life and well-being. If David were to die right now, right here in Engedi, God would remain God and he would die as God's obedient servant.

5   When King Saul left the cave, David followed him and called out,

> *Why do you think I want to harm you? God delivered you into my hand, and some urged me to kill you, but I had mercy on you and told them, "I will not harm my master because he is the LORD's anointed."*

By assuring the king that he would not kill the LORD's anointed, David gave Saul even more of an advantage over him. David then contrasted his merciful treatment of King Saul with Saul's desire to kill him:

> *Here is the corner of your robe that I cut off and did not kill you. It shows that I will neither harm you nor sin against you ... and yet you seek to kill me. The LORD will judge between us and deliver me out of your hand, but my hand will not be against you.*

David's demonstrations of mercy toward his king and of confidence in his God shook Saul. Saul wept and said,

> *You are more righteous than I. You continue to treat me well even though I have rewarded you with evil. Now I know that you will be king and that the kingdom of Israel will be established in your hand. Pledge to me now that you will not kill my family and destroy my name out of my father's house.*

This was a bold request since new rulers who seized power often executed the family and leadership of the previous ruler (McKenzie 45,152). (In future centuries, God directed this as punishment upon three corrupt kings in Israel's divided kingdom to the north. Additionally, a king in Judah to the south would choose to "strengthen himself" by executing his brothers and other rivals when he took the throne.) Maybe Saul remembered Samuel's declaration that a man after God's heart would replace him. In yet another admission that he knew David would be Israel's next king, Saul hoped that David was ready to show even more mercy. David easily pledged to spare the lives of King Saul's family; not only did he love them, but he would also show respect for God's anointed king by doing what Saul asked.

6   This encounter temporarily quieted Saul's passion to pursue David. Saul returned home. But his downward spiral worsened when Samuel died. Even though both God and Samuel had already rejected Saul as king because of his disobedience, Samuel was his only real link to God. Samuel's death would leave Saul in a quandary about what to do when he would be desperate for some direction or for some word from God.

David meets Abigail

7   Even after Saul went home, David and his band of 600 men did not feel safe at Engedi. And safety was not their only concern; this large group of marked men had many practical needs, such as acquiring food. They could not travel in the open, visit public markets, or go door-to-door requesting assistance. Certainly, they could snare wild game and gather edible food, but that effort could take time and become tiresome. One way they could earn some of their daily sustenance would be to provide a service that was out of the public eye. On one occasion, David and his men protected shepherds who were shearing sheep for a wealthy man named Nabal. They likely ate of the shepherd's food during the shearing season. Afterwards, since their security service had been especially valuable to Nabal's shepherds and sheep, David sent ten men to request a gift from Nabal with the words,

> Peace to you and your house. We were with your shepherds and nothing was lost while they sheared your sheep. Ask them and they will tell you how well we served them. Now we ask for your favor and a gift such as you may have with you.

They had volunteered their services without making an agreement with Nabal, but these fugitives had many needs, and David thought that they had earned additional provisions.

8   Nabal was very rich, but he was a fool, as his name meant. He rebuffed David's men and dismissed David, saying,

> Who is David? Who is the son of Jesse? There are many unfaithful servants. Should I give these strangers the bread, water, and meat that I have prepared for my household?

Nabal did not respect David at all, possibly because it was risky not to support the king's passionate opposition to David or possibly because Saul's propaganda had effectively branded David as a fugitive from justice, even as a treasonous rebel. Nabal's antagonistic words amplified the stressful frustrations of being on the run, and David reacted by organizing his men against Nabal. He ordered,

> Everyone get your sword. We have served this man in vain. I swear that no man under his roof will be alive in the morning because he has rewarded my good service with evil.

Wow! This same man had just shown Saul mercy. Certainly, Nabal's disrespectful treatment of David's men was foolish, but David's intended reprisal was unexpectedly harsh. Although Nabal did not have protection as God's anointed, such cruelty could not be justified. Possibly, fugitives responded this way, and his men may have suggested this kind of retaliation. Sadly, David hastily made and acted upon his merciless judgment; he did not call upon God or act as one who trusted that his God was good and faithful in supplying the needs of His servants.

9   Thankfully, one of Nabal's servants rushed to Abigail, Nabal's wise wife, and told her,

> *David sent men to salute Nabal, but he railed on them since he is so cruel that a man cannot talk to him. David's men were a wall about us night and day; nothing was lost while they were with us. Consider what you should do because evil is determined against our master Nabal and his entire household.*

Abigail acted quickly.   She gathered and sent David five whole, ready-to-eat sheep, 200 loaves of bread, 200 fig cakes, 100 raisin clusters, much dried corn, and wine to drink. She did this at great risk. Her husband would definitely not approve, and she would be publicly helping an enemy of the state. In addition, she had no assurance that David would receive the wife of the rude Nabal, who had slighted him.

10   Abigail's gift, with its pacifying power, preceded her, and when she met David, he heard her out. First, Abigail appealed for mercy:

> *Let the iniquity of my husband be on me. He is a cruel man, and he is the fool his name signifies. I did not see the men you sent. Now, please receive this blessing and forgive the sin of your handmaid.*

Abigail then articulated a persuasive argument, giving David good reason to show mercy. She declared to him,

> *The LORD will make your house sure because you fight His battles, and no evil has been found in you. Your life is in the hands of the LORD your God, and He will destroy your enemies.*

These details indicated that she had followed David's career closely and had perceived God's providential purpose for his life. Abigail understood that

(1) God had plans for David's house,
(2) David actively supported God's plans,
(3) David had always done so honorably,
(4) God protected him, and
(5) God Himself would destroy those opposing him.

Abigail also showed insight into David's anointing when she advised,

> *Therefore, when the LORD has done all the good He has promised you and has set you up as ruler in Israel, do not let it grieve your heart or damage your reputation that you shed blood to avenge yourself.*

David both listened and heard. He understood that such an act of personal vengeance would be a repulsive stain on his character and would defile his heart. He humbly received her wise counsel and responded,

> *Blessed be the LORD God Who sent you and blessed be your advice, which has kept me from shedding blood and avenging myself with my own hand.*

David was still growing as God's servant.

¹¹   Abigail expressed an entirely different view of David from that of her husband. Having observed that David had already been fighting God's battles with integrity and that God had protected His servant, Abigail fully expected him to become King of Israel. Her prudent insights broadened David's perspective of his anointing by helping him see that if he were to be king, his actions now, such as taking personal vengeance on Nabal, could adversely affect the kingdom he would have later. David realized that even though he was still a fugitive, having a heart which reacts by striking out in revenge was unacceptable. It may have been common or even desirable for kings of that era to show no mercy to those who resisted them, (McKenzie 22,23,106,107) but as Moses had told Israel, the king whom God chooses must not be a proud king who acts as if he were better than the rest of God's people. David's need for Abigail's wisdom showed that he was still becoming the man who could lead God's people in God's way.

¹²   David accepted Abigail's gift of food and did not harm Nabal. Yet, judgment came quickly. When he learned how Abigail had intervened to save his life, Nabal had a heart attack and died in ten days. Once David heard this, he married the wise Abigail. David had another wife named Ahinoam, but his wife Michal, Saul's daughter, did not flee the palace with David, and King Saul gave her to another man.

David again confronts King Saul

¹³   Unfortunately, Saul still wanted David dead. Acting on current intelligence gathered by the Ziphites, one more time the king and his 3000 elite soldiers came after David. One more time David had a clear opportunity to kill Saul, who was sleeping soundly in the valley below his perch. One more time he refused his men's advice to kill Saul and put an end to this chase. David, of course, respected Saul's life, the life of God's anointed King of Israel, but this time – possibly because of Abigail's influence – he expressed a greater trust in God's ability to fulfill His purposes when he firmly countered his nephew Abishai's desire to kill Saul, saying,

> The LORD will strike Saul, or the appointed time of his death will
> arrive, or he will die in battle.

Saul's death was certain, but David refused any part in taking the king's life.

¹⁴   One more time David passionately pleaded with Saul to stop chasing him. He also appealed for God's protection in his season of great trouble.

> As I have honored your life, so let God honor my life and deliver me out
> of all tribulation.

One more time David's merciful actions humbled King Saul and again caused him to acknowledge David's future triumph, this time in the hearing of Israel's elite soldiers.

> Be blessed, my son David: you will both do great things and prevail.

Although Saul then returned home, David felt extremely vulnerable. If he saw Saul first, he was committed to honor him as God's anointed ruler, but if Saul saw him first ….

Chapter 2

David Becomes King

2-1 The Philistines give David asylum in Ziklag (I Samuel 27 – 29)

David pondered his perilous circumstances and concluded,

It is inevitable that I will die by the hand of Saul.

While this desperate conclusion may indicate a lack of trust in God's ability to protect and provide for him in Israel, the situation seemed hopeless. It was impossible for 600 men to disappear. They could not obtain the substantial provisions needed each day and remain unnoticed by the populace all around them. Since David was a fugitive from the king, and since Saul had great influence as king, many in Israel hoped to receive a reward for their assistance in capturing or killing David. David did not know whom he could trust; even in his own tribe of Judah, the Ziphites twice exposed his location to King Saul. Thus, his resistance to leading a life of constant peril may indicate a wisdom in not tempting God into helping him. Choosing to remain in harm's way could be a careless or presumptuous decision.

2   David found no simple solution to his perplexing predicament, yet there is no record that he asked his good God for direction. Although he may have pleaded for wisdom and guidance, in this situation he did not express an assurance that God was leading him. He decided,

It is best that I quickly escape into the land of the Philistines so that Saul will never find me in Israel.

Determined to be free from Saul's relentless pursuit, David and his band of fugitives left Israel to request asylum from Achish, a ruler of the major Philistine city of Gath. (David had come here immediately after leaving Saul, but the servants of Achish expressed concern that David was a great military leader who had killed tens of thousands. At that time, David feared for his life, but Achish threw him out when he pretended to be insane.) David's reputation now was that of a fugitive and an enemy of King Saul. The Philistines, being Saul's enemies as well, were more receptive to him, and furthermore, because of Saul's pursuit of David, the Philistines were better able to make successful incursions into central and northern Israel.

3   This time Achish accepted him and allowed him to live in the southwestern Israelite city of Ziklag, currently under Philistine control. Ziklag was located in

a barren wilderness, very much out of the way. David's band finally had a safe place to stop and settle down with their families, a quiet place to rest and refresh themselves. While he did not feel like a fugitive in Ziklag, he may not have felt much like a servant of his God, the Almighty God of Israel.

Saul seeks direction from a medium

4   Meanwhile, Saul did indeed stop chasing David, but the king – and Israel – faced a grave danger. The Philistines had grown stronger, and now they mustered their forces deep inside Israelite territory for a major battle against Israel and King Saul. Scouting out a view of the large Philistine army preparing to fight put Saul in such a panic that he did not know what to do. He asked God for guidance, but God did not answer him.

5   In his helplessness, Saul called for a séance to speak with the deceased Samuel. It was not a good idea. God not only pronounced the death sentence on those who attempted to communicate with the dead, He also personally opposed anyone who sought direction from a medium. Even though King Saul himself had a policy to execute those who engaged in such practices, he was desperate for direction and insisted on having the séance.

6   His servants knew of a woman at Endor, and Saul persuaded her to bring up Samuel's departed spirit. However, instead of providing Saul with guidance or support, an agitated Samuel questioned the king,

> *Why have you disturbed me?*

Saul answered,

> *I am greatly distressed. The Philistines have come to fight me, and God neither responds to me nor speaks to me by a prophet or in a dream. I need you to tell me what to do.*

Samuel replied,

> *Why are you talking to me if the LORD has become your enemy? He has done what He said: He has torn the kingdom from you and given it to your neighbor, even to David, because you did not obey Him and administer His fierce wrath upon Amalek. In addition, you will not only lose this battle, but you and your sons will also die.*

Samuel's words during the forbidden séance only added to King Saul's doom. Because of this extreme departure from God's ways, Saul would be punished with death. Samuel's stinging denouncement left the king prostrate on the ground, overwhelmed with fear. With such an impaired leader and such a dire prophecy, this was not a good time to be in the Israelite army.

David temporarily goes with the Philistine army to fight Israel

7   For David and his men, the wilderness village of Ziklag had become like a paradise. But they were not idle; they decimated cities and independent clans in the southern area of Israel. These raids kept this band of warriors battle-ready, provided for their daily sustenance, increased their wealth, and, significantly, cleared more of the vast territory that had been assigned to the tribe of Judah.

When he gave Achish an account of his activities, David reported that he and his men were attacking Judah. Achish believed David and assumed that these fugitive exiles were becoming enemies, not only of King Saul but now also of their homeland. Achish said,

> *He has made his people Israel utterly abhor him; therefore, he shall be*
> *my servant forever.*

8   Because of this perception and the importance of the upcoming battle, Achish wanted David and his men to fight with the Philistines against Saul and the Israelites. For more than a year, David had not joined the Philistines in their battles against Israel. However, for this battle, Achish commanded him,

> *Be certain that you and your men come with me to the battle.*

David was confronted with this troubling opportunity because of his decisions to vacate the land of Israel, to seek asylum with the Philistines, and then to allow Achish to see him as an adversary of Israel. He agreed to join Achish, but answered somewhat ambiguously,

> *You will surely know what your servant can do.*

Achish responded by giving David a position of honor,

> *I appoint you to guard my life as long as I live.*

At the order of Achish, David led his band of 600 to fight with the Philistine army against Israel.

9   In doing so, David appeared to ignore the serious implications of joining the battle against the same armies of God's people that he had so passionately defended when Goliath defied them, against the same armies that he had led in battle as a servant of King Saul! He gave no hint that he was planning to turn on the Philistines and fight instead for Israel. Furthermore, by uniting with the Philistines to fight against King Saul, David risked breaking his own standard of showing respect for God's anointed king.

10   Although David's desire to serve the Philistines seemed sincere, his reply to Achish did not show an eagerness for this battle. He appeared to be uncomfortable with the request and acted tentatively, having neither confidence nor control. In doing what Achish requested, David chose not to risk offending Achish by refusing to support the Philistines in their war against Israel. David's decision raised a question about his priorities. Was he, an anointed servant of God, more concerned about what Achish thought than about the implications of his actions toward God and Israel? Was he about to make another serious mistake, or would God intervene?

11   Thankfully, this disturbing opportunity was thwarted. During the pre-battle inspection of their troops, the Philistine leaders noticed David and his men and asked Achish,

> *What are these Hebrews doing here?*

Achish answered,

This is David, the servant of Israel's King Saul. I have found nothing wrong with him all of the time he has been with me.

The Philistine leaders were angry with Achish and commanded,

Send this man home. He might attempt to reconcile with his master, King Saul, by turning against us in battle. You remember how the Israelites sang and danced that Saul has slain his thousands, but David has slain his ten thousands.

They declared that David's group had good reason to change sides in battle. In addition, many years earlier, such defections had cost the Philistine army a victory when the Israelites fighting with the Philistines changed sides to fight for Saul and Israel. The Philistine leaders allowed no possibility of defection during this important battle.

12   Achish honored David, even as he sent him home:

You have been honest and I admire you for coming to this battle with me. I have nothing against you, but the leaders have forbidden you to join in this battle. Return home peacefully so that you do not upset the leaders of the Philistines.

Although he may have been relieved that Achish discharged his band of warriors, David asserted that he wanted to fight for Achish:

What have I done or what have you found against me to keep me from fighting your enemies?

Achish responded firmly,

I know that you are as good as an angel of God, but the leaders of the Philistines have made their decision – you must leave tomorrow morning at first light.

There was mutual respect, but there was no concession. David and his men must make the three-day journey back to Ziklag without having fought.

2-2 Drama for David at Ziklag. Saul dies.

(I Samuel 30, 31; II Samuel 1; I Chronicles 10; 12: 1-7,19-22)

Ziklag turned out to be vulnerable, especially while the Philistines were calling all available troops to a location far north in Israel. Amalekite raiders saw their opportunity and ransacked cities in the south, including Ziklag. David and his men had been away from Ziklag for at least a week. When they returned from the Philistine battle camp, they found, to their unspeakable horror, that the entire city had been looted and burned. They found no bodies, but their families and livestock were gone, taken captive at best. Neither, it seems, did they find any smoldering embers or other clues to give them a reasonable hope of catching the raiders and rescuing their families.

2   These mighty men of war wept until they could cry no more. Disconsolate in their grief, some were ready to stone David. Having no solution to their grave

plight and having no hope in himself, David was overwhelmed with anguish. For possibly the first time since he fled Israel, he encouraged himself in the LORD his God and poured out his specific needs to God in prayer. Abiathar the priest assisted him as he sought God for the direction he desperately needed:

Should I pursue the raiders? If I chase them, will I catch them?

Hopeless or not, chasing the raiders seemed to be their only option, so David, in his grief, asked God if he should pursue them. God answered,

Pursue them. You will certainly overtake them and recover everything you have lost.

Acting on God's encouraging word, they pursued and, to their great joy, they recovered what they had lost, plus additional loot from the Amalekites.

3   David had much to be thankful for and shared his wealth. He was delighted to send gifts to bless those in Israel who had aided him during his difficult days as a fugitive. Acknowledging his ties to the tribe of his family, David also sent presents to Judah's tribal leaders in thirteen cities with the greeting,

Behold a present for you from the spoil of the enemies of the LORD .

There were no strings attached to the gifts; he asked no favors in return. He showed respect for his tribe and its leaders, whether or not they could welcome back a fugitive living in enemy land.

David learns of the deaths of Saul and Jonathan

4   Three days later, a young Amalekite, who looked as if he had been grieving, came to David in Ziklag with what he thought was good news. David asked him about Israel's battle against the Philistines and he reported,

Israel fled from the Philistines and many died, including Saul and Jonathan.

When David heard this terrible news, he inquired,

How do you know that Saul and Jonathan are dead?

The young man answered,

I found them by chance and saw that Saul had impaled himself with his spear to take his own life, but he remained alive. He saw me and pleaded with me to finish killing him, so I slew him because I was sure that he could not live. Then I took his crown and bracelet and have brought them to you.

The young Amalekite claimed that King Saul was going to die anyway, so it would be best to do as Saul had asked and end Saul's suffering. However, David turned to him and responded sharply,

Why were you not afraid to kill the LORD's anointed?

David immediately ordered his execution. The young man had hoped to receive a reward for his actions, but David had learned that no one could ever harm the LORD's anointed servant for any reason.

5   David's grief was intense; he was especially distressed about the death of his best friend, Jonathan. He and those with him mourned and fasted all day. He expressed his sorrow in a song of lamentation he wrote for Saul and Jonathan:

The beauty of Israel is slain upon thy high places:

> *how are the mighty fallen!*

Tell it not in Gath, publish it not in the streets of Askelon, lest the daughters of the Philistines rejoice ...

Saul and Jonathan were lovely and pleasant in their lives, and in their death they were not divided:

> *they were swifter than eagles;*
> *they were stronger than lions.*

You daughters of Israel, weep over Saul,

> *who clothed you in scarlet, with other delights ...*

How are the mighty fallen in the midst of the battle!

O Jonathan, you were slain in your high places.

I am distressed for you, my brother Jonathan:

> *very pleasant have you been to me:*
> *your love to me was wonderful,*
> *passing the love of women.*

How are the mighty fallen,

> *and the weapons of war perished!*

6   David's passionate grief demonstrated that he did not want Saul to die. This was truly amazing. King Saul had wrongfully displaced him from a fulfilling life and forced him to run just to stay alive. Yet David, at all times, showed respect for King Saul. Later on, in his first act as king, David would pronounce a divine blessing upon the men from Jabesh who gave Saul and his sons a proper burial, because these men had risked their lives to recover the bodies of the royal family from the display wall on which the Philistines had hung them.

7   Certainly, David honored the office of the anointed king over God's people, but he also respected the officeholder, Saul himself. David never took the fight to him in word or action, but, finding refuge in God, he stayed on the defensive – such a difficult response when attacks are undeserved and unprovoked. Although the severe persecution deeply frustrated him, David was learning to take his place as a servant of his good God, trusting Him to accomplish His purposes. It was God Who had exalted Saul to the office of king over His people, and David knew that God would be the only one to put Saul out of office.

8   After the battle and Saul's death, David's ranks began to swell. Several captains, mighty men of courage from the tribe of Manasseh, had actually chosen not to fight with Saul and instead had joined David at the Philistine battle camp. These captains and their men returned to Ziklag with David and helped him

chase down the Amalekite raiders. Additional soldiers from Saul's tribe of Benjamin came to David in Ziklag. Still other highly qualified soldiers came to Ziklag daily to help him until there was a great host. Not so motley, this new bunch. It was quite a population boost for this small, out-of-the-way village. What an encouragement for David; he was neither despised nor forgotten.

2-3 David is crowned King of Judah (II Samuel 2:1-7)

With Saul's death, David was no longer a fugitive, and new options were open to him. He could now move to back into Israel. With a growing military force and an honorable reputation among most of the Israelites, it was possible for him to recruit many more soldiers. Most importantly, the deaths of Saul and Jonathan left Israel without a king. Because Samuel had already anointed him and because Saul, Jonathan, and Abigail had each told him that he would be king, David could proclaim himself the new king over Israel. His ascension to the throne might thrill the entire nation, and, if necessary, his growing forces could quell any resistance.

2   This dramatic change in circumstance elevated the importance of David's next decisions. From Abigail he had learned that his conduct now would affect the quality of his future reign. Significantly, even though he was in a powerful position, he did not force his way into becoming king, and he did not implement a hidden agenda. The mighty men surrounding him may have offered appealing suggestions, but David did not impulsively act on an idea that sounded wise or attend to a situation that seemed urgent.

3   The God-directed recovery of their family and possessions at Ziklag seemed to renew David's confidence in God. He asked the LORD to direct his next step:

Should I move to a city belonging to the tribe of Judah?

It was an important question. Although Ziklag could be rebuilt, living a quiet, easy life would satisfy neither his own dreams nor God's plan for his life. Was God now ready to move him beyond Ziklag and back to his homeland? God answered,

Yes.

David then asked,

To which city shall I move?

God answered,

Hebron.

God honored his specific requests for specific guidance with specific answers. At God's direction, David and his troops moved their families, their livestock, and their possessions northeast to Hebron.

4   After David and all of his supporters arrived in Hebron, the leaders of Israel's southern tribe of Judah publicly anointed him to be their king. No longer on the run, David's position was now established.

Reasons that the tribe of Judah anointed David as their king

5   Alternatively, the leaders of Judah could have united with the rest of Israel's tribes to select and support a successor from the royal family of Saul, the one whom God had chosen to be Israel's first king. But they did not wait and work to install a king over the whole nation. Instead, Judah's leaders anointed David, one of their own, to be king of their tribe only. They could cite several reasons for this decision.

6   First, despite Saul's campaign against him, David had broad support in Israel. Even Israelites from the tribes outside Judah would have accepted him as Saul's successor. When he served King Saul and the entire nation, he did so with great wisdom. He had directed Israel's army to successes in battles against the Philistines, and the Israelites noticed and loved him. And now, after Saul's death, the people of Israel still recalled those times when they celebrated the honor of being an Israelite.

7   Also, in contrast to Israel's respect for David, King Saul had lost his good reputation, largely because of the way he treated David. The Israelites knew that a young David's harp-playing had often calmed a troubled King Saul. The decline of their nation had coincided with David's forced departure from the king's service. The people then watched their king, being consumed by his obsession to kill David, grow increasingly unstable. Saul's ability to rule diminished to the point that he was unfit to lead Israel in his last battle against the Philistines. Defections from an insecure Saul began prior to that battle. Israel's loyalty to King Saul's royal family became even more difficult when three of Saul's sons died with their father in that battle.

8   Transcending all other reasons was the fact that God had chosen David to succeed Saul. After Saul's rebellious disobedience in not destroying every Amalekite possession, God took his kingdom away, but He did not send Samuel to anoint Saul's son Jonathan, who appeared to be highly qualified. The royal standing of Saul's family had to end, and God immediately sent Samuel to anoint David. Samuel knew that he had anointed a new king, but there were no visible changes in Israel's leadership after this early, private anointing. Saul lived and reigned as king for many more years.

9   God, however, had His man, and with that anointing of David, God transferred His Spirit and His blessing from Saul to David. God's action was unseen, but its effects on a troubled Saul and a blessed David were soon evident. Saul was actually the first to realize that David was God's choice to replace him, but that realization made him clutch his throne more tightly. Saul did not want David to have it; he did not want anyone to have his throne except his son. His intense efforts to oppose God's man were all in vain. As God protected David and the Philistines gained strength, Saul lost all control of his destiny. God was working out His purposes, and Judah's leaders anointed David, the choice of both Israel and God, to replace Saul as king.

2-4 **Northern tribes crown Saul's son king** (II Samuel 2 – 4)

Nevertheless, Abner, the commander of Israel's army under Saul, took Saul's son Ishbosheth and installed him as king over all of the tribes of Israel, except Judah. Despite the widespread support for David, these Israelites followed Abner, the most powerful and respected leader of the northern tribes, and recognized Ishbosheth as their new king; they accepted the right of Saul's royal family to continue its rule.

2   But several problems plagued Israel and its new king. First, Ishbosheth, also called Eshbaal, was a weak king who depended heavily on Abner. Abner's strength blessed Ishbosheth, but Ishbosheth was afraid of him. Ishbosheth received this support even though Abner knew that God had planned for David to rule over the entire nation.

3   Another problem was that the Philistines were now even stronger after their resounding victory in the last battle against Saul. Israelites in the north fled many of their cities, and the Philistines were so securely in control of this territory that they came to live in the abandoned cities. The strength of the Philistines forced Ishbosheth to base his kingdom in Mahanaim, a city across the Jordan River to the east, far from Gibeah, where Saul had reigned and his family had lived.

4   Still another problem for these northern tribes of Israel was the competition with the southern tribe of Judah. Since many of their soldiers were with David in Hebron, and since many in Israel still admired David, Judah had the clear advantage. But this competition did not just weaken Israel in the north; recognizing two different kings split the Israelites in two and weakened them all. God had chosen the entire family of Israel to be one nation, not two. Its strength and influence as God's people in the world required unity. As a divided nation, neither Israel nor Judah could challenge the dominance that the Philistines now exerted over them. Yet, while the Philistines maintained their strong position in the north, they did not aggressively seek to expand their control; they seemed content to let the divided people of God struggle separately and even fight, further weakening each other.

5   Initially, since there was no peaceful agreement to unite the house of Saul and the house of David, war between them was inevitable. Israel's forces led by Abner squared off against Judah's forces led by Joab, who was David's nephew and one of his captains. During one of the battles, Joab's fleet-footed brother Asahel chased down Abner. Not wanting to kill a brother of Joab, Abner pleaded with Asahel to chase someone else. Asahel, however, was determined to fight Abner, who then killed him.

Abner makes a treaty with David

6   Over the next two years, Judah grew stronger while Israel, under King Ishbosheth, son of Saul, grew weaker. Nonetheless, Abner continued to press the war against Judah and David. The end came quickly after King Ishbosheth foolishly accused his commander Abner of a misdeed:

Why have you gone in unto my father's concubine?

Abner was incensed and retorted,

Who do you think I am that you charge me with a fault concerning this woman? Is this how you repay my kindness to your royal family in standing up against David and Judah?

After setting up Ishbosheth as king, Abner expected to be treated with more respect. Following Ishbosheth's accusation, however, Abner ended his support for Saul's family and pledged,

I swear that I will do as the LORD has sworn to David to transfer the kingdom from the house of Saul and set up the throne of David over all Israel.

He would oppose God's plan no more. King Ishbosheth was afraid of Abner and could not even answer him.

7   Abner then sent a messenger to David and offered,

Make a treaty with me, and I will bring all Israel under your rule.

David accepted Abner's offer, with one condition:

I am willing to make a treaty with you; however, I will not meet with you unless you bring my wife Michal, Saul's daughter to me.

Abner agreed and met with the leaders of Israel. He reasoned with them:

There was a time when you wanted David to be your king: do it now because the LORD said of David, "By the hand of My servant David I will save My people Israel from the Philistines and from all their enemies."

This proposal resonated with Israel's leaders, including those from Saul's tribe of Benjamin. With their support, Abner journeyed south to confer with David in Hebron and arrange a procedure to bring all of Israel under David's rule. They settled on a peaceful, diplomatic solution to the dispute among God's people, and Abner promised him:

I will go and gather all Israel unto you, my lord, so that they may make a treaty with you and that you may reign over all Israel as your heart desires.

David then sent Abner on his way to carry out the agreement.

Joab murders Abner

8   Unfortunately, Abner did not live long enough to implement the agreement. Joab, who had been away pursuing raiders, reacted violently when he heard that Abner had come to Hebron and had left in peace. Joab questioned the wisdom of David's strategy, labeled Abner a deceitful spy, and then, without David's knowledge, hastened to meet with Abner. Abner, having made peace with David and Judah, was caught off guard. Joab and his brother Abishai avenged their brother's death by killing Abner with a sword under the 5th rib – exactly how Abner had killed Asahel. Of course, this murder was an act of revenge, but Joab

may also have been concerned that David would make Abner his official military commander. David was livid. He publicly condemned Joab and pronounced a grim curse on his family:

> *I and my kingdom are guiltless before God from the blood of Abner: let the blood-guiltiness rest on Joab and on all his father's house and let everyone born to Joab be destitute or die an early death.*

9 Joab and Abishai were David's nephews, sons of his sister Zeruiah. They frustrated him at other times with their spiteful desire to retaliate against those offending them. David sighed,

> *I am weak, even though I have been anointed king: the sons of Zeruiah are too hard for me. The LORD will reward the evildoer according to his wickedness.*

This was an early sign that it was more difficult for him to face family problems than to rule as king. His unsettled family issues would affect the nation adversely.
10 David mourned for Abner and expressed his grief openly. He ordered all of the people, especially Joab, to show their respect for Abner, commanding,

> *Rend your clothes, put on sackcloth, and mourn before Abner.*

He took his grief one step further and swore,

> *Before God, I will not eat anything until the sun goes down.*

This was a memorial for the man who had led the forces opposing Judah, but David respected him as a strong and wise commander. In addition, he deplored the way Abner had died and complained,

> *Did Abner die like a fool?*

He continued as though addressing Abner,

> *Your hands and feet were not bound: you died like a man that falls before wicked men.*

Certainly a warrior like Abner would have preferred death in battle to an unexpected stabbing by someone considered to be an ally. David also said,

> *Everyone should know that a prince, a great man, has fallen in Israel today.*

With these words, Judah's king communicated to Israel's army and people that he did not desire or plan Abner's death. Such a tragedy might escalate the civil war and prevent a peaceful reunion of the nation. The Israelites observed David's grief for Abner and his leadership in the memorial. His actions pleased the people; actually, everything he did pleased the people. Indeed, it was a honeymoon season for the new king.
11 Now, without Abner to lead the forces of the northern tribes of Israel, Ishbosheth's weakness became obvious, and the people of the northern tribes became anxious. By and by, two of Saul's captains assassinated King Ishbosheth, ending his reign after just two years. They brought his head to David, selfishly expecting a

reward or great honor. Even these military leaders who had served under Saul attempted to please David, albeit motivated by their greed for power and prestige. But David, far from thinking they deserved a reward, had them executed with this judgment:

> *The man who told me of Saul's death expected a reward, and I had him executed: how much more when wicked men like you have murdered a righteous man on his bed? Is it not right for me to require his blood of your hand and have you executed?*

2-5 Northern Israel temporarily without a king

Now, both the powerful captain Abner and the king of the northern Israelite tribes were dead. In addition, without Abner to carry out his agreement and bring all of Israel under David's rule, Israel and Judah remained separated. Israel's leaders had approved the treaty and believed Abner's glowing assessment of David:

> *The LORD said of David, "By the hand of my servant David I will deliver Israel from the Philistines and from all their enemies."*

Would they still submit to David after Joab's cold-blooded murder of their captain Abner, or would they attempt to set up another of Saul's royal seed to be king?

2   They did not submit themselves to David, but the Bible does not mention anyone else attempting either to lead the northern tribes or to ratify the treaty that Abner had negotiated with David. Factors that may have caused a reluctance to accept David's authority were the lingering effectiveness of Saul's negative propaganda, dissatisfaction with David's failure to punish Joab properly, and objections that Joab remained David's captain.

3   Even so, Israel should have pursued this union. Militarily, not only were the northern tribes weaker after their commander Abner's death, but their soldiers also continued to defect to David. Politically, they had no clear leader. Such an uncomfortable situation would surely stimulate the people to unite with Judah and make David their king.

4   But, in actuality, they waited five and a half years. David was 30 years old when he was anointed king in Hebron; he reigned there solely over the tribe of Judah for seven and one-half years. Following Ishbosheth's two-year reign, however, the northern tribes of Israel had no king.

5   For all of those years, David showed no selfish ambition to extend his power and authority. He could have done so. During the two years of war against Israel, Judah's military grew stronger, and now, the end of the civil war left Joab free to drill and equip Judah's burgeoning troops. They were certainly strong enough to take over those parts of northern Israel not controlled by the Philistines. But the Israelites in the north were also God's chosen people and posed no military or political threat; David did not attempt to control their ter-

ritory in any way. Besides, he had made an agreement with Abner, and – at least in private conversation with leaders in Israel – he could make clear his continued desire for a peaceful reunion.

6   Furthermore, the Philistines' firm control of much of northern Israel and their occupation of many Israelite cities complicated any plans to reunite Israel. The northern tribes were clearly too weak to regain control, but neither did David wage war against the Philistines and attempt to remove them from the occupied territory. He appears to have maintained a peaceful, even cooperative, relationship with the Philistines, perhaps in gratitude to the Philistine leader Achish, who had provided him asylum.

7   Because the Philistines used their advantage to confiscate Israelite harvests, as they had done in Keilah, the situation became still more unpleasant for the Israelites in the north. Such oppression should have been unacceptable to the Israelites, especially if they remembered Abner's telling them that the LORD had promised to liberate them from the Philistines by the hand of David.

8   But Israel waited. The people remembered the good times they had experienced when David led them as a servant of King Saul. Still, they did not submit; his being their king was different.

9   David, too, waited. He was learning how to rule; his heart to bless and serve as king was still developing. The many challenges he faced as Judah's king were opportunities to grow in his leadership and administrative abilities. As the years passed, those in the northern tribes of Israel could notice that Judah had a strong servant-leader, an organized army, and a safe, free people.

2-6 All of Israel crowns David king
(I Chronicles 11:1-3; 12:23-40; II Samuel 5:1-5)

Finally, after five and a half years without a king, the northern tribes of Israel were ready to unite with Judah as one nation under King David, and he was ready to rule all of Israel. Observing David and remembering how he had honored Abner assured the Israelites that there would be no retribution for their opposition to him or their delay in accepting him as king. They now desired to be a part of the unity, strength, peace, and freedom that those in Judah were experiencing. With a single heart and purpose, all of Israel united to make David king; there were no voices of dissent.

2   Soldiers in Israel's army had no problem joining those who were already with David and probably looked forward to the opportunity of serving under David again. The listing below, from I Chronicles 12:23-37, is by tribe; it shows the numbers and the various qualifications of the vast company of prepared warriors and leaders now with David in Hebron.

Judah: 6800 armed soldiers who came with shield and spear, ready for war
Simeon: 7100 mighty men of courage
Levi: 4600 soldiers and 22 captains

Benjamin: 3000 soldiers (This is Saul's tribe. Most had stayed with the house of
    Saul.)

Ephraim: 20,800 mighty men of courage and renown

Manasseh (in Canaan): 18,000 who came to make David king

Issachar: 200 leaders, who understood the times to know what Israel should do,
    with their troops

Zebulun: 50,000 who could keep rank, single-hearted and expert in using all
    weapons of war

Naphtali: 1000 captains and 37,000 who had shield and spear

Dan: 28,600 who were expert in warfare

Asher: 40,000 who went to battle, expert in warfare

Gad, Manasseh, Reuben: (3 tribes east of Jordan River) 120,000 men with all
    kinds of weapons who were of a perfect heart and could keep rank

3   The people of Israel made no demands of David; in fact, they came to
Hebron with a speech designed to encourage him to be their king. They offered
him three strong reasons:

> *(1) We are of the same flesh and bone.*
>
> *(2) Moreover, even when Saul was king, you were the one who led us.*
>
> *(3) In addition, the LORD your God told you, "You will feed my people
> Israel and you will be ruler over Israel."*

4   David accepted their persuasive reminders. He had no vengeful motives, and
he certainly desired the union of God's people. Leading and serving the whole
nation would give him the opportunity to bring all of the people of Israel to the
place where God could bless and honor them. David and the Israelites were of
the same mind; he received them graciously, heard their words gladly, and made
a covenant with them to be their king.

5   The leaders of Israel anointed David king. The host of soldiers together with
Israelites from every tribe helped to make his coronation a huge, national celebration. Israelites brought bread, fig cakes, meal, clusters of raisins, wine, and oil.
For meat, they cooked oxen and sheep in abundance. The enthusiastic crowd
continued the festivities for three days. The celebration was the beginning of
David's reign as king over all of God's people; it was a memorable time of reunion
for their nation.

Chapter 3

David Confirmed King in Jerusalem

3-1 Jerusalem becomes Israel's capital

(I Chronicles 11:4-9; II Samuel 5:6-10)

Now that he was king over the entire nation of Israel, David could pause and reflect on the dramatic changes in his life. As a shepherd, he had faithfully served his family and God outside the public eye, until the errand to his soldier brothers resulted in his celebrated defeat of the Philistine warrior, Goliath. His future seemed bright after Samuel had anointed him and King Saul had appointed him to lead Israel's troops.

2 But that future turned dark during David's time as a fugitive, when his energies were focused on surviving one more day. After learning that he must respect King Saul's life, he was left with no way out of his constant peril. He remained obedient to God, but at times he did not wait on God's direction and acted instead on naïve assumptions or with reckless immaturity. God dealt with David, and David grappled with God – a necessary part of becoming the man who could rule God's people in God's way. When King Saul died in battle, David's intense struggles ended and a different man emerged. He had grown more humble as God's servant, less confident in his own abilities and more confident in the good God he served.

3 This maturing David also learned to be patient. He waited many years before he was anointed by the tribe of Judah, and then for another seven and a half years until the other tribes of Israel accepted him as their king. And even now, having more control as king over God's people, he was not aggressive in using his new power and authority. His being king was God's astonishing plan, which God had worked out in His Own wise way and time. With this perspective, he did not hasten to act upon what he thought might be God's purpose or to pursue his own agenda for Israel. David had seen firsthand how King Saul had disappointed God, Samuel, and Israel; he hoped instead to please God and Israel with his service.

The capture of Jerusalem

4 King David's official activities began rather quietly. Having many more people to serve and much more land to rule, he needed to determine the current opportunities and needs in the added territory. David headed north from Hebron with his troops. They came to a hilltop stronghold, a heavily fortified

citadel that the tribes of Benjamin and Judah had failed to capture after Israel had conquered the land of Canaan under Joshua. This stronghold was located in a section of the city of Jerusalem named Jebus for the Jebusites who controlled it. (The Jebusite clan descended from Noah's grandson Canaan.) When David came into the area, the Jebusites taunted him, thinking that he could never capture their fortress. David offered the top army position of chief captain to the valiant soldier who seized the citadel from the Jebusites. His nephew Joab led a group up a water gutter, captured this stronghold, and attained the position of chief captain.

5   The citadel impressed David; he renamed that portion of Jerusalem the City of David. He then made Jerusalem the capital of Israel, and in doing so, he moved Israel forward in several ways. Militarily, the newly captured citadel was a natural fortress; Israel's army would be better able to defend its new capital. Politically, Jerusalem was closer than Hebron to the center of the reunited nation of Israel, thus making the capital more accessible to the people. In addition, because the Jebusite castle in the City of David was a residence worthy of a king, David and his family moved in and made it their home. Israel's king no longer needed to reign from a family homestead. Relocating the capital to Jerusalem spawned many infrastructure projects, such as repairing the city, setting up walls, and erecting buildings for the activities of Israel's government. This significant progress showed that Israel's young monarchy was growing up.

3-2 David's finest fighters (I Chronicles 11:10-47; II Samuel 23:8-39)

When Joab, David's nephew, captured the citadel and earned his place as chief captain, there was no family favoritism. Because Joab proved himself worthy of that honorable position, David did not need to choose a favorite from among the many qualified candidates who had strengthened themselves with him during their years together as fugitives. In fact, thirty of these men merited the position of captain in Israel's army, with the following three receiving the highest commendation:

Jashobeam, also called Adino, who killed hundreds at one time with his spear

Eleazar, who stayed with David to defend a barley field from the Philistines after the people of that area had fled

Shammah, who, in similar fashion, stayed alone to defend a bean field from the Philistines after the people had fled

2   Notably, two of these captains took valiant stands in order to defend Israelite harvest fields from Philistine raiders. Since they controlled much land in northern Israel, the Philistines oppressed Israelite farmers and expected some or all of the produce of their farms. Although the Israelites did not willingly give up their harvests, the Philistines were usually able to extract what they desired, and, if necessary, strong enough to overcome any who resisted. But Shammah and Eleazar, with David, successfully resisted. By his personal involvement in protecting an

Israelite farm, David may have emboldened other Israelites in their opposition to Philistine pillagers. Not only did the king's action demonstrate his displeasure that the people under his rule were being oppressed, it may also have damaged his friendship with the Philistines.

3   While he reigned over Judah in Hebron, David respected the Philistines, even as allies, and they respected him. Though he may have known that the Philistines were taking produce from Israelite farms, it was not until he reigned over Israel that he assumed the responsibility and authority to defend their fields. Additionally, Jerusalem, Israel's new capital city, was in the midst of land which the Philistines had occupied or controlled for more than seven years. David's relocation to Jerusalem put him closer to the problem, closer to many Israelite farmers whose ripening crops had been vulnerable to Philistine raiders for so long. King David did not ignore the complaints and misery of the Israelites; he and at least two of his captains actively opposed this cruel Philistine activity.

4   The Philistines, of course, did not appreciate David's efforts to defend Israel's harvests. On one occasion, David found refuge in the cave of Adullam, which had been one of his hiding places when he was running from King Saul. The Philistines then sent their army to the valley below the cave. This threat provided three other captains, who came to David in the cave, an opportunity to demonstrate their loyalty. The elevated cave may have provided a far-off view of Bethlehem, David's hometown, which was then under Philistine control. Trapped and thirsty, David uttered,

O that one would give me a drink from the well of Bethlehem.

His utterance may have been more a cry for peace and security in Israel than a desperate desire or a selfish demand for a drink. But to his nephew Abishai, David's words were a call to action. Abishai, with two unnamed captains, broke through the Philistine army watching the cave and through the Philistine garrison guarding Bethlehem to bring David the drink he requested. It was an unnecessary risk to take for a simple drink of water.

5   Although these three captains seemed to act irresponsibly, David poured this water out to the LORD, an act which looked even more foolish and wasteful. Knowing that his captains had faced life-threatening challenges, he declared,

God forbid it that I should drink this water: shall I drink the blood of
these men who put their lives in jeopardy?

This precious gift had been bought at the price of men risking their lives. The cost to obtain this special water was, of course, too high, but once his men brought it, why did David seem to squander their selfless effort and not drink the water?

6   To these three men, blessing David with a drink was only part of the reason they put their lives in jeopardy. As warriors who thrived on the challenge of doing perilous deeds, they perceived that hazarding their lives to acquire this special water was a great opportunity for them to gain their king's favor and esteem.

He did not waste their effort in pouring out the drink; he dramatically and gratefully acknowledged its value. He showed all the soldiers that their lives were more valuable to him than a drink. Even as king, he would not selfishly take advantage of a person's dedicated service by making frivolous requests that might endanger lives. When he poured this water out to the LORD, David honored his captains. They understood and would gladly risk their lives again and again for him.

7   Several other notable names appear in the listing of David's thirty captains:

Benaiah was honored among the thirty captains and would become the chief of security in Israel. Much later he served as the commander of the Israelite army under King Solomon.

Asahel, the brother of Abishai and Joab, was killed by Abner.

Two other captains foreshadow dark days ahead for David:

Uriah the Hittite, known for being Bathsheba's husband, is famous in David's story. His loyalty was so extraordinary that he would deliver his own death warrant in a sealed letter, a letter in which King David instructed chief captain Joab to make certain that Uriah died in battle. This vicious crime would happen as a part of the diabolical scheme that David had devised to cover up his adultery with Uriah's wife.

Eliam, the son of Ahithophel the Gilonite, was also among the thirty captains. Ahithophel was David's exceptional counselor, who would later conspire with Absalom, David's son, in a coup to wrest the kingdom of Israel from his father for a short time. II Samuel 11:3 states that Bathsheba was the daughter of Eliam. If this is the same Eliam, then Ahithophel was Bathsheba's grandfather, further twisting the complex and difficult days looming for David.

3-3 King of Tyre builds a palace for David

(I Chronicles 14:1-7; II Samuel 5:11-16)

The days were bright for King David when he took his place in Jerusalem, which was beginning to look and function like the capital of a nation. His priority was to exalt God, but before he could act on that desire, two of Israel's neighbors knocked on his door.

2   First, Hiram graciously welcomed David. Hiram ruled the nation of Tyre, Israel's neighbor to the northwest. He may have visited Israel's new king in Jerusalem and received a royal tour of the capital and the newly captured castle in the City of David. Although the castle may have been an excellent military stronghold, Hiram knew that the castle was not a proper palace or a suitable home for David's family.

3   Hiram sent his messengers to David and offered to build a house of cedar wood for the king of Israel. Cedar wood from the forests in Tyre was in great demand, and Tyre boasted of having highly skilled carpenters and masons. David

accepted the offer, and Hiram built an impressive palace in the City of David, which blessed David and Israel and showed off Tyre's remarkable resources as well. A generous and practical gift, the palace allowed King David to host Israel's guests and to conduct official business with royal flair. An elegant home was also a welcome gift for his growing family. While he lived in Hebron, David had fathered six sons, each one by a different wife. After he moved to Jerusalem, he took additional wives and concubines; he would have thirteen more sons.

4   With this gift, Hiram not only congratulated David on becoming the King of Israel, he also demonstrated that he accepted King David as a peer and the nation of Israel as an ally. Hiram built this palace at a time when Israel's young monarchy did not yet merit respect and was largely unable to secure its borders or its people. In addition, since he had done little to distinguish himself thus far, David personally did not deserve such respect or generosity. With thoughts of gratitude and amazement, he perceived that the LORD had confirmed him king over Israel, God's chosen people.

5   As he pondered such an honor, David was humbled to realize that the LORD had exalted him as king because of Israel. At this personally significant moment, he caught a glimpse of God's purpose to put him in a position to bless the people of God, something he himself had earnestly desired to do. His exaltation pleased God as well; in David, God had a man to lead His people in His ways.

3-4 Victories over the Philistines.
(I Chronicles 14:8-17; II Samuel 5:17-25)

Unfortunately, Israel had a neighbor to the west that did not offer David a congratulatory gift. The Philistines had provided him asylum from Saul's pursuit, and Israel had not been at war with the Philistines since Saul's death; their mutual respect and support continued for many years. But David's recent defense of Israelite harvests cast a shadow over their good relations.

2   In addition to resisting Philistine control, Israel held and built up Jerusalem inside the territory that the Philistines had taken from King Saul. Holding the citadel there made Israel stronger. Even though Israel's forces captured it from the Jebusites, not the Philistines, establishing Israel's government in Jerusalem was an additional threat to the Philistines. With Israel under David growing in confidence, the Philistines could not wait any longer to make certain that David and Israel remained under their control. Instead of sending a diplomatic envoy to resolve the tension, the Philistines sent their army after David. He countered by taking Israel's army to a secure stronghold overlooking a valley. The Philistines assembled in that valley and organized themselves for battle.

3   David hesitated for at least two good reasons. First, a war with the Philistines was not David's idea; peaceful relations, such as those he had had with Tyre, were more desirable. Involvement in war could reduce King David's ability to address Israel's needs. Yet, peace with the Philistines might be impossible while they

retained control in Israel and oppressed Israelite farmers. At the very least, the presence of powerful Philistines in the land would make it more difficult for David to bless Israel, which was one reason that God made him king.

4   The strength of the Philistine army was another reason David hesitated. Israel's united army was not battle tested; a defeat could give the Philistines control of Jerusalem and negate Israel's notable progress. David must be certain that God wanted him to engage them in battle. The eager warriors with him had no fear and relished this kind of challenge, but David needed to know God's way. If this battle were the LORD's, as it was with Goliath, he could wage war with confidence; otherwise, he risked a disastrous outcome.

5   To learn how he should proceed, David asked God two questions:

Should I go to battle against the Philistines? And will You give us the victory?

His second question was somewhat bold, but he would not assume that the direction to fight meant victory. Maybe he remembered what occurred during the time Israel was ruled by various judges. Twice the Israelites had asked God if they should fight, and twice God had said to fight – yet they lost both battles! God's direction to fight without the assurance of success could mean that Israel or the intended battle-plan had a flaw that needed to be corrected. David would not order his troops to leave their defensible position and charge down into the valley where the enemy was prepared for combat simply because a battle looked to be inevitable. Victory was essential. David required both God's guidance for the conflict and God's promise of victory. God graciously answered both of his questions plainly, saying,

Go. I will deliver the Philistines into your hands.

David received God's promise, believed it, and, in obedience to God's word, led the army of Israel to triumph over the Philistines in the valley below.

6   God gave the Israelites an amazing victory over the Philistines, but they did not have much time to celebrate. The Philistines, knowing that they were strong enough to defeat Israel's fledgling army, regrouped and came back to the valley, possibly with a new strategy to assure victory in the next battle. David again led Israel's army to their defensible position overlooking the Philistine army. Although God had just guided them to victory in a similar situation, David showed great wisdom when he did not automatically attack as before. Once again, he asked God if he should fight. This time God answered,

No. Do not go after them. Turn away from them.

7   God said no, but He did not tell Israel to be satisfied with one victory over the mighty Philistines. God directed David to fight using a new strategy:

Gather by the mulberry trees and listen for a sound of movement in the tops of the mulberry trees. Attack when you hear this sound because I have gone before you to defeat the Philistine army.

David followed God's instructions with precision. The Philistines saw Israel's army retreat and assumed that Israel did not want to fight this time, but Israel's soldiers had taken up new positions among the trees. The Philistines began the march back to their base camp, quite unaware of the ambush ahead. The sound in the trees was David's signal to order the attack. Believing that God had gone before them according to His word, Israel's army surprised the Philistine army; it was not at all prepared for battle at this time and place. The attack split the stunned Philistine army; its soldiers scattered and ran. David's forces chased them in at least two directions and routed them.

8   Because the Philistines had a mighty army, putting its soldiers on the run like that was no small feat. In addition, Israel had waged and won the second battle in an exceptional manner. The exciting story spread quickly. These two back-to-back victories over the powerful Philistine forces became an epic tale that was told and retold. David became famous in all countries: God even made nations fear him. International fame and respect – a reputation David had not sought! He was grateful that Israel had defeated the Philistines, but his focus was neither battle success nor fame. He was becoming the man who actively honored God and blessed His people. God also demonstrated His gracious heart toward David by guiding him, defending him, and exalting him.

9   With the sudden prominence he gained from this victory, David faced a difficult challenge to his character. The peril lay in his becoming proud, independent, and selfishly abusive of the power inherent in his worldwide fame. He had remained humble when he was elevated from shepherd boy to successful servant of King Saul. His response to King Hiram's generosity and his receptivity to God's battle directions indicated that he also remained humble when he was exalted from a fugitive criminal to become the anointed king over the nation of Israel. In circumstances of triumph or trouble, David had so far remained a faithful servant of God. But receiving international celebrity status was beyond his imagination. Great successes and unexpected popularity could lead to a self-confidence that effectively replaces God-confidence. This character challenge was the new danger confronting David in his widely honored position.

Part Two

God's Revelation
Concerning David's House

Chapter 4

David Attempts to Move the Ark of the Covenant

4-1 David's first priority: the Ark of the Covenant (I Chronicles 13:3)

Because of his enormous popularity in Israel and his prestige internationally, David could now do almost anything he wanted. His army was gaining confidence and developing into a formidable force of highly capable warriors. Yet Israel was not secure. Putting the mighty Philistine army on the run reduced the threat in the area around Jerusalem, but oppressive Philistines still possessed or controlled many of Israel's northern cities. Important benefits could be realized if David went on the offensive and attempted to drive the Philistine occupiers out of Israel and back into their own land. If successful, Israel would be more secure and exalted among the nations, changes which God too might support and desire.

2   Nevertheless, David did not immediately seek to strengthen Israel's new monarchy or to increase his influence by waging a military or political campaign. His priority to worship and glorify God did not change with his initial success and fame.

3   David demonstrated his deep desires to honor God before His people and to encourage all Israelites to honor God. He proposed – as his first order of business in a safer Jerusalem – a celebration to bring the Ark of the Covenant to himself and to Jerusalem, the capital of Israel.

4-2 Summary of the movements of the Ark of the Covenant

Prior to the reign of David, the Israelites kept track of the Ark of the Covenant. Each time the Ark moved, it received a great deal of attention in Israel. The following table summarizes the movements of the Ark of the Covenant:

2   The Israelites revered the Ark and associated it with their God; to the people of Israel, nothing on earth was holier or more powerful. Many dramatic stories were associated with it. A detailed overview of Israel's turbulent history with the Ark of the Covenant will help explain why it was so special to Israel and why bringing the Ark to Jerusalem became David's top priority.

Location of the Ark	Length of Stay	The Ark's Movements
Mt. Sinai	1 year	Built at Mt. Sinai per God's design
Wilderness: Sinai to Jordan	40 years	Remained at the center of the traveling Israelites
Middle of Jordan River	A day or two	Held by the priests while Israel crossed the dry riverbed
Various parts of Canaan	7 years	Traveled with Israel as Canaan was conquered
Shiloh: a city in Canaan	About 375 years	Chosen to be the tabernacle's permanent location
At a battle against the Philistines	1 day	Taken by Eli's sons from Shiloh to help Israel in battle
Several Philistine cities	7 months	Captured by the Philistines in battle, then causing plagues
Bethshemesh: a city in Israel	Days or weeks	Returned on a Philistine cart, causing many deaths in Israel
Kirjathjearim: a city in Israel	20 years	Sent from Bethshemesh to Abi-nadab's house
Jerusalem: David's tent	About 40 years	I Chronicles 15, 16
Jerusalem: Solomon's temple	About 360 years	II Chronicles 1 – 7
?	?	Location not mentioned after Solomon's temple is destroyed

4-3 Israel's history with the Ark of the Covenant
The Ark built at Mt. Sinai and put in the most holy place

At Mt. Sinai, God personally gave Moses a pattern for building a tabernacle of worship. God did this immediately after He freed the descendants of Israel from slavery in Egypt and guided them across an arm of the Red Sea. The pattern contained the specifications for every item in the tabernacle, including the Ark of the Covenant. The Ark was an extremely ornate gold-plated box, having a cover of pure gold known as the mercy seat. Two golden angels, molded into each end of the mercy seat, stretched their wings over the Ark. God said that He would meet with Moses above the mercy seat and between these angels, called cherubim. This "box" was called the Ark of the Covenant because it contained a copy of the actual covenant God had made with Israel. (This covenant, sometimes referred to as a testament or a testimony, was similar to a contract, but it was not negotiated. God graciously made covenant agreements, which included both conditional and unconditional promises to His people.) God's law formed the basis for His covenant with the family-nation of Israel. At Mt. Sinai, God covenanted with the Israelites to make them His special people and to guide them in His ways while the Israelites covenanted with God to worship only Him as their God and to obey His law. God Himself, with His finger, wrote His commandments on two tablets of stone and gave them to Moses. God told Moses to write out a copy of His law and then to put the stone tablets inside the Ark.

2   One year after their redemption from slavery in Egypt, the Israelites finished making the all of the items specified for the tabernacle of worship. When God told Moses to set up the tabernacle, Moses first verified that every item had been fashioned precisely according to the God-given pattern. The tabernacle was an elaborate, rectangular tent surrounded by a large courtyard with an outside border fence of white linen curtains. A bronze altar for offering sacrifices and a washbasin, called a laver, were placed in front of the tent. An exquisite veil divided the tent into two rooms, designated as the holy place and the most holy place. Moses placed the Ark of the Covenant behind the inner veil into the most holy place. Only Israel's high priest could enter this room containing the Ark and then only one day every year. On that day, Israel's annual Day of Atonement, God's law required the high priest to bring the blood of the animal sacrificed for Israel's sin into the most holy place. The high priest also carried burning incense, which filled that holiest of rooms with a smoky cloud. God chose Aaron, Moses' brother, to be Israel's first high priest and his four sons to be the priests who ministered to God on behalf of the Israelites. Two of Aaron's sons died in God's presence when they did not follow His rules in His holy tabernacle. David and the Israelites knew the awe and holiness of that sacred place. No one was to come into the presence of the Holy God, except in the precise way that God had provided.

The Ark central to Israel for forty years in the wilderness

3   The new nation of Israel left Mt. Sinai and journeyed through a vast wilderness to Canaan, the land that God had promised them. (The land of Canaan lay between the Jordan River and the Mediterranean Sea.) During the nation's time in the wilderness, the Ark of the Covenant was a highly visible focal point because a cloudy pillar came down from the sky and remained connected to the holy rooms of the tabernacle. God established this connection when Moses initially assembled the tabernacle, and His glory filled the holy rooms; a cloud completely enveloped the tabernacle. By this cloudy pillar, God directed the Israelites through the barren wilderness; when it moved, they traveled; when it stopped, they camped. With this cloud, God also protected His people; during the day it shielded them from the sun's heat, and during the night it was a fiery pillar to give them light, heat, and protection.

4   This prominent cloudy pillar coming down upon the tabernacle – this observable presence of God – was always at the center of the nation. When Israel set up camp, the tabernacle, the Ark, and the Levites (the tribe of Moses, Aaron, and the priests) all camped in the center area. The other twelve tribes of Israel camped in four groups, three in each compass direction around the Ark. (Joseph's family had two portions, making a total of thirteen. See the Background Appendix, Section 3 and Paragraph 4, for further details on Israel's tribes.) While the nation journeyed, the Levites, who transported the Ark and the holy items of the tabernacle, were positioned in the midst of the long column of Israelite travelers. After two years, God brought the Israelites to the southern border of Canaan, their promised land, but a 40-day search of this good land found the Canaanites to be strong and intimidating. The people of Israel refused to enter Canaan. Despite their constant experience of His visible presence among them and of His miraculous provision for them, most of the Israelites did not believe that God could lead them victoriously into the land He had promised to give them. Because of their unbelief, God led His people to wander in that dreaded wilderness for another 38 long, drawn-out years. When the unbelievers had died, God brought Israel back to Canaan – this time to its eastern border.

The Ark leading Israel across the Jordan River into Canaan

5   Before the Israelites entered Canaan, their revered leader Moses died, and Joshua was installed to lead them into their promised land. Israel's entrance into Canaan was a dramatic one, as the Ark of the Covenant led them west across the Jordan River. Although the river was in flood stage, its waters stopped flowing and accumulated upstream when the priests carrying the Ark stepped into them. The Israelites were impressed that their God, Who was present between the cherubim on this Ark, stopped the waters of the Jordan River. As a result, they honored Joshua as God's chosen man to succeed Moses and to lead their nation in possessing their promised land. The nations living in Canaan were dismayed as they watched Israel's spectacular crossing. They already knew that the God of

Israel had promised Canaan to His people. The Canaanites knew that Israel's God, visibly distinguished by this Ark, had shamed all of Egypt's gods when He freed the Israelites from slavery. They knew that this God had given His people dry passage through an arm of the Red Sea. They also knew that Israel, helped by this God, had just conquered two powerful kingdoms east of the Jordan River. As the harlot Rahab informed the Israelite spies who scouted the Canaanite city of Jericho,

> The knowledge of what you and your God have done has melted our hearts and sapped our courage, because the LORD your God is God, in heaven above and on earth.

Even more, when they saw the Ark of this God make a dry-way for His people to cross a river that had been overflowing its banks a day earlier, the Canaanites knew that Israel would conquer Canaan and lost all hope. The nations living in Canaan could only wonder what would happen to them if they stood in the way of Israel's God. He was different from all other gods. Israel's God did not demand blind allegiance; He revealed Himself in unmistakable ways and clearly communicated what He wanted from them. Israel's God acted powerfully, visibly, and purposefully. Israel's God cared for His people – in acts of justice as well as in acts of mercy and grace. The Canaanites saw that the people of Israel were greatly honored to have such a God living among them – a real God to trust and obey.

The Ark set up in Shiloh after the conquering of Canaan

6   The Ark of the Covenant moved with the Israelites while they conquered Canaan under Joshua's command. In seven years, Israel had defeated the threatening regional kings and tribal nations in Canaan. Although pockets of strong Canaanites remained to be cleared, Israel had gained firm control of its promised land. The tabernacle with the Ark of the Covenant was then set up in Shiloh, which was centrally located north of Jerusalem. Not only did the Israelites worship at Shiloh, but the people also gathered there, in the presence of their all-wise God, to make national decisions, such as dividing the land of Canaan among Israel's tribes.

The Ark, taken to battle and captured by the Philistines

7   The Ark remained at Shiloh about 375 years, from the days of Joshua through the time that various judges led Israel and until Eli was Israel's priest-leader. Then, in a foolhardy action, the two unscrupulous sons of Eli, being priests, took the Ark to a battle against the Philistines. God had not directed this. Eli's sons treated the Ark of the Covenant like a magic box that would surely crush the enemy. Maybe they thought that the Ark itself had helped Israel when the priests carried it into the Jordan River and stopped its flow. But the box alone had no power, and these two priests had no heart to trust Israel's Almighty God. The Philistine soldiers rallied themselves to oppose this box, this revered "god" of the Israelites. The Philistines won the battle and captured the Ark of the

Covenant. Eli's corrupt sons died in the battle, and then the 98-year-old Eli died when he heard about the Ark's capture. It was after this that the prophet Samuel, who had been a respected servant of Eli at Shiloh, took over as the leader in Israel.

8   The Philistines celebrated the defeat and capture of Israel's "god"; their victory proved the superiority of their god Dagon ... or did it? The Philistines brought the Ark of the Covenant into the house of Dagon and set it beside their great god, but Dagon was unable to rule in his own temple. On two successive nights, the sculpted image of Dagon fell down and broke apart before the Holy God of Israel. In addition, a severe plague broke out upon the residents of this holy Philistine city. Quite understandably, these Philistines did not want the Ark of the God of Israel with them, so they sent it to two other major Philistine cities. At each of these locations, the residents were plagued before the holy presence of Israel's God. The Ark of the Covenant was not a magic box, but it was certainly much more than an ornate box. Although it had no special power to be controlled by some special person, the glory and presence of the Holy God was connected to the Ark.

The Ark returned to Israel on a driverless cart
9   Afraid of the Ark of the God of Israel, the Philistines put the Ark on a cart pulled by two dairy cows, which had never been yoked to a load. In an act of reverence giving glory to the God of Israel, the Philistines also sent an offering of golden jewels made to represent the plague He had brought upon them. The Philistines then watched as these cows left their calves behind and, with their heads bowed low, pulled the cart directly to Bethshemesh, a Levite city in Israel. Evidently, these animals were humble and obedient in God's holy presence. The Ark of the Covenant had stayed in Philistine land for just seven months.

The Ark sent to Kirjathjearim
10   The people of Bethshemesh were surprised and overjoyed when they recognized the Ark of the Covenant. Although they celebrated by offering sacrifices to the LORD, they foolishly looked into the Ark and over 50,000 died at the hand of the LORD. The inhabitants of Bethshemesh lamented,
Who is able to stand before this holy LORD God?
Once again, God's people did not properly respect His holy presence. They quickly arranged to have the Ark brought to Abinadab's home in Kirjathjearim, a village west of Jerusalem. Abinadab's son, Eleazar, was sanctified to care for the Ark in his father's house. It remained there for 20 years but had little impact on life in Israel.

The Ark of the Covenant separated from the tabernacle
11   The Ark of the Covenant was back in Israel, but it was not in the holiest place of the tabernacle still at Shiloh. The Ark belonged there and had been there for hundreds of years until Eli's sons took it into battle. Some years later, soon after he had become king, Saul demanded that the Ark be brought to a battle, but he changed his mind and hurried to join the fight already in progress (Section 1-

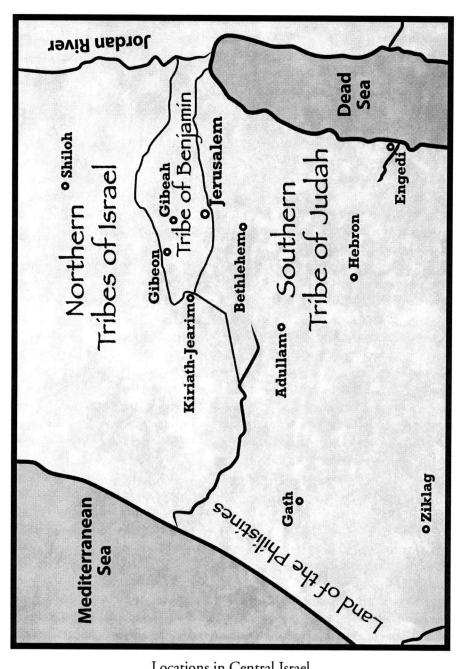

Locations in Central Israel

1:17-19). During Saul's reign, the tabernacle was moved from Shiloh to a high place of worship in the Canaanite city of Gibeon, just northwest of Jerusalem. Gibeon, by deceiving Joshua and Israel's leaders, had been the only city to make peace with Israel while it conquered Canaan. Even though the Gibeonites were not Israelites, Gibeon was selected as one of the 48 cities given to the Levites. When Canaan was apportioned, the territory assigned to the tribe of Benjamin included the city of Gibeon. (Sections 7-5 and 9-3 contain further details about Gibeon.)

12   Hopefully the tabernacle was not moved from Shiloh because Gibeon was thought to be a holier location for worshipping God. From the days of Joshua to Samuel, the nation of Israel honored Shiloh as a holy city. The prophet Jeremiah would say that God had set his name at Shiloh – but only temporarily. Jeremiah would also say that God had punished Shiloh and had made it desolate because of Israel's wickedness. Possible reasons to move the tabernacle from Shiloh included protecting it from a Philistine incursion or bolstering a desire to bring the Ark of the Covenant back into the tabernacle. Although moving the tabernacle from Shiloh to Gibeon put it closer to the Ark at Kirjathjearim, the Ark was never returned to the place designed for it in the tabernacle built at Mt. Sinai.

13   While the presence of their Holy God had been associated with the Ark of the Covenant, the nation of Israel had avoided, ignored, and carelessly handled the Ark. There is no record of any public use of the Ark while it stayed in Abinadab's home. Meanwhile, the tabernacle at Gibeon remained in use. The priests continued to offer ritual sacrifices on the altar, even though the Ark was not in the tabernacle's holiest room. Ceremonial activities had been safe as long as they did not deal directly with the presence of their Holy God. These opportunities for cleansing, forgiving, and thanksgiving easily blessed both the ministers and the worshippers. God's people could follow God's rules and continue their rituals, apparently unconcerned whether or not the God Who resided between the cherubim of the Ark was actually present.

The Ark of the Covenant required on the Day of Atonement
14   According to God's laws for Israel, the Ark of the Covenant itself was required on only one day every year, on the Day of Atonement. On this solemn day, the high priest brought the blood of the sacrifice offered for Israel's sin into the tabernacle's most holy place and sprinkled the blood on the mercy seat cover of the Ark. At that time, God accepted (hopefully) the offering. However, if the Ark were not in the holiest place of the tabernacle, the high priest could not do this exactly as specified in the law; he could not sprinkle the blood on the mercy seat. Was God present even if the Ark were not there? Did God accept that offering for sin even if the high priest did not sprinkle its blood directly on the mercy seat?

15   Apparently the Israelites tolerated this uncertainty even though their relation to God depended on the effectiveness of the Day of Atonement. On that day, because of the sins of the people, God provided that certain blood sacrifices could atone for the high priest, for his priestly family, for all the people of Israel, and for the tabernacle as well. The atonement enabled God to maintain His covenant relationship with Israel. This atonement was essential since neither the nation of Israel nor any Israelite obeyed God's laws completely; they all failed and sinned against God. Sin always distorted the covenant relationship; sin kept God and His chosen people apart. Yet, with the atonement He provided, God assured His people that He Himself had properly dealt with their sin; God's atonement-based mercy enabled them to live confidently in His presence as His people. In addition, God could live among His people as their God, when they carried out His instructions for the Day of Atonement and received His mercy in His way.

4-4 David prepares to move the Ark (I Chronicles 13:1-4)

Although Israel had suffered serious consequences from its haphazard dealings with the Ark, moving it to Jerusalem was a priority for David. Having the Ark in their capital would help the Israelites to be more aware of God's presence. Certainly, God was holy and many of His people were afraid of His presence, but to David, it was worth any risk to receive the great benefits that would come from properly honoring Him. Throughout his life, he had been personally learning about the value of worshipping and trusting God, and now, as king, he could lead God's people to benefit from the presence of their great God. He decided to move the Ark of the Covenant from Kirjathjearim to the City of David in Jerusalem. But why Jerusalem? The tabernacle, with the most holy place already built for the Ark, was located in Gibeon. Nevertheless, David chose to bring it to a location close to his home.

2   David had to decide how to relocate the Ark of the Covenant. Since the Ark had been tucked away in Abinadab's home and had been neglected for any public or ceremonial use for at least 20 years, one option could have been to move it quietly and casually like a piece of common furniture. Using the priests and others to maintain the necessary protocol, David could have had the Ark brought to Jerusalem without bothering many people. The king's desire to bring the Ark close to him might have impressed the Israelites and even caused them to appreciate God's presence among them.

3   But David did not make his royal actions the focus; he wanted to exalt God, and he wanted the people to exalt God. Although the Israelites knew the name of their God as "the LORD Who dwells between the cherubim," most had little more than a ceremonial knowledge of Him. This move of the Ark of the Covenant would help assure them of the reality of God personally present among them. Then, if Israel's neglect of the Ark of God's presence were corrected, God would be exalted even more. Therefore, David planned to make the actual moving of the Ark a

national celebration honoring God before the people – a grand occasion designed to lift the people's hearts and thoughts toward God and to inspire a greater desire for His presence.

David asks for counsel before moving the Ark

4   David wanted the processional for the Ark of the Covenant to happen quickly, but he did not simply exercise his royal authority to make it happen. Instead, he first consulted with all of Israel's military and civil leaders, even those having minimal authority. In seeking their consent and support, he honored this large group of leaders and received the benefit of their wisdom concerning this important initiative.

5   The king prefaced his proposal by saying,

> *If this sounds good to you, and it is of the LORD our God....*

Two conditions must be met before the Ark could be moved. First, Israel's leadership must concur that relocating the Ark was a worthy national endeavor and commit to it – it must be more than compliance with the king's order. He gave them an opportunity to suggest modifications or even to overrule his plan. Second, David needed this assembly of leaders to recognize that this project was from God – it must be more than agreement with the king's good idea. He expected his leaders to know their God well enough to seek Him and to learn whether or not He wanted the Ark moved to Jerusalem.

6   David next presented the details of the plan he wanted this leadership assembly to consider.

> *Let us send invitations to our fellow citizens everywhere in the land of*
> *Israel that they may join us. Make sure to include the priests and Levites*
> *who live in cities and suburbs throughout Israel.*

Expecting so much more than a simple relocation, he proposed that all the people of Israel participate in the Ark's move. His language was inclusive:

> *Let **us** bring the Ark of **our** God to **us**.*

Together, as one people having one purpose (no distinction was made by home location, by gender, by race, or by age) the citizens of Israel would bring the Ark of the Covenant to Jerusalem. David also recommended a special effort to assemble the priests, who ministered to God on behalf of the Israelites, and the Levites, who supported the priests in their work.

7   Moreover, this project addressed a long-standing problem. The king explained,

> *We did not inquire before the Ark when Saul was king*

When they ignored the Ark of the Covenant, Israel also disregarded the reality of God personally present among His people. David's unexpected and unprecedented decisions during and after this celebration would begin to correct this deficiency.

⁸   Having finished his presentation, David waited for this assembly of leaders to respond. To his delight, Israel's leadership deemed his plan to be right. They agreed to hold a national celebration and to move the Ark of the Covenant from Kirjathjearim to the City of David in Jerusalem.

⁹   All of this preparation showed David's respect for the Ark of the Covenant. His international fame did not dull his mind or heart to the significance of this monumental enterprise or to its potential impact upon the nation of Israel and beyond. The king did not take this project lightly.

¹⁰   Nevertheless, while David's priority to make the Ark of God's presence accessible was admirable, while his desire to inquire before the Ark was noble, and while his request for the support of Israel's leaders was wise, he later admitted that he did not seek God for specific direction or search God's law for instruction on his project. David invited the priests and Levites, but, apparently, the exalted king neither sought advice from Israel's priests nor received appropriate divine and legal counsel from the priests or anyone else. Ominously, he seemed to treat the relocation more like a civil enterprise that he could manage than a spiritual work that required God's help. Since the leadership agreed that God wanted the Ark moved, David may have presumed that a good and godly project done with the right motives would turn out well.

4-5 The procession of the Ark of the Covenant begins
(I Chronicles 13:5-8; II Samuel 6:1-5)

David and Israel began to carry out the agreed-upon plan. The call went out for all of the people to gather at Kirjathjearim for the specific purpose of taking the Ark to the City of David, the citadel of Jerusalem. David did not merely invite them to watch a parade; he asked each Israelite to participate in moving the Ark of the Covenant, one simple objective behind which the nation could unite.

²   To David, this meaningful event was far more than a relocation; the Israelites were coming together to restore the Ark of the Covenant to its place at the center of their life and worship. The people might also see that they had a personal invitation to come into God's presence. God's covenant promise was to be their God, to live among them and guide them in His ways; they no longer needed to fear or neglect the Ark of the Covenant.

³   From Lebanon to the north and Egypt to the south, a huge throng of Israelites accepted the invitation and joined the festivities. The people rallied behind Israel's leaders and their unified commitment to this national endeavor. The priests, the Levites, and Israel's thirty thousand select military men assembled as specially invited groups. Expectations were high as the Israelites lined the streets for the ten-mile journey from Kirjathjearim up to the City of David.

⁴   King David went to the house of Abinadab to start the processional. The Ark of the Covenant was to be transported to Jerusalem on a new cart pulled by oxen and driven by Uzza and Ahio, two of the sons of Abinadab. (The Levites

had always carried the Ark of the Covenant and other holy items on their shoulders. Some Levites did use carts for their work at the tabernacle, but the family responsible for moving the Ark did not. The Philistines were the first to put the Ark on a cart twenty years before.)

5   The cart carrying the Ark began to move, and the huge throng of Israelites overflowed into the streets around it. Coming together with one clear focus helped unite the people's praise, yet their praise was undirected. They sang and played cymbals, trumpets, and stringed instruments as their hearts, minds, and bodies desired. With individual expressions of worship, these Israelites exalted the God Who chose them to be His people and chose to live among them. King David and the people were in the presence of God; they praised Him with all of their strength. It was a jubilant celebration … while it lasted.

4-6 God interrupts the Ark's procession
(I Chronicles 13: 9-13; II Samuel 6:6-10)

Although the roads were not always smooth, there was no need to hurry, and the Ark traveled just fine on the cart. In Jerusalem, near the end of its journey, the processional passed over a threshing floor where farmers crushed stalks of harvested grain to separate the seed kernels from the chaff. The floor was a smooth, hardened surface on which the oxen and stone cylinders broke the husks of the grain to release the edible seeds inside.

2   Because this level threshing floor was built onto an uneven path, possibly now on a narrow ascent to the City of David fortress, the oxen pulling the cart stumbled, and the cart itself shook. Being aware that the cart was about to be pulled over this same rough spot, Uzza put his hand on the Ark to stabilize it. Uzza, one of the two driving the cart, cared for the Ark; he took his responsibility seriously and did not want the Ark to be damaged. He was the one in the right place to perform this ministry of ensuring the safety of Israel's holiest item. When Uzza reached out his hand to steady the Ark, he did a good job, right? Actually, no. God was angry with Uzza and struck him dead on the spot. God did so because Uzza put his hand on the Ark.

3   Uzza's death was not an accident. David immediately recognized that it was God Who had struck Uzza. The procession stopped. The Israelites' rejoicing turned to mourning, and questions filled David's heart and mind. Did Uzza – or did I – do something wrong? Was it wrong to move the Ark at all? He was now afraid of God and groaned,

How will I bring the Ark of God to me?

4   This incident was disastrous for David's plans. Uzza's death crushed his hopes for changing the way that Israel related to the presence of God. God's judgment fell on Uzza, even though David, with all of the Israelites, praised God and rejoiced at the Ark's coming to Jerusalem. Apparently, his idea for the Ark to be at the center of the nation would not work. David wanted all of

God's people to be free to come to God and worship Him, but the inherent risks seemed too great and thus prevented direct access into the presence of the Holy God connected to the Ark of the Covenant.

5   As king, David had further questions to answer. Was God's presence safe for only a few special people like Moses or the high priest? Historically, Israel had had great difficulty relating to its Almighty, Holy God in an acceptable manner. Should he make the safer choice and accept the necessity of restricting access to the Ark of God's presence?

6   Even though the Ark was now in Jerusalem, David did not bring it the short distance remaining to the City of David. Under the cloud of Uzza's death, David did not want the Ark near him, but he did not bring it to a priest or any other Israelite. Possibly fearing another catastrophe, he took Israel's holiest object to the nearby home of Obededom the Gittite, a man from the Philistine city of Gath.

Chapter 5

David Completes the Move of the Ark of the Covenant

5-1 David prepares to move the Ark … again

(I Chronicles 13:14; 15:1-24; II Samuel 6:11)

This situation baffled David. Even while Israel honored the holy presence of the one Almighty God, He demonstrated His power by striking a key participant dead. This great God had promised to be Israel's God, yet He halted His people's exuberant worship by a judgment against them. Even as the people blessed God with their joyful praise, He caused their happy hearts to grieve and turned their joy into mourning. The king and many in Israel questioned how God could do such a thing.

2   For three months, while David mourned Uzza's death and pondered the distressing turn of events, God noticeably blessed the household of Obededom because of the presence of the Ark of the Covenant in his home. This news jolted the king out of his grief and self-pity; if God were blessing the family of a man of Philistine descent, then surely He would bless His Own chosen people.

3   David sprang into action, sure again of God's purpose for him to relocate the Ark. If the Ark of God's presence were with him in the City of David, near the center of Israel's government, then he would have God's blessing to lead the nation, and all of the people could experience God's blessing, not just Obededom. It was time to complete this task and to do it correctly.

4   But what had he done wrong? His heart and his preparation for the first move seemed to honor God, yet that processional ended in a tragedy. He had sought the counsel and agreement of a large assembly of Israel's leaders, but one or more crucial details had not been right. Having faced many other perplexing circumstances in his life, David had been learning to pour out his heart to God and humbly trust Him to help; his misery and confusion would linger if he stubbornly harbored bitterness and complaint against God.

5   While his broken heart lamented Uzza's death, David sought God and obtained the critical answers he needed. First, he realized that, in the excitement of the event, he had neglected to make specific plans for the Ark after its arrival in the City of David. This time he designated a specific location at his palace and pitched a tent there to house the Ark of the Covenant; choosing a resting-place for the Ark would not be a casual or last minute decision.

David enlarges upon a Levite ministry found in the law

6   Another correction concerned a critical function of the Levites. While David had specifically invited the Levites to the Ark's first move, they were not set apart in that celebration; no distinction was made between the Levites and the rest of the Israelites. Now, three months later, he stated,

No one but the Levites ought to carry the Ark of God because the LORD has chosen them to carry the Ark of God ....

Even though David and many in Israel may have known that the Levites had carried the Ark in the wilderness, they attempted to move it on a cart. David now understood that the Levites **must** carry it on their shoulders; the method of transport was not optional. God had even warned Israel that the Levites must not touch the holy items of the tabernacle or they would die. It was a humbling realization for the king; if he had followed these instructions the first time, Uzza would not have died.

7   In addition, David discovered in God's law and now declared to the people that it was the Levites' place

... to minister unto the LORD forever.

He understood this ministry to include more than their clearly commanded duties of caring for the tabernacle and helping the priests. Acting on this discovery, he gave the Levites several distinct roles during the Ark's second processional. Furthermore, after the Ark rested in its tent, he gave the Levites a continuing new ministry unto God.

8   Armed with a greater knowledge of God's ways, David again called the Israelites to gather at Jerusalem and to help bring the Ark of the Covenant to the place he had prepared for it. This time, however, he counted 862 Levites, organized them in six family groups, and set them apart from the other Israelites.

9   David called a meeting with the head of each Levite family group, plus the two priests, Zadok and Abiathar. He gave these eight men two specific tasks. First,

You are the chief Levite leaders: sanctify yourselves, and your brethren, so that you may bring the Ark of the LORD God of Israel to the place I have prepared for it.

Each Levite participating in this processional was to cleanse himself as needed and stay away from anything unclean. David explained further,

Because you did not bring the Ark the first time, God halted that move with the death of Uzza. We did not seek God according to the order established in His law.

This was a humbling admission. During the first move, the Levites were not properly cleansed and the Ark was moved on a cart. This time, all the Levites sanctified themselves as instructed. With the Levites thus prepared, the eight leaders could carry the Ark by inserting wooden poles through rings in the Ark and lifting the poles onto their shoulders.

¹⁰   Secondly, David instructed the eight Levite leaders:

Appoint your Levite brethren as singers, lifting up their voices with joy and playing instruments of music, psalteries, harps, and cymbals.

When they had moved the Ark three months ago, the king and the people individually expressed their praise. This time the Levites were to take the lead and exalt God with their music. It was a new task. Except for the trumpet, the law God gave to Moses did not mention the use of instruments or singing during Israel's regular rituals. The priests blew silver trumpets to call an assembly, to begin a journey, or to rally the army for battle. The priests also sounded their trumpets at many sacrifices and on certain holy days. On the other hand, singing and the playing of instrumental music were done spontaneously during the ministry of prophets and at times of celebration. Moving the Ark was certainly a time of celebration, but the Levites had never been responsible for singing songs or playing psaltery and harp. Yet, because David understood that God had chosen the Levites to minister to the LORD and bless Israel in His name, and because David personally knew that music aided such worship, he instructed the Levites, not just the priests, to worship God with music and to lead the people in song and dance. Much later, at the end of his reign, David organized the Levites in an expanded ministry of music (Chapter 11 of this book), a ministry which continued for many centuries.

¹¹   The eight leaders of the Levite tribe followed the king's instructions and appointed singers and musicians. They knew or could determine who among the Levites had the necessary talents and skills. The Levite leaders appointed Asaph, Heman, and Ethan to be the chief music leaders, using cymbals to direct the sections of musicians and to keep the beat. Leadership positions under Asaph, Heman, and Ethan (later called Jeduthun) were assigned by the eight Levite leaders; a Levite named Obededom, received one of these positions. Gifted instrumentalists were given a place in the orchestra. The eight leaders also chose a choir of talented singers and appointed Chenaniah to direct the choir because he was a skilled conductor who had had music training. Leading the way for the Ark would be the priests, blowing their trumpets. The eight leaders chose Jehiah and still another Levite named Obededom to be doorkeepers or porters for the Ark of the Covenant. Porters, another new Levite position, controlled access to the Ark and to Israel's holy places.

David does not bring the Ark to the tabernacle

¹²   But David did not change Jerusalem as his destination for the Ark of the Covenant. He could have placed the Ark where God designed it be, in the holiest room of the tabernacle then located at the high place of worship in Gibeon. Bringing the Ark there would solve the serious problem that occurred on the Day of Atonement, when the high priest carried out God's requirement to sprinkle the sacrificial blood on the Ark's mercy seat. Because the Ark was missing, it remained uncertain if the God Who dwelt between the cherubim of the Ark were present to accept this offering for sin.

13   But David did not mention bringing the Ark back to the tabernacle in Gibeon, nor bringing the tabernacle itself to Jerusalem, nor reuniting all the holy items at Shiloh, Israel's first holy city situated further north in lands under Philistine control. Why did the Holy God, Who exacted punishment upon Uzza when he touched the Ark of the Covenant, allow David to bring the Ark to a tent in Jerusalem instead of uniting it with the tabernacle? Indeed, the location of the Ark of His presence was extremely important to God, but David and Israel were not ready for His word on that. God's word, specifying a permanent location for the Ark, would come many years later, when David would consider sacrificing at the tabernacle at Gibeon; it would be the time of God's second momentous revelation to David (Chapter 9 of this book).

5-2 The Ark of the Covenant is carried to the City of David
(I Chronicles 15:25-29; 16:1-3; II Samuel 6:12-23)

Now, three months after the first attempt, David and Israel were ready to bring the Ark of the Covenant up to the City of David. Just a short distance remained, so the huge throng of Israelites, once again alive with anticipation, packed the streets of Jerusalem. David, the leaders of Israel, and the captains of Israel's army accompanied the eight Levite leaders to get the Ark from the house of Obededom, the Philistine from Gath. When these Levite leaders carried the Ark out of the house, the celebration began again in earnest with singing and shouting and playing and dancing. All of Israel joined in.

2   After those carrying the Ark of the Covenant had taken six steps, David offered seven bulls and seven rams to God, Who helped the Levites now carrying the Ark. Three months earlier, God had broken in and halted the procession with a stunning act of judgment. This time, it was David's choice to interrupt the celebration and lead the people in offering sacrifices.

3   Also new to this processional was the distinctive clothing worn by some of the Levites. First, those carrying the Ark wore robes of fine linen. The people's focus was drawn to the striking sight of the Ark of the Covenant on the shoulders of specially robed Levites. The chosen singers, along with their director Chenaniah, were also prominently arrayed in linen robes. Being set apart in this way helped the choir unite the multitude of celebrants in singing praise to Israel's great God.

4   King David wore the same robe, along with a linen ephod. The ephod was an elaborate skirt designed to be worn over the robe of Israel's high priest. Attached to the high priest's ephod were stones on which the names of Israel's tribes had been inscribed. The high priest thus brought the names of the children of Israel with him when he ministered in the presence of God. With David arrayed in priestly vestments, the people could easily identify him as he danced and played an instrument with all of his might in God's presence. Animated and even extravagant in his worship, David encouraged the people, by his example, to

give thanks and praise to the LORD with their whole hearts. They brought the Ark to its new home with singing, shouting, playing, and dancing.

5   Sadly, not everyone in Jerusalem praised God that day. As David's wife Michal watched him from a window, she despised him in her heart. To her, David did not look very dignified or kingly as he celebrated the Ark's coming with unbridled enthusiasm while wearing priestly attire. After David returned home, Michal mocked him, saying,

> How glorious was the King of Israel today, who exposed himself in the sight of his servants and behaved shamelessly like a worthless man!

But he did not show embarrassment, as Michal had hoped, about the way he honored God; instead, he became even more resolute and responded,

> It was before the LORD who chose me to rule over Israel. I will continue to worship freely in the presence of the LORD and be even more contemptible in my own sight.

Here was David's heart. He was not showing off or even thinking of himself. He did not dishonor the Holy God of Israel. Quite the contrary, he praised God so extravagantly because he was in the presence of God. He lost himself in his God, his gracious and merciful God; he honored God with no thought for his own reputation or the dignity of his office as King of Israel. David's first concern was God – His reputation and His glory.

6   With the king leading the way in his selfless worship of God, the Ark of the Covenant at last arrived in the City of David. To David, the end of the processional was just the beginning of the benefit and blessings. With the Ark now publicly accessible, the entire nation could honor God and enjoy His presence among them. And the God of the Ark could bless the household of every Israelite, as He had blessed the household of Obededom the Gittite. David placed the Ark in the tent he had prepared for it, but the celebration was not finished.

7   David, and those celebrating with him, sacrificed again, this time at the new home for the Ark of the Covenant. Here, in the presence of their Holy God, they offered whole burnt offerings, thus giving themselves completely to God. They also burned the fat of the peace offerings, acknowledging God and His goodness with praise and gratitude. David then blessed the people and gave each celebrant a loaf of bread, a portion of wine, and an ample piece of meat from the peace offerings. God's people ate and drank together as they took in the meaning of this spectacular event. God was with them and accepted them this time. They, in turn, received God and committed themselves to honor and glorify Him.

8   God's presence among His people – an essential part of His covenant relation with them – carried risks that became obvious during David's first attempt to relocate the Ark. But he did not give up; he received instruction from God's law and made the necessary corrections to complete the relocation. A summary of differences between the two processionals highlights the many changes David made.

The Failed Move	The Successful Move
David offered the Levites a special invitation.	The Levites were organized and given a special place.
The Ark traveled on an ox-driven cart.	Sanctified Levites carried the Ark on their shoulders.
All of Israel helped move the Ark together, as equals.	The Levites led Israel in bringing the Ark to its place.
The people praised God before the Ark with one purpose but with many voices as each desired.	The Levites led united praise in the singing, playing, and rejoicing before the Ark.
There was no distinctive clothing.	Certain Levites who ministered at the celebration wore linen robes.
There were no sacrifices.	The Israelites sacrificed many burnt offerings and peace offerings.

5-3 David appoints Levites to praise God daily

(I Chronicles 16:4-7, 37-43)

After the Ark was in its place, David appointed 68 Levites to minister before the Ark of the LORD every day, to record the goodness of God, and to thank and praise the LORD God of Israel. Asaph, with his cymbals, led this group, which sang and played the psaltery or harp. David also appointed two priests to play trumpets continuously in the presence of the LORD. Their music blessed and exalted God by giving Him the honor due His holy name.

2　　In addition, the family of Obededom, porters during the Ark's second processional, was among those chosen to work as porters here at the Ark. All of these Levite ministers blessed the Israelite worshippers as well by facilitating their praise to God in His holy presence. In making these appointments, David honored the calling of the Levites to minister to God and bless in His name.

3　　Next, David set priests and Levites to minister before the tabernacle at the high place in Gibeon. Since the altar was there, the priest Zadok and his family offered the daily, weekly, monthly, and annual sacrifices required in God's law. While some Levites supported the priests, David appointed many Levites to work as musicians at the tabernacle. Heman and Jeduthun (earlier called Ethan), with their trumpets and cymbals, led this group in giving praise to the LORD. Yet another group of Levites, the sons of Jeduthun, were selected to be porters at the tabernacle. None of these Levites were part-time volunteers; they were specifically chosen by name to minister daily before the LORD, Whose mercy endures forever.

4　　David was greatly blessed. The expanded ministry of the Levites occurred step by step as he adapted to each change in circumstance. Initially, he acted on his desire to establish the presence of God among His people. Then, after Uzza's death, he appointed Levite musicians to minister during the Ark's second processional. Lastly, when the Ark was in its place, David appointed the Levites to a permanent service of worship at two locations. Being able to write songs, play instruments, and even craft instruments, he could support and encourage the Levites in their new ministries of worship. These musical skills along with his personal desire to exalt God made David the right man in the right place to establish appropriate new ways for the Levites to honor God and give Him praise.

God's effective judgments

5   David and Israel rejoiced – but was God pleased or did He merely tolerate David's activities? If God saw anything good in these events, why did His harsh judgment fall upon Uzza when David and Israel were united in praising Him with all their hearts? At five other key historical times, when God had been revealing His glory and power in spectacular ways, His severe and holy judgment resulted in deaths that cast a shadow upon the radiance of those days.

(1) Shortly after the new nation of Israel had left Egypt, while Moses was receiving God's law on Mt Sinai, which was visibly ablaze with the glory of His presence, Aaron and the people crafted idols. The people of Israel then worshipped those idols, giving them the credit for their deliverance from Egypt. Thousands died as God plagued the people for their idolatry and as Levites stood with God and slew their fellow Israelites with the sword.

(2) Within one year of that event, God twice showed the glory of His presence. God manifested Himself when the tabernacle was initially assembled and then again during the first ceremony in the tabernacle when the nation anointed Aaron and his four sons to be priests. But two of Aaron's newly-anointed sons foolishly entered the new tabernacle in their own way and died in the presence of the Holy God.

(3) God again demonstrated His greatness when Joshua led Israel in an awe-inspiring crossing of the Jordan River and then in a sensational victory over the city of Jericho. Because one man, Achan, disobeyed God's command not to loot Jericho, God left Israel to fight its battles – unsuccessfully – without His help until the entire nation humbly submitted to His shocking judgment that Achan, his family, and all that he possessed be stoned because he had taken loot from Jericho.

(4) Many centuries later, God's Holy Spirit came upon the new church of Jesus' followers and filled them with His power. While God was multiplying this new church and expanding its influence, a husband and wife among them died dramatic, public deaths after they had agreed to present a dishonest offering to the church.

6   As with all of God's actions, the mortal judgments that took place at these highly significant times were just and righteous. Intentional and unintentional error stood out against the backdrop of God's holy activities and could

not be tolerated. But God, by His judgments, does more than implement His holy standard of living and accomplishes much more than the punishment of sin and the correction of error.

(5) Never did error stand out more than when Jesus carried the sin of the world, and never was the judgment so severe or the shadow so dark as when he died for our sins.

7   God acts out of His boundless wisdom, and His judgments are always appropriate, both to the historical situation and to His purposes. This occasion, the relocation of the Ark, held great possibilities. One of God's purposes has always been to establish praise among His people, but the first move of the Ark yielded only voluntary, individually expressed praise, which would stop after the move was complete. To David's dismay, God halted that processional. Yet, David was God's man; he came to understand God's purposes and then acted to support them. God Himself orchestrated these events; He directed David to give the Levites their special and intended place, ultimately instituting daily praise at the Ark of His presence and at the tabernacle. Not only was God's judgment against Uzza just according to His law, but this judgment also advanced His purposes, both for Israel and for King David.

God advances His eternal purposes

8   Even more, God was working out some of His universal and eternal purposes. By His prophet Moses, God said to a resistant Pharaoh,

> *For this purpose I have raised you up ... that My name may be declared throughout all the earth.*

And that is what happened; God made for Himself an everlasting and glorious name when He delivered His people from slavery in Egypt and brought them safely across the Red Sea. Two years later, when an unbelieving Israel refused to go in and take the land of Canaan, God declared to an interceding Moses,

> *As truly as I live, all the earth shall be filled with the glory of the LORD.*

The prophet Isaiah saw a vision of God on His throne, with angels above the throne crying out to each other,

> *Holy, holy, holy is the LORD of Hosts: the whole earth is full of His glory.*

Human eyes see few, if any, places on earth that are full of God's glory, yet these angels proclaim as a fact, "the whole earth is full of His glory." They know that God's eternal purposes are sure to be fulfilled.

9   Even though it is God's purpose for His name to be declared in all the earth and for His glory to fill all the earth, He does not force that reality on the world. God does not compel the earth's inhabitants to believe in Him or to worship Him. Rather, He asserts,

> *This people have I formed for Myself; they shall show forth My praise.*

God has chosen to build up a people who praise their most mighty and worthy LORD. God will have a believing people who fill the earth with His glory, not a fearful, unbelieving people like the soldiers who ran from Goliath's challenge. When David moved the Ark of the Covenant and gave it a central place in Israel, he acted in harmony with God's covenant plans. When he then established daily worship at the Ark, David accomplished important works toward the fulfillment of God's eternal purposes. God's people were now giving Him more praise in more ways and in more places.

5-4 David's psalm of thanksgiving to God
(I Chronicles 16:8-36. See Psalms 105:1-15, 96, and 106:47,48.)

It had been a great celebration, and David humbly gave thanks and glory to God for all of it. David's first song for Asaph was one of thanksgiving to the LORD. His psalm for this occasion was a medley of mainly two psalms, which honored God in wide, glowing terms and proclaimed His glory, which was filling the earth.

> Give thanks unto the LORD, call upon His name,
>> make known His deeds among the people.
> Sing unto Him, sing psalms unto Him,
>> talk of all His wondrous works.
> Glory in His holy name:
>> let the heart of them rejoice that seek the LORD.
> Seek the LORD and His strength,
>> seek His face continually.
> Remember His marvelous works that He has done,
>> His wonders, and the judgments of His mouth;
> O ye seed of Israel His servant,
>> ye children of Jacob, His chosen ones.
> He is the LORD our God;
>> His judgments are in all the earth.
> Be mindful always of His covenant;
>> the word which He commanded
>> to a thousand generations;
> Even of the covenant
>> which He made with Abraham,
>> and of His oath unto Isaac;
> And has confirmed the same to Jacob for a law,
>> and to Israel for an everlasting covenant,
> Saying, "Unto thee will I give the land of Canaan,
>> the lot of your inheritance;"

When ye were but few, even a few, and strangers in it.
　　　And when they went from nation to nation,
　　　and from one kingdom to another people;
He suffered no man to do them wrong:
　　　yea, He reproved kings for their sakes,
Saying, "Touch not Mine anointed,
　　　and do my prophets no harm".

Sing unto the LORD, all the earth;
　　　show forth from day to day His salvation.
Declare His glory among the heathen;
　　　His marvelous works among all nations.
For great is the LORD, and greatly to be praised:
　　　He also is to be feared above all gods.
For all the gods of the people are idols:
　　　but the LORD made the heavens.
Glory and honor are in His presence;
　　　strength and gladness are in His place.
Give unto the LORD, ye kindred of the people,
　　　give unto the LORD glory and strength.
　　　give unto the LORD the glory due unto his name:
Bring an offering, and come before Him:
　　　worship the LORD in the beauty of holiness.
Fear before Him, all the earth:
　　　the world also shall be stable, that it be not moved.
Let the heavens be glad, and let the earth rejoice:
　　　and let men say among the nations,
　　　"The LORD reigns."
Let the sea roar, and the fullness thereof:
　　　let the fields rejoice, and all that is therein.
Then shall the trees of the wood sing out at the presence of the LORD,
　　　because He comes to judge the earth.

O give thanks unto the LORD;
　　　for He is good; for His mercy endures forever.
And say ye, "Save us, O God of our salvation,
　　　and gather us together

and deliver us from the heathen,
that we may give thanks to Thy holy name,
and glory in Thy praise."
Blessed be the LORD God of Israel for ever and ever.
And all the people said, "Amen," and praised the LORD.

Chapter 6

David's Heart for God and God's Heart for David

6A God Reveals Some of His Eternal Purposes to David

6-1 David wants to build a house for God
(I Chronicles 17:1, 2; II Samuel 7:1-3)

This shepherd boy made king began his reign very effectively. Israel had in Jerusalem a capital city worthy of God's people. A neighboring king encouraged David in his place as king over God's people when he generously erected a magnificent royal palace in Jerusalem. A major battle victory demonstrated the increasing readiness of Israel's army and provided peace and security around Jerusalem. The Levites now led Israel in offering praise to God daily at two locations. For Israel and for David, such obvious progress produced an atmosphere of joy and gratitude. The nation was growing up as God's people.

2   While this growth demonstrated God's blessings upon His people, it blessed God as well. In fact, this was a special moment for God, and David was His man. The deep desire of David's heart for God's glory became God's opportunity to speak a great new word of revelation in the earth, but He did not speak directly to David.

3   This remarkable occasion began as a time of worship for David. God had so clearly blessed him. His palace provided an abundance of luxury to enjoy. The national celebration to relocate the Ark of the Covenant was a wonder-filled event for him to dwell upon. At the nearby Ark, Asaph led musicians in offering praise to God. With such clear expressions of God's goodness available to occupy his meditations, David was inspired with a way to bless God, a way to give back to his gracious God. He told the prophet Nathan,

> I live in a grand cedar house, but the Ark of the Covenant of the LORD
> is in a tent.

David wanted to build a house for God. Not only could he honor God with a magnificent dwelling place, but he could also impress the people of other nations with the greatness of Israel's Almighty God. He waited to hear what Nathan thought.

4   (Nathan appeared abruptly onto this scene without a known history. He was a trusted advisor to David and likely to Solomon as well; the Bible mentions that

Nathan wrote about the reigns of both David and Solomon. God could talk to
Nathan and trust him to deliver His message clearly. He appeared during two
other events in the Bible. One of those was the tragic time when Nathan faced
the king with God's convicting word after David's multiple sins regarding Uriah
the Hittite and his wife Bathsheba. Nathan also aided in the urgent installment
of Solomon as Israel's next king. Two of Nathan's sons became officials in
Solomon's court.)

5   Nathan saw the best motives in David's desire, so he urged the king forward
by responding,

> Do all that is in your heart because God is with you.

When Samuel anointed him, David received God's Spirit. Nathan noticed that
God had remained with David personally; if such a spiritual man wanted to do
a work for God, how could he oppose that desire? Nathan was confident that, as
David carried out his plan, he would seek God humbly, accept direction or correction as needed, and bring more glory to God.

6   Nathan, God's prophet and David's advisor, told David exactly what he
wanted to hear and gave him total freedom with this building project. As a service to God and with the support of Nathan's word, David could commit himself to building THE house for the Ark of the Covenant; God's house was worthy
to receive all of his time, attention, and resources.

6-2 God says that David cannot do it

(I Chronicles 17:3-6; II Samuel 7:4-7)

But God did not want David to build His house, and Nathan's advice had to
be corrected immediately. Although David needed a strong, clear word to stop
him, God did not personally speak to David. Instead, God came to Nathan that
very night and sent Nathan to deliver His message. God commanded Nathan,

> Go and tell David my servant, "Thus saith the LORD, You shall not
> build a house for Me."

A surprising word – but God's word. The response recorded in II Samuel provides additional perspective. In that passage, God did not directly tell David no,
yet He seemed to question why David thought that he should be the one to build
such a house. God asked,

> Shall you build a house for Me to dwell in?

2   Next, God gave Nathan two reasons for not allowing David to build. First,
He noted,

> I have not lived in a house from the day I brought Israel out of Egypt
> until now.

He further pointed out,

> I have gone from tent to tent and from one tabernacle to another.

God had only temporary and portable places of residence. God could never be locked into a time or space. Solomon would later acknowledge,

> *The heavens cannot contain God; how much less an earthly dwelling that I build.*

Having a tent for an earthly house did not bother God.

3   In fact, God honored the tent that David had prepared for the Ark of the Covenant. The prophet Amos would declare a future rebuilding of the "tabernacle of David." This tent, however, is not described; the Bible records neither its dimensions nor any of its materials. Additionally, the ability to come to David's tent and worship in God's presence was apparently unrestricted; no mention is made of any required cleansing, atoning sacrifice, cloud of incense burning, or any other necessary ritual. Such priestly services were performed at the tabernacle in Gibeon. Thus, during the remainder of David's reign, access to the holy place of Moses' tabernacle required holy men and legal rituals while access to David's tent with the Ark of the Covenant – that is, access to the most holy place of God's presence – was freely available to all, without restriction and without prerequisite deed, gift, or sacrifice. James, an early church leader who expounded on the prophecy of Amos, declared that David's "tabernacle" – not Moses' tabernacle and not Solomon's temple – would be repaired and restored to give all people a way to seek God. (Interestingly, soon after he became king, Solomon demonstrated that David's tabernacle was a special site for making offerings. Immediately after God had promised him remarkable, unexpected blessings, Solomon purposely traveled from Israel's official altar of sacrifice at Gibeon to Jerusalem in order to offer sacrifices of commitment and thanksgiving before the Ark of the Covenant.)

4   God gave Nathan a second reason for telling David no:

> *In all my travels with Israel, did I ever ask any judge or leader in Israel, "Why have you not built Me a house?"*

Not only did God not need a house, He had never asked for one. God did command Moses to make a tabernacle where He could live among His people, but that tabernacle was a tent patterned after the tabernacle in heaven. God had in heaven a house better than an exceptional residence that David, or anyone else, might design and build.

5   God did not tell David to build Him a house; the project was David's idea. Solomon was later to say,

> *God told my father David, "You did well for having the idea in your heart to build a house for My name."*

Very significantly, God both recognized and commended the deep desire of David's heart – it was God's desire as well. He too wanted a house built to His name, but not now and not designed by David. God would reveal that part of His plan to David later in his life and under much different circumstances

(Chapters 8 and 9 of this book). For now, God sent Nathan to deliver an emphatic no.

You shall not build a house for Me to live in.

6-3 God reminds David what He has already done
(I Chronicles 17:7, 8; II Samuel 7:8,9)

But God did not end with no. Here and now, God had an opportunity to declare some of His vast eternal purposes, which included David. God prefaced this revelation in His words to Nathan:

Now say to My servant David, "Thus saith the LORD of Hosts."

The God of this far-reaching revelation had hosts of resources, servants, and armies at His command. David had experienced that the LORD of Hosts was well able work out some of His incomprehensible plans, and now, before telling him even more, God told Nathan to review what He had already done for David.

Three reminders:

2   First, God reminded David of the change He had made in his life and said,

I took you from your shepherding responsibilities in order that you should be ruler over My people Israel.

From leading sheep to leading God's people: what a promotion! God did it. Next, God reminded David,

I have been with you everywhere you walked.

Every step of the way, he had the benefit and blessing of God's presence, even during those trying times when he did not see or feel it, but felt instead the trouble surrounding him. And finally, God reminded David,

I have given you victory over all of your enemies and have exalted your name like the names of the earth's great men.

Saul made himself David's enemy, but even with his authority to use Israel's resources, King Saul could not kill him. The mighty Philistines also made themselves David's enemy, and were routed. He had other enemies too, but the LORD of Hosts had been with him to make him a victorious and internationally renowned king.

3   Significantly, God twice referred to David as His servant. God said to Nathan,

Go and tell David My servant.

And again,

Say to My servant David.

David had been maturing. As a young man learning to serve in the household of his father Jesse, he was also learning to serve God. After Samuel had anointed him, David continued to grow as a servant who learned to trust God, not only when he was blessed and obedient, but also when he was perplexed and distressed with difficult situations or serious mistakes. As God advanced His purposes in the earth and did great things for Israel, He found David to be a servant whom He could trust with abundant blessings, many of which were beyond what David or anyone else could conceive. He was a man in whom God had already demonstrated His grace and great glory.

Three reasons to remember

4 David needed these reminders. His power and success could easily corrupt his heart. Basking in the glory of being King of Israel, he could begin to think that he belonged there. As he began to grasp his great authority and all of the good he had already done, he might think himself quite worthy and deserving of such power. His memory of his narrow escapes, timely deliverances, and spectacular victories could give him a feeling of invincibility. However, such thoughts would drastically disfigure the reality of David's situation. Apart from God, he belonged at home as the youngest son. Apart from God, he deserved to be a shepherd. Apart from God, he would be dead. David needed to remember that his power and success resulted from God's anointing, God's calling, God's merciful care, and God's gracious provision.

5 David also needed these reminders because he was famous. He faced a strong and dangerous temptation to trust in his influential status and abuse the respect that people had for him. He needed to remember that God had exalted him and had given him great influence in the world, and in doing so, God had extended His Own glory on the earth. David did not choose or earn his prominent place in the world or in God's purposes; God and God alone had placed him there.

6 Finally, David needed these reminders because God was about to reveal some of His eternal plans, including some of His future purposes for His people and His Own kingdom. And God was about to give David some important roles. When he did not understand what God was doing, he could remain God's servant and, in every circumstance, trust the LORD of Hosts to carry out His purposes for the future. These reminders of what God had already done would help foster the humble, dependent frame of mind that David needed as he moved forward.

6-4 God says that He will do more for David
(I Chronicles 17:9-14; II Samuel 7:10-16)

With Nathan's next words, God revealed some of His plans to David, declaring,

> *I will appoint a place for My people Israel and plant them there. They will live in their place and never again be moved; neither will wicked people be able to plunder them there.*

God had great plans for Israel; He promised to give the nation of His chosen people a fixed place and a protected place. Such a security for his nation would thrill any king. Not only would this promise give David more confidence in his desire to act for Israel's blessing, its fulfillment would also become a crucial part of his calling (Sections 7–1 and 10–1 of this book).

2   God continued,

>*I will subdue all of your enemies.*

This assurance, too, would delight any leader. David had many powerful enemies yet to face; both Israel's enemies and God's enemies would actively oppose him. Yet God had spoken victory; David could trust Him and be at peace.

Eight promises for David's family and kingdom

3   Next, God elaborated on what He planned to do for David and his family with a list containing eight separate promises, one of which He repeated. God said that He would

(1) build David a house,

(2) raise up David's seed after his death,

(3) establish the kingdom of David's son, and

(4) establish the throne of David's son forever.

4   It is noteworthy that God promised,

>*The LORD will build you a house.*

This is what he wanted to do for God. God reflected David's very desire back on him as a huge blessing. David was thinking of a material building, but God wanted to build him a family and a kingdom.

5   Providing a glimpse of what He had designed for David's house, God continued,

>*After you die, I will raise up one of your sons and establish his kingdom.*
>*I will establish the throne of your son forever.*

David himself had no power or control after his death, and his activities while he lived could guarantee nothing. But God promised to set David's son on the throne of the kingdom after him. Once again, God had spoken, giving David further reason to trust Him and be at peace.

6   God not only promised that David's son would be king, He also promised that He would establish the throne and kingdom of David's son. By God's power and purpose, the kingdom of David's son was to be stable and secure, rooted as firmly as any kingdom on earth had ever been. Even more, God said *forever*. Forever! That was not an exaggeration. God declared that the throne of David's son would outlast the earth and all of its kingdoms.

7   God briefly interjected,

>*Your son will build a house for Me.*

God chose a man, a son from the royal house that He had just promised to build for David, to do the great work of building His house. Although David might be thrilled that his son would do this great work, he may have wondered why he could not build God's house himself, especially if it were to be built anyway. Years later, a persistent David would ready himself to build the house for God. Once again, but for a new reason (described in Section 10–1 of this book), God would not allow David to build His house. While He honored David's desire and idea, God had His Own plan. Near the end of David's reign, God would give him a second extraordinary revelation, which energized him to carry out vital preparation tasks in advance of his son's work of building God's house (Chapters 9 and 11 of this book).

8   But the focus of this revelation was the house that God had in mind for David. Its extent was already inconceivable, yet God continued by promising to

(5) be a father to David's son,

(6) never take His mercy from David's son,

(7) set David's son in God's house forever,

(8) set David's son in God's kingdom forever, and

(4 repeated) establish the throne of David's son forever.

9   God became personally involved in the life of David's son and said,

   I will be his father, and he shall be My son.

With this promise, David could relax and trust God with the growth and development of his son. While David would prove to be a faulty father, the wise, loving God would provide the perfect combination of nurture, instruction, and discipline. Even more, David's son would be God's son, a part of the royal family of the great King over all!

10   God graciously continued,

   I will not take My mercy from him as I took it from Saul.

God had rejected the rebellious King Saul and his good sons too, but He promised never to reject David's son. Because of God's mercy, the place of David's son in God's plan was secure. Such a reassuring word was important since David's son, and David himself, would often need great mercy. Indeed, all daughters and sons of all time would need great mercy – all except one, all except Jesus, who never sinned.

11   God concluded this revelation by assuring David,

   I will settle your son in My house and in My kingdom forever; his throne will be established forever.

God immediately confirmed His remarkable promise to establish the throne of David's son! With an additional promise to settle him in God's house and in God's kingdom forever, He provided a secure place and future for David's son. The house and kingdom of David's son would work together with God's house and kingdom, aiding and supporting each other's growth.

12   Three times God declared that His eternal purposes for David's son were to continue forever – an exceptional guarantee.

6B Fulfillment Preview and David's Response

[Note: The narration in 6B slows to dwell on God's revelation and consider parts of it more deeply.]

6-5 Scope and gospel fulfillment of God's promises to David

Forever … God's son … God's kingdom. God revealed some truly amazing plans in response to David's simple desire to build a house for the Ark of the Covenant. David could not comprehend them. Even though he knew God well and meditated on how he could bless God extravagantly, his imaginations were largely confined to the family and the world he knew. David might think that God's kingdom meant the kingdom of His people in Israel, and his understanding of forever would be extremely limited. The scope of God's promises to David extended far beyond what could ever be fulfilled in any earthly kingdom or by the physical offspring of David's royal seed. Why did God express purposes that were incomprehensible to anyone in time or space?

2   David, in his desire to build a house for God, was in harmony with God, and his heart of worship opened the way for God to speak a great, new word in the world. God often speaks to those who hear Him, and each time His word can affect one or many lives. But here, in this special moment with David, God expressed some of His vast, eternal purposes affecting the whole earth.

3   God had previously spoken great, universal words to Noah, to Abraham, and to Moses. Special words from God also came to others, including many of the prophets. Later, on a personal and exalted level, God's eternal word came to the world in Jesus. As the rain and snow both water the earth and make it fruitful, so God's word prospers in the world and accomplishes His purposes. Since God's Own authority is behind every word He speaks, all of His declarations on these grand occasions will be fulfilled when the time is right.

4   For a noteworthy example, Abraham could never have imagined the vast scope of the promises God made to him. Many centuries before David lived, God had declared to Abraham,

In you and your seed shall all nations of the earth be blessed.

God also told Abraham,

I have made you the father of many nations.

An aged Abraham had no idea how God might fulfill these promises, but Abraham believed God. Abraham's faith pleased God, and it became a model of belief. Yet God had even more in mind than giving visible blessings to all earthly nations; God also purposed to give abundant spiritual blessings to the vast family of those who would follow Abraham's example of believing God.

5   Likewise, when God spoke to David, He had much more in mind than David's physical family and earthly kingdom. For instance, the peace and security He promised Israel were a part of God's far-reaching purposes for all of His people called by His name.

Jesus: the Son of David

6   Most significantly, God had Jesus in mind. From his birth in the lineage of David to his eventual reign on the throne of David, key aspects of Jesus' life and calling were set in motion or advanced by God's potent word. In this revelation,

God promised to be a father to David's son. When He made this promise, God not only spoke of a son whom David would personally father, He also spoke of Jesus. Twenty-eight generations (about 1000 years) later, Jesus would be physically born into David's royal family as the son of Mary and her fiancé Joseph prior to the consummation of their marriage. The Scriptures often give Jesus the title Son of David, and Jesus declared himself to be the offspring of David.

Jesus: the Son of God

7   Additionally, God said that David's son would be His Son. This promise too was ultimately fulfilled in Jesus, Who was God's Son in both a literal and an eternal sense. Although Jesus was born in the same manner as any other person, his conception was unique. Jesus was supernaturally conceived in his mother Mary by God's Spirit. At Jesus' birth, he was called Saviour, Christ the Lord, and King – titles that embody God's purposes for His Son. During his life on earth, Jesus was clearly revealed to be the Christ, the Messiah, and the Son of the living God. Jesus came as the King of the Jews with the divine calling to save God's people from their sins.

God's purpose to save the world

8   God's plans for this promised Son of David included more. Since God loved the world – because God loved the whole world so much – His purpose was to save the world. The whole world needed saving because sin had entered the earth when Adam, the first man God created, disobeyed Him. As God had warned, Adam's sin resulted in death – a slavery to sin, a relentless decay, and an end of life. This death affected all of God's good creation, as well as Adam and his wife Eve. In addition, because Adam is the father of the whole human race and because each individual has also sinned, this death was passed to every person conceived with the seed of a man.

Two universal problems

9   The effects of sin are deeply personal. Every person is guilty of sin; each individual fails to live up to God's law and to the internal standard residing in his or her own conscience. Additionally, no one is able to stop sinning and start living a life perfectly acceptable to the glorious God. These two problems, sin-guilt and imperfection, have plagued the entire human race. The tragedy is that no person with either problem can ever come into the presence of God. Yes, God had provided mercy and forgiveness for sins on Israel's annual Day of Atonement, but this provision did not permanently deal with the sin problem; the ceremony had to be repeated every year. Furthermore, no one, not even the priest who offered the blood of the sacrifice, could ever attain God's requirement of perfect righteousness – neither by offering sacrifices nor by performing activities of worship. As it was with Israel's priests, so it is with every person on earth. No one can ever do enough or give enough either to make amends for sinning or to become acceptable to the entirely Just and Holy God. But God provided the permanent solution to both of these universal problems when He sent Jesus, His Son and

David's son, to earth. Jesus did not come to condemn sinners; all have been condemned by their own sin and unbelief. Every person needs the solution God has provided in Jesus.

Jesus suffers an unjust and undeserved crucifixion

10   As the Son of David, Jesus lived a human life on earth and had a natural, physical body, even though he had been conceived without the seed of a man. Because of his unique conception as the Son of God, Jesus began his life without being corrupted by the sin and death passed down from Adam to every other person. Jesus then lived without sinning against God or man; he never needed mercy or forgiveness. Nevertheless, the rulers of his own people convicted him of blasphemy against God and sentenced him to die. By framing Jesus and then making certain that the Roman authorities crucified him, these religious leaders unwittingly participated in God's plan. Yet, in the face of this unmerited opposition, Jesus did not defend himself, appeal his conviction, or resist the harsh death sentence. In fact, his part in God's profound plan to save the world included suffering these injustices. Acting on the steadfastness of his faith in God, Jesus faced the shame of his wrongful conviction and endured the horror of his undeserved crucifixion. Exhibiting the strength of his meek and lowly character, Jesus remained humble and obedient to his calling, all the way to his death on the cross.

Jesus solves the sin problem

11   But his death was infinitely more than an unjust end to his life, a martyrdom, or a selfless sacrifice. Having no sin of his own, Jesus was able to take our sins in his own body when he was nailed to his cross. Instead of confronting sin, he bore it; instead of engaging a cosmic struggle against the forces of evil, Jesus allowed them to do their worst to him. His enemies mistakenly thought they were defeating the God-sent Saviour when Jesus willingly offered his life to be sacrificed as the unblemished Lamb of God Who takes away the sin of the world.

12   In a legal action, God condemned the sin that Jesus bore in his flesh. God's mortal judgment against sin – the sin Jesus carried, the sin passed down from Adam, and the sin corrupting humanity – His judgment against sin was just. Throughout history, sin has incriminated itself by its dreadful misuse of God's holy law. Sin actually uses the just mandates of the law to deceive and frustrate the efforts of people who want to live right – until even their good desires to obey God's law are extinguished. Carrying this condemned sin to his cross, Jesus put away sin forever by the sacrifice of himself. Since that day, God has not needed, desired, or accepted any further sacrifice for sin. In addition, Jesus Christ came in the flesh as a man and experienced human death in order to destroy the devil, who had the power of death, along with his evil deeds.

13   After Jesus poured out his life unto death, he brought his precious life's blood into God's presence. This priceless sin offering, made by a man who was also a flawless high priest representing humanity, satisfied the Just God and His justice. In God's presence, Jesus obtained eternal redemption, the release from the

bondage and effects of sin that each person needed so desperately. When sin controls a person, the end result is death, but when God's grace reigns, the end result is life eternal. Each person who believes that the sin-bearing Jesus died for his or her sins is free from guilt, justified by God's grace. Each believer is also redeemed, cleansed, and forgiven through Jesus' blood. The entirely good God shows off the riches of His grace, the grace that enables all who believe in Christ Jesus, both Israelites and non-Israelites, to live with purpose and to be at peace with God and with each other. The universal problem of sin and guilt is now solved.

Jesus solves the imperfection problem

14   At the same time he offered his blood, Jesus offered himself to God. Jesus' perfect, human righteousness <u>satisfied the Holy God and His holiness</u>; it was the very perfection that people needed. In the same spiritual way that Adam's sin makes every person a condemned sinner, Jesus' perfect obedience makes every believer righteous in Christ Jesus. God Himself was active in solving this problem; it was God Who made Jesus to be sin for us. And now, having fully accepted Jesus' redemptive work, God also credits Jesus' perfect righteousness to believing sinners. Since this righteousness meets God's perfect standard, the second universal problem, imperfection, is now solved.

God establishes His covenant relationship with believers

15   The amazing solution to these two universal problems was but the beginning of what was accomplished when God sent His Son and David's son to earth. Jesus gives believers eternal life. Additionally, Jesus gives believers the Holy Spirit of God to dwell in them, to empower them, and to seal them permanently in Christ. Justified believers are one body in Christ Jesus. When Jesus offered himself to God, he also opened a way for all believers to enter the holiest place of God's presence. God now accepts believers into His holy presence in the same way He accepted Jesus, the world's Saviour. Since Jesus' saving work has completely dealt with their sin, believers can be confident in God's presence. Correspondingly, God now lives in and among believers as their God because they have received the mercy, forgiveness, and righteousness effected by Jesus' saving work. Thus, the two-way covenant relation that God has wanted with His people has been established forever.

Jesus still working for believers

16   After Jesus offered one sacrifice for sins forever, God raised him up from the dead. This is eternal victory over death; Jesus can never die again. God then exalted Jesus to sit at His side as the Lord of heaven and earth with authority over all creation. By God's gracious, spiritual work, each believer in Christ Jesus has been crucified with Christ into the death that mortally judged sin, has been raised with Christ into the life that is free from sin's power to enslave, and has been seated with Christ into the authority that is above all earthly powers and demonic forces. From heaven, Jesus prays and works to complete God's purposes for believers. Two of God's purposes for all of His people, individually

and collectively, are to be united as one body conformed into the image of His Son, Jesus, and to be a temple, worshipping God in His presence. Jesus, as the head of the church of God's people, is now implementing both purposes. God continually supplies the gifts and grace needed by believers who assemble together for mutual exhortation and encouragement, and who serve together for the blessing and growth of the whole body of believers. The effectiveness of his intercession and the continuing power of his sacrifice are two other ways Jesus works to accomplish the purposes of God for His people.

Jesus destined to rule on David's throne

17   Additionally, as the Son of David, Jesus is destined to sit on the throne of David. When God promised to establish the throne and kingdom of David's son forever and to settle it in His Own kingdom, He also expressed purposes for His Own Son to rule His kingdom. Every power and authority in heaven and on earth will be subdued under His Son's authority. Jesus shall reign over all of his enemies, over all of the earth's kingdoms, and over all of creation as God designed. At the end of time, when he is ruling as God's completely obedient servant, Jesus will formally yield himself and all of his authority to his Father God. Jesus is the final fulfillment of the prophet Jeremiah's proclamation,

> *Thus saith the LORD, "If you can break My covenants with the day and with the night, to stop the orderly cycle of day and night, then might My covenant with David, My servant, be broken, to stop him from having a son to reign on his throne."*

6-6 David says, "Wow!" (I Chronicles 17: 15-22; II Samuel 7:17-24)

How would David react to such an astonishing revelation? God's perspective in using words like *forever* and *My son* were outside anyone's grasp. Yes, David had often experienced the wonder of God's plans. In a variety of perplexing situations, he had been learning to trust God and to serve God obediently, regardless of how little he understood. Nevertheless, the wide-ranging scope and all-encompassing effect of the purposes God had just revealed to him were unimaginable. Certainly, David could never have envisioned their fulfillment in Jesus and His eternal work.

2   This extraordinary revelation was God's response to David's desire to build a house for the Ark of the Covenant. Although Nathan had been speaking, David received the message directly from God. Stunned at this seemingly incredible word, he sat down before the LORD, and possibly beside the nearby Ark of God's presence. When David brought himself to reply, he spoke – not to Nathan, but to God – and wondered,

> *Who am I, O LORD God?*

David, in true humility, did not feel deserving. Though he was king, he did not mention that to God. God had blessed David continually and bountifully, but David gave no hint that he expected additional blessings. His heart's desire was to give back to God, yet God gave him even more. When he attempted to bless God, God added to David's blessings. When David sought to glorify God, God spoke and acted in the world for His Own glory.

3 (It must be noted that at a later time David would experience the negative side of this principle. He would then act proudly in grave sins against God and Uriah. God would again send Nathan, but this time to declare His plans to curse David and his family. Sadly, the just God would then act less to honor David and more to shame him. The more serious David's sins as the head of his household were, the more forcefully God had to intervene to preserve His Own glory and holy name. Although David would confess these sins, repent, and receive mercy, he and his family would suffer severe consequences. The historians authoring I Chronicles chose not to repeat these disgraceful events.)

4 On this blessed occasion, however, David honored God. Remembering his family roots, he asked,

What is my family that You have brought me so far?

David was amazed that God had made him king, but he went on to acknowledge that God's newly revealed purposes were so much greater.

Yet this was small in Your sight, O LORD God, since You have now spoken of Your servant's house for a great while to come.

He humbly continued,

You have regarded me like a man born into royalty, O LORD God.

By making David king and then making these grand promises, God was treating him as though he were of royal birth.

5 David was almost speechless before God and said,

What more can David say to You?

Then, he found the ability to say,

You know your servant.

While he grasped for words, he took his place as God's servant. In his heart, he did not see himself as a king or a member of royalty who is entitled to great blessings. In order to accept promises that seemed unnecessarily extravagant, he rested in his God Who knew him and knew how to deal with His servant. He felt extremely blessed, and credited God, saying,

For Your servant's sake, and according to Your Own heart, You have done all this greatness in revealing all these great things.

The phrase, "according to Your Own heart," not only offers a reason that God gave this revelation, it also helps explain the vast scope of the revelation. In addition, David's words show that he knew something about God's heart.

6 Still overwhelmed, David exalted God even more highly:

O LORD, there is none like You. There is no God beside You, according to everything we have heard.

His thoughts lingered on his marvelous God, Who had done more than respond to His servant's temple-building desire: God had expressed His eternal purposes. No other god could compare to the God Who gave this revelation.

7 David next took special note of the promises God had made to Israel and marveled,

> *What one nation on earth is like Your people Israel, whom You redeemed to be Your Own people?*

By redeeming the descendants of Israel from slavery in Egypt and making them His people, God not only made a great name for Himself in the earth, but He also exalted the nation of Israel above the nations of the earth. David then recalled,

> *You made Israel to be Your Own people forever, and You, LORD, became their God.*

Considering His covenant agreement with Israel, God's speaking great plans for them did not surprise David.

8 With his humble acknowledgements and tributes to God, David displayed a pure heart that would remain a servant of God, even if God chose to bless him over and over again. He accepted God's word and wisdom without expressing any unworthiness. He made no implication that God had made a mistake in choosing him, in blessing him, or in speaking such glorious promises to him. David rested in the knowledge that the great God Who knew him was the God Who made these promises and spoke this revelation.

6-7 God includes David in His plans

Such a reply validated God's decision to speak this great, eternal word to David. At this special time, when David's heart longed to bless God in a tangible way, God proclaimed His far-reaching purposes for David's house.

2 As vital as God's declarations were, David's heart offered God more than an opportunity to express eternal purposes in the earth. David had actively supported God's plans. From his opposition to Goliath's defiance to his moving the Ark of the Covenant and establishing daily praise to God, he had become a man who would join with God and act for His glory. Even if he did not understand God's ways, David would do as he was directed, such as enforce respect for God's anointed king Saul, who was also his persecutor.

3 Now that God had expressly linked His Own Son and eternal kingdom to David's son and kingdom, God had in mind to give His servant David a significant part in advancing the plans He had just revealed. (*In fact, God gives all of His people, not just David, a role in the fulfillment of His purposes. God measures out gifts and grace, which enable each individual to do his or her part. Every deed done actually works together for good to those who, along with being called to fill a role, love God.*

⁴   Because God sees all of history clearly and understands every event that has caused the present circumstance, He knows exactly what each person can do in this present moment to work for His eternal, unchanging purposes. As God guides and assists people who trust Him, He works out His purposes for the earth and for humanity.

⁵   At the very beginning, God delegated the responsibility over the earth to the human race. God created Adam with the ability and the authority to care for the needs of the entire earth, including all life created in the earth. God and Adam communicated regularly; Adam received the instruction and guidance he needed to carry out his responsibilities. Beginning with Adam, the very first man, any person can learn what God is planning and eagerly join in on the tasks to be done.

⁶   After Adam's sin, however, tending the earth became quite challenging, even impossible at times. Adam's sin and its consequences have been passed to all humanity in all succeeding generations. These consequences have made it more difficult for each person to find out what God is doing and to join in as He directs.

⁷   Furthermore, many people now adamantly oppose God's plans, but He is never surprised. God is so wise that He actually causes such rebellion to increase His glory. God is aware that many others, maybe most, will not consider His purposes; they will not care that their actions on the earth in this present moment can work for the fulfillment of God's eternal purposes.

⁸   But God is patient. He speaks and acts from heaven within the scope of the authority and responsibility He has given to the human race. God does not intervene to accomplish what He wants done on earth just because someone does not learn His ways or participate as He directs. He does not need to. If "a Saul" does not obey Him, "a David" is prepared to follow God's direction and more than make up for Saul's lack.

⁹   Although God does not arbitrarily decree a "fix" to miserable circumstances on the earth, He is not a mere coach or cheerleader to instruct and inspire those serving Him. God acts in countless ways every day throughout the whole earth. With many seen and unseen works, God effectually moves His purposes forward. He is effective in visible public judgments or blessings, and He is just as effective in private responses, when He grants personal assistance, provision, or direction to His people who humbly cry out to Him in faith. God always looks for and encourages such faith. God has even made covenant commitments, giving His covenant partners and future generations still more reason to believe, obey, and trust Him to keep His promises.

¹⁰   While an oft-rebellious humanity has drastically slowed the fulfillment of His purposes on the earth, no person or power will ever be able to stop the eventual fulfillment of God's word. Through many stops and starts, God is forming a people who praise Him. God is calling a people who trust that He is working out His purposes in every situation.

¹¹   As God moves His plans forward, He waits for, and He finds, those individuals who will commit themselves to Him. To such people, God communicates His will, provides what is needed, and guides them as they work to do His will. Admirably,

many of God's servants have a wide view of His work; in faith they take their stand with God and call upon Him for His kingdom to come and His will to be done on earth as it is in heaven.)

¹²   At the time of his anointing by Samuel, David was a man already committed to God, resolute in taking a stand for His glory, and as he matured, he demonstrated that he was willing to expand his view of God's purposes and able to act accordingly. At this moment, when He sent Nathan to David, God did far more than direct one of His servants not to build a temple. God also took advantage of the desire within David's heart toward Him both to speak this mighty, eternal word and to direct His committed, obedient servant toward the fulfillment of parts of it.

¹³   Yes, God had important roles for David, his reign, and his kingdom to fill in advancing some of the purposes He had just revealed. In fact, David's actions done in the light of this great revelation would be necessary in order for his son to build God's house. God would reveal the details of this plan to David near the end of his life (Chapter 9 of this book).

¹⁴   Although he would also display regrettable errors that would adversely affect Israel, David's kingdom demonstrated certain qualities that provided a glimpse of God's eternal kingdom and the eternal reign of His Son, Jesus. Thus, in spite of failure and in the face of extreme opposition, God moves His plans forward. With His people filling their various roles throughout the coming millennia, God has continued to work out His word to David along with His other eternal purposes – however long the way and however long the wait.

6-8 David says, "Let it happen"
(I Chronicles 17: 23-27; II Samuel 7:25-29)

Yet, in this great word to David, God did not immediately give him a role to fill; instead, God actually prevented David from acting on his personal desire to bless Him with a house. Amazingly, David himself did not know what to do in the light of these new, unimaginable promises. He typically responded with obedient action when God spoke to him. He sought God and immediately obeyed His counsel in delivering Keilah, in chasing down the Amalekite raiders, and in fighting the Philistine army. By these deeds and many more, David demonstrated his faith in God and His word.

²   But there was no demonstration here. This man of action knew of no great feat that he could perform to exhibit his faith and gratitude toward God. He simply sat down in God's presence and wondered at the greatness of this revelation. Remarkably, David's unrehearsed reply to God cast light on the depth and quality of his heart in a way that his many notable deeds could not show.

³   When David continued, he asked God to do what He had just promised:

Therefore now, LORD, let the promises You have spoken concerning Your servant and concerning his house be established forever, and do as You have said.

In fact, David made essentially the same request a total of five times. David asked of God:

(1) Let the promises You have spoken … be established forever. (v23)
(2) Do as You have said. (v23)
(3) Let it even be established. (v24)
(4) Let the house of David Your servant be established before You forever. (v24)
(5) Let it please You to bless the house of Your servant. (v27)

David's developing heart for God

4   By asking God to do what He had promised, David displayed his heart for God in at least four ways.

(1) He showed that he accepted what God had said even though most of God's words were beyond his understanding.
(2) He testified to his agreement with God's plans, being assured that they were good and right.
(3) He took his stand with God and demonstrated his strong, personal desire for God's purposes to be accomplished.
(4) He uttered his faith that God was able to fulfill every promise He had just spoken.

5   David also voiced his confidence in God when he stated the obvious:

> LORD, You are God, Your words are true, and You have promised this goodness unto Your servant.

David did not question or resist God's generosity, knowing that God Himself had made these promises. After all, He is always a gracious and giving God, not only toward David but also toward all of His needy, trusting servants.

6   Although he was a clear beneficiary of God's promised goodness, David's five requests for God to do as He had said were not greedy pleas for more blessings. His earlier words showed that he was truly grateful, and now he continued to take his place as God's servant. David was not selfishly seizing a chance to get in on these promises; God had made the choice to include him. Neither did David expect God to bless him because he had asked so many times; he expected these promises to be fulfilled because God Himself had spoken them.

7   Additionally, beyond exhibiting his heart for God, David's reply also shed light upon qualities that made him a man after God's heart. Each of the traits listed below developed while he cared for the sheep, served King Saul, faced difficulties as a fugitive, and reigned as King of Israel.

(1) His immediate and unqualified acceptance of God's word showed that David had listened to God speak, learned to recognize His voice, and matured to receive His entire message.
(2) David's agreement with God demonstrated that he had reflected on God's plans and choices and that he had taught his heart that they were good and right.

(3) When David took his stand with God, he gave evidence that he had labored to embrace God's purposes in his heart and mind. Even more, he had resolved, as much as possible, to make God's purposes his own purposes and to transform his own plans to be exactly the same as God's plans.

(4) David's faith in God to fulfill His word showed that he had himself trusted God and found Him faithful.

Each one of these qualities was a part of David's growing intimacy with God; each one required focused effort to become ingrained into his life. When God called David "a man after My Own heart," it was a singular and meaningful commendation made for good reason.

David's faith is exercised

8   Yet, God's word at this time tested David's faith. After stopping David's building plans, He made promises that were almost too overwhelming for David. This word appeared to stagger him at first; but he settled back on what he knew and said,

> You, O my God, have told Your servant that You will build him a house;
> therefore, Your servant has been able to pray before You.

David took special notice of God's extensive plans for his house and clung to his place as God's servant. The fact that his God had spoken enabled him to pray.

9   David met this challenge to his faith. Like Abraham before him, he did not dwell on the impossible circumstances or limited resources he saw, nor did he stagger in disbelief at the astounding promises of God. David too gave glory to God by being strong in faith and being fully persuaded that what God had promised, He was able also to perform.

10   David wanted God's name to be glorified.

> Let it be established that Thy name may be magnified forever, saying,
> "The LORD of Hosts is the God of Israel, even a God to Israel."

11   Another reason that David asked God to keep His promises was his own deep desire for his house to be blessed as God had spoken. Three times in his reply, David specifically asked God to do what He had promised for his house. In one instance he said,

> Let it please You to bless the house of Your servant that it may be before
> You forever because when You bless, O LORD, it shall be blessed forever.

12   But God had more than a physical family and royal bloodline in mind, therefore David prayed for more. Whether he realized it or not, when he trusted God to bless his family, David aligned himself with God's ultimate purpose to bless and establish all of His people forever. In addition, when he prayed generally for God to do as He had said, David acted in support of the eternal purposes God had spoken. Even though an overwhelmed David did not specifically ask God to establish the promised kingdoms or thrones – neither his own nor God's – his believing words for God to do as He had spoken supported those promises as well.

[13]   Such a prayer of faith is not unique to David. Any servant of God can coop-erate with God in this way: each person who prays in faith for God to meet a vis-ible need can trust that these requests and their answers will also advance eternal purposes, which may be unknown to the one praying. Corporately too, since the time of Jesus, God's people have repeatedly supported and blessed inconceivable divine purposes when uniting to plead in faith, "Thy kingdom come."

[14]   All in all, although he was yet maturing as God's servant, David's reply to God showed a heart fit to receive this divine revelation of promise and purpose. He showed this heart by

- accepting God's words completely. He did not filter out the best promises or the ones he could understand.
- accepting God's words unconditionally. He did not require an explanation or ask for more information.
- agreeing with God's word wholeheartedly. He made no objection, proposed no bargain, and offered no "better" way.
- asserting his support for God and His purposes to be fulfilled. He did not hold back because he might face great difficulty or because he did not know how God would fulfill His promises.
- asking God in faith to do everything exactly as He had promised. He was not afraid that some promises were too grand and glorious to be fulfilled.

[15]   Upon receiving this revelation, David had no task to perform, but his recep-tive, believing heart blessed God far more than his service to build a magnificent house for the Ark of the Covenant could ever have done. Soon, as God's servant, David would again know how to act in light of this revelation. He was not lazy, and he did not go about his separate business while God went about His. As much as possible, David made it his business to do God's business.

Chapter 7

David's Military Conquests and Administration

7-1 David conquers and subdues the surrounding nations
(I Chronicles 18:1-13; II Samuel 8:1-14)

Some of ways that God had abundantly blessed and greatly honored David were these:

- David was established and famous as king over all of Israel.
- Jerusalem was secured and built up as Israel's capital.
- The Ark of the Covenant of God's presence was now close to his new royal palace in Jerusalem.
- Best of all, David had now received an extraordinary revelation containing some of God's magnificent purposes for himself, his family, Israel, and God's eternal kingdom.

Without a doubt, this revelation gave David great confidence that, as king over Israel, he was exactly where God wanted him to be and that God had more for him to do. What might that be? He knew that neither he nor one of his sons – all under 10 years old – could immediately build a house for God.

2   Although his heart was committed to the worship and glory of God, David often found himself serving God in a military setting. And now, while he had not been aggressive in war since being anointed king, he focused his next efforts on advancing God's purposes to subdue his enemies and to plant Israel securely in its land. The fulfillment of these grand promises would require further military efforts.

3   First, a showdown with the Philistines, Israel's neighbors to the west, was inevitable. Their possession of cities and much land in the north had confined Israel for more than seven years. Although David still had a tenuous alliance with the Philistines, he had begun to resist their oppressive activities. Certainly, the Philistines would want to maintain their control in Israel, and the increasing strength of Israel's army was a serious problem for them. David had already defeated them twice as he followed God's specific battle instructions. Although the Philistines may have strengthened their positions after these two losses, they did not again attack Israel.

4   David, however, acting in the light of God's promises to him, attacked the Philistines in order to drive them out of Bethlehem and the other cities they had captured from Israel. This conflict with the Philistines became the first major test

of Israel's military might under David. When the fighting ended, Israel's armies under David had defeated and subdued the Philistines. The nation of Israel repossessed its northern lands, and its armies forced the Philistines back into their own territory. David even took control of Gath, a major Philistine city with a strategic location near its eastern border with Israel.

5   Significantly, David did not require the Philistines to demonstrate their subservience to him, as he did later on with most of the other nations he would defeat. He neither required gifts from the Philistines nor punished them. The Philistine king at Gath, Achish, had given him asylum, and a man from Gath, Obededom, had housed the Ark of the Covenant for three months. Later, during Absalom's revolt, Ittai, a Philistine captain also from Gath, brought 600 soldiers to aid David. This support indicated that there was a continuing respect and at least a cooperative relationship between David and the Philistines (Halpern 152), who nevertheless were annoyed that David had now retaken control of northern Israel.

6   Next, in a somewhat surprising move, David attacked the nation of Moab, located on the east side of the Dead Sea. Throughout its history, Moab had rarely been a military threat to its neighbors. In addition, David had trusted the king of Moab to keep his parents safe while he was running from King Saul. The Bible does not record how the nation of Moab treated David's parents, but if it had properly cared for his parents, it should have received a blessing. Instead, David did not just attack and defeat Moab's army, he dealt the Moabites an unusually harsh punishment. The people of Moab became his servants and brought him gifts.

7   David then conquered nations to the north of Israel and established his dominion all the way to the Euphrates River. He defeated and subdued Hadarezer, the powerful king of Zobah, as well as the cities under his rule. During that campaign, Syrians from Damascus joined in the fight, but David subdued them as well and left occupying garrisons in Damascus. David received gifts from all of the northern cities he defeated.

8   David's success was not blind, accidental luck, nor was it mere military genius ... "the LORD preserved David wherever he went." As He had promised, God was securing Israel in its land, subduing David's enemies before him, and extending David's kingdom. Certainly, these campaigns were dangerous as Israel's army faced strong armies having many fierce and fearless warriors, but God kept David safe and blessed his military efforts. For his part, David was on God's side, believing His word, taking his stand with God and His purposes, and then trusting Him as he went to battle.

9   David increased his dominion still further. To the east, it included the nation of Ammon. David and Ammon's King Nahash maintained an existing respect and appreciation for each other. To the south, Edom and Amalek were defeated. For unrecorded reasons, David, with his nephews Joab and Abishai, treated the

Edomites harshly. This severe punishment produced an adversary of Israel, one that later rose up to harass Solomon. David also set up military garrisons in Edom to maintain peace and control.

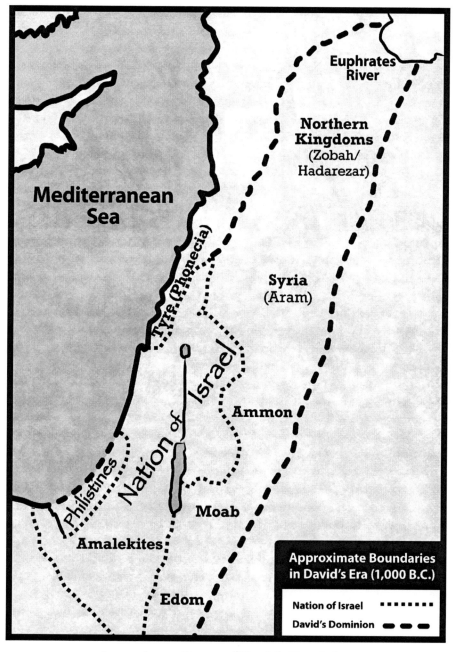

Approximate Extent of David's Dominion

God aids the expansion of David's dominion

10   With God fulfilling His promises, preserving David, and giving him victory after victory, David's dominion extended north to the Euphrates River and south to the edge of the Red Sea – a vast area. Some may have questioned David's interpretation of God's promises for Israel to be secure and wondered if he were presuming on God's protection in places where God was not leading, or if part of David's success was his own doing rather than God's.

11   David, however, purposely went to the Euphrates River to establish his dominion. God had specified to both Moses and Joshua that Israel's borders were to extend to the Euphrates. Certainly, David would be guided by that repeated word of God. In addition, other neighboring rulers may have made themselves David's enemies. Any nation which actively opposed the strength and security of Israel would need to be subdued. (Notably, there is no mention of the neighboring nation of Tyre. David made no effort to subdue his supportive friend, King Hiram, who apparently did not join in any battle for or against Israel.)

12   And God, who set Israel's borders, did not question the expansion of David's authority; He aided it. The statement that "the LORD preserved David wherever he went" was repeated. The same God Who raised David up to be the king of Israel also directed and protected him in these many battles. As God's servant in his military campaigns, David distinguished himself from other powerful conquerors of his era (McKenzie 152). Although he controlled a vast area, he did not seek to extend his kingdom beyond the limits of God's direction, such as into Egypt or beyond the Euphrates River or into nations where there might have been a power vacuum. He even maintained peaceful relations with his closest neighbors, the nations of Tyre and the Philistines, and did not attempt to control or rule over them.

13   By preserving David wherever he went, God also made it clear that His presence and protection were not limited to the location of the Ark. He was with David, even when David ventured far from the Ark of the Covenant in Jerusalem. Because David proceeded in the light of God's revealed purposes and personally rejoiced in God's plans for the security of Israel, it is not surprising that he enjoyed this protective presence of God.

Military victories also bring prosperity

14   As David extended his dominion, Israel became more prosperous. Plunder from battle, such as shields made of gold, immediately increased the wealth of the nation and of King David. In addition, the conquered nations accepted their place as David's servants, and most of them brought him "gifts." The gifts included many items made of gold, silver, and brass. One northern king, grateful to David for defeating the neighboring tyrant Hadarezer, sent his son as an ambassador of peace bearing many valuable treasures. As a continuing acknowledgement of David's rule and authority, conquered nations likely paid an annual tribute. These tributes were more like a tax based on the benefits and services

they received from David, such as military, social, or legal support. David dedicated battle loot, gifts, and tributes to the LORD.

[15] David's military success did not change his desires for God's glory and for a house of worship for the Ark of the Covenant. The knowledge that his son would build the temple kept the project close to David's heart. He regularly set aside gifts and tributes for his son to use. Specifically, an abundance of brass, known to have come from certain cities of subdued northern nations, was later used to make several particular items for that new house of God. This itemization of the plunder showed that David did not randomly stockpile the treasures he had collected. In fact, he assigned three wealth managers with separate areas of responsibility: 1) The wealth of the nation, 2) The treasures dedicated to the LORD, and 3) The wealth that David had personally accumulated. In conducting military campaigns and in managing the spoils of war, David acted in harmony with God's purposes.

7-2 David's leadership and administration
(I Chronicles 18:14-17; 27:1-22, 25-34; II Samuel 8:15-18; 20:23-26)

David had now gained authority over many surrounding nations; he was widely known to be a great military leader. But how would he rule Israel as king? Though he had occasionally dealt ruthless punishments to conquered nations, David did not control the people with fear and a heavy-handed use of power. King David distinguished himself yet again by ruling Israel with judgment and justice. These two qualities, working in conjunction with one another, have always been essential to God. In fact, when Jesus, David's greater son, sits on David's throne, he too will establish his kingdom with judgment and justice. As God's servant and Israel's king, David applied these two characteristics of God's kingdom.

[2] First, David ruled with judgment. Judgments made by human rulers are typically based on a whim, a law, or a personal agenda. God's judgments, however, transcend human judgments; they proceed from His holy and merciful character, confirm His righteous standards, and implement His eternal purposes. Significantly, with an increasing understanding of God, His ways, and His purposes, David's judgments gave the world a glimpse of the rule of God's kingdom. For instance, after years of learning to respect his persecutor Saul, David advocated a greater respect for God's anointed king by blessing the men of Jabesh who honored King Saul and executing young Amalekite who did not (Section 2-2). Actions such as these demonstrated how judgment teaches righteousness by both encouraging those doing right and opposing those doing evil. Without proper judgment, the wicked are emboldened. Having received a revelation of God's purposes and heart to bless His people and having embraced God and His promises by faith, King David ruled with judgment – a judgment patterned after God's.

3   In addition to judgment, the quality of justice, characterized by compassion and truth, marked David's reign. Ruling with justice required showing mercy and caring for the victims, as well as mandating appropriate punishment for the guilty. Because David had been unjustly oppressed himself, he knew first-hand the need for equitable and transparent justice, according to God's high standard. As an example, David and some of his men boldly defended the harvest fields of Israel's farmers. Also, both those who fought and those who were too weak to continue across a stream to help with the Ziklag recovery received equal portions of the loot recovered and taken from the Amalekite raiders. David overruled the objections of some selfish warriors to make this gracious distribution, which became a new standard of fairness. Additionally, acting on a clear purpose to bless and preserve the family of Jonathan, King Saul's son and his best friend, David brought Jonathan's lame son into the palace and gave him a permanent seat at the king's table. He also arranged for the preservation and care of the lands of Jonathan's family. Delivering the oppressed from the oppressor and preventing the rich from taking advantage of the poor were important objectives in David's kingdom.

4   With David's increased rule and influence, God was expanding the knowledge of Himself and His ways. As David applied consistent judgment with justice, he aligned himself with God's ways of ruling a kingdom, and in doing so, David worked toward the eventual fulfillment of God's purposes. Of course, David did not rule alone; he surrounded himself with many qualified and responsible leaders to help administer his kingdom. Key members of David's official administrative team and their possible job descriptions are listed below. [Note: This listing contains some fresh background information as well as a few obscure names and details.]

David's sons – <u>Chief around the king</u>

5   Because all of David's sons were born after he had become king over the tribe of Judah, they were young when they began their time around the king. This privilege allowed his sons to become accustomed to the ways of the palace and the king as they grew up. David delegated part of the responsibility to care for his sons to Jehiel, who was with David's sons to assist and to guide them as they matured.

6   Three of David's sons, each having a different mother, became somewhat notorious. In the years ahead, David's first-born son Amnon would rape and further mistreat his half-sister Tamar, who was the sister of Absalom, David's third-born son. Two years later, Absalom had his half-brother Amnon killed, partly because David did not punish Amnon for defiling and degrading Tamar. Furthermore, while David was still living, both Absalom and David's fourth-born son Adonijah would separately attempt unauthorized takeovers of their father's kingdom. These horrid events put on display some of the effects of the curse pronounced upon David's family because of his cruel sins against Uriah the Hittite. Later in David's reign, a man named Ira was designated chief ruler, serving the king in the palace.

Joab, David's nephew – <u>Commander over Israel's armies</u>

7   Joab earned this military rank by leading a group of soldiers to capture the citadel of Jerusalem from the Jebusites. Though a masterful battle general, Joab was a maverick who frustrated David on several occasions. When David began to look to Abner, and later to Amasa, for military leadership, Joab personally murdered both men. In defiance of David's direct order, Joab also killed David's son Absalom to end the coup that Absalom would lead against his father's kingdom. Although David and Joab did not always see eye to eye, Joab, at times, gave good advice that David needed to heed. He was faithful to David through Absalom's rebellion, but in the end, he supported Adonijah instead of Solomon. As a punishment, Solomon had Joab executed.

Benaiah, one of David's thirty mighty men – <u>Director of Security</u>

8   Benaiah's security forces were separate from the military forces under Joab. They made up David's bodyguard and were responsible to maintain peace and safety in Jerusalem. Some security forces, called garrisons, were used to maintain control in sensitive or dangerous areas across the kingdom, such as Edom and Damascus. After Solomon was anointed king, he promoted Benaiah to Joab's position of commander of the military.

Zadok, Abiathar, and Abimelech – <u>Priests over Israel's worship ministries</u>

9   The priests offered the daily, weekly, monthly, and annual sacrifices or feasts, in addition to the many voluntary sacrifices brought by the Israelite people. Abiathar loyally supported David when he was a fugitive and often helped David receive direction from God. Like Joab, Abiathar endured hardship with David, aided him during Absalom's rebellion, and in the end, foolishly allied with Adonijah. As a punishment, Solomon removed Abiathar from serving as priest and retained the priest Zadok, who had served faithfully. In the temple described in Ezekiel's prophecy, Zadok's priestly line will be exalted even more. The priest Abimelech was Abiathar's son.

Shavsha – <u>Scribe and legal counselor</u>

10   Shavsha, also referred to as Sheva or Seraiah, helped David make laws for Israel. Knowing the laws of God and the laws of the kingdom, he was qualified to give advice about gaps or conflicts in the policies or decisions that David considered. As a technical writer, Shavsha was responsible for making official documents out of the decrees of David and the kingdom.

Jehoshaphat, son of Ahilud – <u>Recorder</u>

11   Jehoshaphat recorded information so that David did not have to worry about remembering who said and did what. With his detailed journal, Jehoshaphat made David aware of scheduled items and unresolved issues. His office kept track of the needs mentioned, the decisions made, and the steps planned or taken for the resolution of each issue. Jehoshaphat must have done his job well because he continued in this position during the reign of Solomon.

I Chronicles 27 lists other administrative duties and noteworthy names.

The king's monthly servants – <u>Twelve groups of 24,000 for a total of 288,000</u>
12   These twelve groups were similar to a military reserve called up to serve the king just one month each year. These groups may also have served David in the daily care of his household and administration in Jerusalem. The leader of each monthly group was one of David's captains. Jashobeam, the foremost of David's mighty men, was given the first group. Benaiah, who was David's security chief, was in charge of one of the groups. This system of monthly service was established within two years of David's being anointed king over the tribe of Judah because Asahel was designated as a group leader even though he died in battle soon after David became king. Zebadiah, Asahel's son, led this group in place of his father.

Princes over the tribes of Israel
13   I Chronicles 27:16-22 names thirteen men chosen to rule the tribes in the family-nation of Israel. One of the princes was Elihu, or Eliab, David's eldest brother, who ruled in Judah. Eliab was a handsome, confident man who had chastised David for speaking out against Goliath. David apparently did not hold a grudge and honored his brother by placing him over Israel's largest tribe. Another notable prince was Jaasiel, son of Abner, who ruled in Benjamin. David honored Abner, Saul's cousin and commander of Israel's army, both with eulogies at his funeral and then with this appointment of his son to a key administrative position.

Caretakers of David's personal wealth
14   I Chronicles 27:25-31 names eleven caretakers with specific areas of responsibility: (1) Inventory and care of the king's treasures, (2) Inventory of all of the warehouses in Israel, (3) Care and operation of the vineyards, (4) Storage of the vineyard's harvest production in wine cellars, (5) Care and operation of the olive and sycamore trees, (6) Storage of oil in cellars, (7) Care of the herds in Sharon, (8) Care of the herds in the valleys, (9) Care of the camels, (10) Care of the mules, and (11) Care of the flocks.

Jonathan and **Ahithophel**, then **Abiathar** and **Jehoiada** – <u>The king's counselors.</u>
15   Ahithophel was very powerful; receiving his counsel was like getting counsel directly from an oracle of God. Soon after aiding Absalom in his conspiracy, Ahithophel took his own life because Absalom did not follow his advice. Ahithophel was replaced by Jehoiada, Benaiah's son, and Abiathar, David's confidant. Jonathan, David's uncle, was a wise man and a scribe who was able to give David good and godly counsel.

Hushai the Archite – <u>The king's companion</u>
16   Hushai was a wise old man and an excellent friend to David. When David fled from Absalom's plot to take over the kingdom, he left Hushai in the palace to gain Absalom's trust and hopefully to negate Ahithophel's good counsel.

Hushai was successful. Absalom's decision to follow Hushai's advice instead of Ahithophel's led to the end of his coup.

Adoram – Tribute manager

¹⁷ Appointed late in David's reign, Adoram managed the non-Israelite resources under David's dominion. The duties of his office included organizing and accounting for the annual tributes paid by the subservient nations and overseeing the foreign labor pool available for David's projects. Adoram, also called Adoniram, likely continued in this position through the entire reign of Solomon. Early in reign of Solomon's son, Rehoboam, Adoram was stoned to death by a mob of angry workers.

7-3 The nation of Ammon foolishly offends David
(I Chronicles 19 – 20:3; II Samuel 10 – 11:4; 12:26-31)

In addition to the neighboring nations of Tyre and the Philistines, David maintained peaceful relations with the Ammonites, a nation located east of the Jordan River. Nahash, the king of Ammon, had reached out to support David – perhaps to spite King Saul who, very early in his reign over Israel, rescued an Israelite city from King Nahash and decisively defeated the Ammonite army.

² When Nahash died, David expressed his desire to honor Nahash.

I will show kindness to Hanun, his son, because his father showed kindness to me.

David sent messengers to Hanun, the new king of Ammon, to express condolences. But Ammon's ruling princes did not trust David's envoy and told Hanun,

Do you think that David honors your father? Are not his messengers actually spies sent to search the land in order for David to overthrow Ammon?

Ammon's princes knew that David was strong, and they may have assumed that he, like other conquerors of that time, would aggressively pounce on a vulnerable nation with an inexperienced ruler on the throne (McKenzie 152). Hanun believed his advisors and turned away David's messengers, greatly shaming them in the process. Hanun made an ill-advised decision.

³ Hanun's action meant war to David, and the leaders of Ammon knew it. They hired mercenary fighters out of Mesopotamia to the east and out of Zobah to the north. David sent Joab to lead Israel's army in attacking Ammon, but the mercenaries surprised Israel from behind and forced Joab to wage war on two fronts. Joab chose Israel's best warriors to fight the mercenaries and sent his brother Abishai to lead the remainder of the soldiers against the Ammonites. This battle plan worked well for Israel. Joab's elite force put the mercenaries on the run, and when the Ammonites realized that they were on their own, they too retreated from their battle against Abishai and returned to their cities.

⁴ The battle advantage shifted back to Ammon when the mercenaries themselves recruited much additional help from northern nations; joining the battle

were both the Syrian armies and Hadarezer, the powerful ruler whom God had previously subdued before David. When David heard this, he called up all available fighting men in Israel and brought them to the battle. David led these soldiers against the newly recruited armies to the north. It was a rout. Israel decimated the Syrian chariot force and killed 40,000 soldiers, including the commander of the Syrian forces. Hadarezer suffered such severe losses that many cities he had controlled switched their allegiance and began serving Israel. Syria refused to help Ammon anymore.

5   Without either the mercenaries or Syria to help the Ammonites, David did not feel obligated to participate further in this retaliatory war. David again sent Joab to lead Israel's army to subdue the nation of Ammon and conquer its well-fortified capital city, Rabbah. It was a long campaign.

6   "But David tarried at Jerusalem." Such ominous words. "It was a time when kings went to battle" – but not David. In fulfillment of God's revealed purpose, God had subdued all of David's enemies before him. Did David now presume upon past victories and assume that he did not need to finish this campaign? In fulfillment of another promise, Israel had peace in its land. Did David think that he no longer needed to work to maintain that peace? After years of laboring for God and experiencing God's blessings, did David feel it was time to relax and enjoy the rewards of having been a highly valued servant of God? Was he already harboring thoughts about forbidden, costly delights in Jerusalem? The treacherous ideas that overpowered David's mind at this time are unclear. Also uncertain is the process which brought David to the brink of destruction before adversaries that were far more threatening than the Ammonite army.

7   There was great trouble when David stayed in Jerusalem while Israel's army fought Ammon. This was that appalling time when David, by his dark decision and devilish determination, committed adultery with Uriah's wife and then had Uriah, one of his 30 captains and one of Israel's most devoted and elite soldiers, killed in battle. This was that shameful time when God sent Nathan to David with a condemnation and a curse, both of which worked against God's promises and blessings for David's family.

8   After Joab's forces had overrun the country and conquered Rabbah, Joab called for David to complete the victory. David removed King Hanun's crown and severely punished the Ammonites. Ammon's alliance with David was restored through Shobi, who was the son of Nahash and the brother of the deposed Hanun. Later, Shobi came to aid David when Absalom revolted.

7-4 Timeline and later encounters with Philistine giants
(I Chronicles 20:4-8; II Samuel 21:15-22)

David was now a powerful monarch. He had conquered and gained dominion over the land extending north and east to the Euphrates River and extending south to Edom and nearly to Egypt. As God had promised, Israel was secure in its land, and David's kingdom was established. There remained strong nations that did not like the expansion of David's authority and would challenge Israel, as in the expanded battle with Ammon. Nevertheless, David and Israel maintained control over this vast territory.

2   The main turmoil in David's kingdom for much of his reign was in his home. He had more difficulty ruling his own family than he did ruling Israel. Aside from a few conflicts with the Philistines, the history of the remaining years of his reign includes only events related to his family struggles and internal issues in Israel. God worked with an internal problem and a tragedy resulting from David's obstinate decision to bless a contrite David with a second extraordinary revelation near the end of his reign. When he acted on that revelation, David would bless Israel and honor God's purposes.

3   Before continuing to those dramatic events, some key points of David's life are listed by his approximate age at the time they happened. Building an exact timeline is very difficult, so the listing below uses the clues in the history of the books of Samuel as literally as possible. For example, the Ark of the Covenant remained at the house of Abinadab in Kirjathjearim for 20 years. Those 20 years include all of the time Samuel judged Israel by himself, as well as the entire reign of King Saul, plus almost 10 years of David's reign before he moved the Ark to Jerusalem. These details indicate that Samuel and Saul did not lead Israel long, but the books of Samuel record neither their ages nor the length of time they ruled. However, since the priest Eli lived to be 98 years old, Samuel could have been quite old when he officially began to judge Israel. And since Jonathan was already a mature leader for Israel's army in just the second year of his father's reign, Saul himself could have been fairly old when he became king. Making use of these and other clues, which are listed in the reference section, here is a possible timeline using David's age to order the events of his life:

Age 18: The Ark is captured and Eli dies at 98 years of age.
Age 19: The Ark of the Covenant is brought to Kirjathjearim.
Age 21: Saul is crowned as Israel's first king at about age 55.
Age 23: David kills Goliath.
Age 24: King Saul disobeys; David is anointed and serves Saul well.
Age 26: David escapes King Saul and becomes a fugitive.
Age 28: David takes up asylum in Ziklag.
Age 30: Saul dies in battle and David becomes king over Judah.
Age 31: David's first son, Amnon, is born.
Age 32: Israel and Saul's son Ishbosheth are defeated.
Age 33: David's third son, Absalom, is born.
Age 37: Israel and Judah are united. David reigns from Jerusalem.
Age 39: The Ark of the Covenant is moved to Jerusalem.
Age 40: David begins to expand his dominion.

[Note: I Chronicles does not record David's family troubles, and this book does not walk with David through the tragic events listed below. The Bible Reference appendix summarizes more of this period of David's life.]

Age 43: David sins against Uriah during the campaign against Ammon.

Age 51: Solomon, the fourth son of Bathsheba, is born.

Age 53: Amnon sins against Absalom's sister Tamar.

Age 55: Absalom has Amnon killed for harming Tamar.

Age 64: Absalom attempts to overthrow his father as king.

Age 70: David dies after 40 years as king. Solomon becomes king.

4   An alternate timeline applies the 40-year period mentioned by Paul in Acts 13:20,21 to the combined time that Samuel and Saul ruled after Eli's death. (Some translations of I Samuel 13:1 say that Saul reigned for 42 years, but the word for *forty* is not found in any old Hebrew text. Apparently the Hebrew is difficult, and *forty* is added because of Acts 13:21.) In this case, the Ark's 20-year stay in Abinadab's home, specified in I Samuel 7:2, might refer to the time that elapsed until an unspecified event closed that 20-year period. This would mean that the Ark actually remained with Abinadab for about 50 years, and his sons, though quite old, could still participate in David's move of the Ark of the Covenant. Giving Saul a reign of 22 years, this scenario might expand the above timeline of David's early years as follows:

Ten years before David's birth, the Ark is captured, Eli dies, and Samuel begins to judge Israel by himself.

One year later, the Ark of the Covenant is brought to Kirjathjearim.

Age 8: Saul is crowned as Israel's first king at about age 45.

Age 16: David kills Goliath.

Age 20: King Saul disobeys; David is anointed and serves Saul well.

Age 24: David escapes King Saul and becomes a fugitive.

Age 28: David takes up asylum in Ziklag.

Age 30: Saul dies in battle and David becomes king over Judah.

5   Another text potentially affecting the timeline is II Samuel 12:24, in which Solomon appears to be Bathsheba's second son, born within a few years of David's adultery with her. If this were the case, the birth of Solomon could have happened earlier, or David's adultery during the military campaign against the Ammonites could have happened at a later date. Yet, the ordering of the sons born to David in Jerusalem lists Solomon fourth, and I Chronicles 3:5 adds that Bathsheba was the mother of these four.

Certainly, knowing the sequence of the events in David's life is helpful, but building an exact timeline is, again, very difficult.

⁶   Some of the skirmishes during the latter part of David's reign happened with the nearby Philistines. The strategic border town of Gath was contested. Gath was Goliath's hometown, and Goliath's family produced other mighty giants. Israelite warriors who defeated one of them had their names recorded in I Chronicles 20 and II Samuel 21. Any who failed were not listed; but one near-failure is mentioned. Even though David was well past his prime fighting years, he would not back down from a tough opponent. He faced one of Goliath's sons, but this time David was an old warrior with a sword instead of a young shepherd with a slingshot. Goliath's son may have been fighting to restore the honor of his father's name; this giant was defeating David until Abishai came to rescue his uncle the king.

⁷   One other contest is notable. During a battle at Gath, an especially powerful, towering giant, another son of Goliath, defied Israel, much like his father had done about forty years earlier. At that time, no one in Saul's army would face Goliath, leaving the opportunity open for a young David to kill him. Now again, this son of Goliath reproached God's people. What would be the response this time? This army had the benefit of David's extensive leadership in the ways of Israel's Almighty God. In addition, the oft-told testimony of David's legendary defeat of Goliath was an example for Israel's warriors of what their glorious God would do when His servants trusted Him. Shimea or Shammah, one of David's older brothers, was in Saul's army the day David killed Goliath. This time, forty years later, Shimea's son, Jonathan, fought and killed Goliath's formidable son when he defied Israel. What a great reason for David to praise the LORD of Hosts! Someone, one of his nephews, took a victorious stand for God and His glory in Israel.

7-5 Israel endures famine for an action of King Saul (II Samuel 21:1-14)

During the latter part of David's reign, Israel also faced a natural enemy. There had been very little rain, and Israel had been under famine conditions for three years with no relief in sight. Seeking help from God, King David inquired, "Lord, why have we not had rain for so long? You have promised the early and late rains, and we desperately need them. We ask You to help us."

²   God answered David directly and said,

> *Saul and his royal house caused the famine. Blood remains on them because he killed the Gibeonites.*

More than thirty years earlier, Saul had attacked the Gibeonites and had attempted to annihilate them. This created three critical problems that Israel could no longer ignore. First, Saul's family had Gibeonite blood on their hands. Second, the surviving Gibeonites still remembered what Saul had done and did not bless Israel; they and the blood of their slaughtered ancestors cried out for justice. Third, the famine in Israel showed that the land itself was corrupted, having absorbed the innocent blood of the slain Gibeonites.

3   Historically, at the time Joshua led Israel to conquer Canaan and destroy all of its inhabitants, Gibeon had been a major city in Canaan. Because the Gibeonites living there knew Israel's purpose and feared Israel's God, they made peace with Israel. Although they tricked Joshua and Israel's leaders to get them to agree to a peace treaty, Israel was bound by its oath to the Gibeonites. The treaty required Israel not merely to allow them to live, but also to protect them. Because of their deception, the Gibeonites had to serve Israel by doing heavy and menial tasks, such as chopping wood and hauling water. Several Canaanite kings in the region saw the treaty between Gibeon and Israel as a threat and united in an attack against Gibeon. Even after being deceived, Joshua kept the agreement by leading Israel's army to assist Gibeon and defeat these kings. Though they were not Israelites, the Gibeonites continued to be peaceful and supportive of Israel. For centuries, until the reign of King Saul, they were thankful to remain alive and to be favorably integrated with Israel. Even many centuries later, the Gibeonites would join Nehemiah and help rebuild the wall of Jerusalem. For its part, the nation of Israel consistently honored its treaty with Gibeon – except for Saul.

4   Saul justified his ruthless action by claiming a nationalistic zeal for Israel. Yes, the Gibeonites had tricked Joshua, but Saul had no right to punish them for their deceit. Yes, Israel under Joshua had been commanded to conquer Canaan and destroy all of its inhabitants, but Saul had been given no such command. And yes, under Joshua, each tribe had then been responsible to complete that conquering work in its own territory. But King Saul had no authority to anni-hilate the Gibeonites, even though he was king and even though Gibeon was located in the territory of his own tribe of Benjamin. The Bible does not record the attack on the Gibeonites, and neither does it record the move of the taberna-cle from Shiloh to Gibeon, both of which occurred during the reign of King Saul. If Saul had coordinated these two events, he may have reasoned that this racial cleansing of a "better" place for the tabernacle – a place not far from his home in Gibeah – would be good for Israel and blessed by God.

5   Whatever his rationale, King Saul possessed strong motivation to kill the Gibeonites. His passion here was so very wrong. Sadly, he carried out his depraved desire; King Saul attacked Gibeon with the goal of completely wiping out its people. The attempted genocide was a proud, racist action. The blood spilt in this hostile campaign damaged Israel's relations with Gibeonite people. The blood of these innocent lives cried out for justice; it also stained Saul's fam-ily and defiled the land.

6   Time did not heal the wounds or repair the damage; some thirty years later, the whole nation was infected and suffering with no end in sight. The conse-quences of Saul's irresponsible attack were now causing a famine so severe that King David had to get involved. But the savage deed was not simply Saul's indi-vidual sin or personal campaign. Saul acted in his capacity as the King of Israel.

It was as King of Israel that Saul had embraced the idea to kill the Gibeonites, and it was as king that Saul had led the army of Israel to carry it out. At the king's command, an established national treaty was broken. King Saul's action was a national sin, and Israel was judged guilty. Until atonement could be made for the national sin, the whole nation endured punishment.

7   The King of Israel must solve these long-standing national problems caused by his predecessor. The solution was for King David to make atonement so that the Gibeonites could again bless the nation. Many Gibeonites had vivid memories of Saul's atrocities and likely echoed the cry of their ancestors' blood in dirges and ceremonies remembering their dead. Understanding his responsibility to stop the cry of the massacred Gibeonites and their descendants, King David went to the Gibeonites to find out what to do. He did not delegate this job; the king himself acted for Israel to resolve the problems created by King Saul's national sin.

8   David asked the Gibeonites,

What shall I do for you and how shall I make the atonement so that you can bless the land of Israel?

The Gibeonites first told David what would not suffice, saying,

We do not want silver or gold from Saul or his family; neither do we want you to kill any man of Israel.

David replied,

Whatever you say, I will do for you.

The Gibeonites answered,

The man who killed us and devised to exterminate us from Israel is responsible. Give us seven of his sons, and we will hang them in his hometown of Gibeah unto the LORD who chose Saul to be King.

Requiring King Saul's immediate family to suffer capital punishment for his crime was a grave request. But David had no choice – atonement must be made. He responded,

I will give them to you.

This atonement would cleanse the ground and Saul's family, both of which had been defiled by the blood of the innocent Gibeonites who had been slain. In addition, the Gibeonites' ability to trust the God of Israel had been shaken. They took notice that God Himself had chosen, as Israel's first king, a man who would plan their destruction; they held the God of Israel partly responsible for Saul's tragic action. Now, to the relief of the Gibeonites, God had chosen a king to act on their behalf, one who would not offer excuses or a defense for the actions of the previous king, but one who would make atonement.

9   David himself chose the seven men who were to die and in making his decision, he spared the family of his friend Jonathan. He selected the two sons of Rizpah, Saul's concubine, and five men whom Michal, Saul's younger daughter and David's wife, had raised for Adriel, the husband of Saul's older daughter Merab.

How these men must have pleaded for their lives! They had nothing to do with
Saul's attempted genocide, which had happened such a long time ago. Although
the solution was indeed costly, the effects of King Saul's action continued to grow
as a festering wound to the nation. David acted in his capacity as King of Israel
to make the atonement required for the Gibeonites to be reconciled with Israel
and with Israel's God. Only then could God again bless the land.

10   King David brought the seven descendants of Saul to the Gibeonites. Just as
Saul had gone to their home of Gibeon to destroy them, so here the Gibeonites
went to Gibeah, Saul's city, to hang his sons. They hanged them on the hill
before the LORD; the God of Israel was their God. It was a deep, solemn ceremony, an atonement to effect reconciliation, not revenge to stir up hatred. This
ceremony was healing a 30-year-old wound, and it was silencing the cries for justice emanating both from the innocent Gibeonite blood absorbed into the
ground and from those living Gibeonites who still remembered the tragedy. This
ceremony not only restored the treaty with Israel, but it also restored the
Gibeonites' place in the nation. As a result, the Gibeonites reconciled with Israel
and were again able to trust the God of Israel and to bless the nation.

11   But David realized that this grave and costly ceremony was not sufficient to
resolve the national crisis when he learned that Rizpah protected the remains of
the men who had been hanged. Out of respect for the royal house of Saul, David
gathered the remains of the seven hanged men, together with the bones of Saul
and his son Jonathan, and buried them all in the graveyard of Saul's father. With
this official act, David, King of Israel, completed all that was required to make
atonement for the nation. God then answered the many prayers for rain and
healed the land.

Part Three

God's Revelation Concerning
His Own House

Chapter 8

David Orders a Disastrous Census

[NOTE: Chapter 8 builds upon the concepts of a national act brought out in Section 7-5.]

8-1 God and Satan oppose Israel (I Chronicles 21:1; II Samuel 24:1)

Israel endured another punishment near the end of David's reign. "Satan stood up against Israel" (I Chronicles 21:1). "And God 's anger was kindled against Israel" (II Samuel 24:1). What was going on here?

2   Satan's opposition to Israel in David's time was not surprising. He hated the way David was ruling his vast dominion with judgment and justice, thereby expanding the knowledge of God's ways. Satan, having sought for himself the glory that belongs to God, has continued to contest the authority of God violently and to oppose the knowledge of God vigorously. Satan had been created as the most glorious angelic being, yet he attempted to exalt himself above his Creator God. Satan convinced many other angels (demons) to join in his rebellion, and God threw them all out of heaven. From the time God created Adam and Eve, Satan has used his power to pressure or deceive people into blaspheming, denying, disobeying, and ignoring God.

3   Nevertheless, Satan still had access to God. In God's presence, he took his stand against Israel as a nation. He continued to make accusations against God's people, as he did when he questioned the integrity of Job's service to God, even though he found nothing wrong with Job. Satan did not torment Job until God told him that parts of Job's life were available to him and to his devilish assault. Likewise, despite his persistent opposition to Jesus, Satan could not touch him until Jesus took the sin of the world, until God made His Son to be sin for us and forsook Jesus on the cross. These examples show that Satan cannot harm God's people at his own discretion.

4   On this occasion, Satan could only stand against Israel and accuse the nation before God. While the nation and its citizens were far from perfect, Israel was progressing toward those magnificent purposes that God had revealed to David by the prophet Nathan over twenty years before. In spite of this, Satan apparently brought up a problem that kindled God's anger against Israel as a nation.

5   Although God was aware of the problem, He is merciful, gracious, slow to anger, and ready to pardon. Thus, even with a valid, Satanic accusation, God's

anger did not seem to fit His merciful character. God desires to bless His people and to see them live in ways that allow Him to multiply those blessings. God's anger here also seemed to be in opposition to the great promises He had given David and Israel for their future. The blessings contained in these promises fit His character and gave God ways to act graciously toward His people. Additionally, in being angry with Israel, God did not appear to respect the growth of the nation of Israel. Even though Israel needed much improvement, the spread of judgment and justice during David's reign was in harmony with God's purposes for His Own kingdom.

6   Moses had warned Israel against activities that could provoke God to anger. These included worshipping idols and gods of other nations or forgetting God by selfishly seeking vain pleasures and treasures. Indeed, on many occasions, the people of Israel provoked God by national failings such as these. Beginning with their deliverance from Egyptian slavery and their formation as a nation, through forty years of travel in the wilderness, and during centuries of living in their promised land, the Israelites provoked God to anger many times. Also, in the future, Israel and its kings would often make God their enemy by choosing to depart from the ways in which He had instructed them to live.

7   But these national departures from God's ways did not happen with David or with Israel under King David. He had set his heart and his kingdom to obey God and to give Him glory. Each day, at two places of worship, the Levites led the nation of Israel to honor and praise God. There was no sanctioned or accepted worship of any other god. While David was king, any idolatry or departure from God's commands beyond that of isolated individuals would have been difficult. It seems that all of this should have pleased God and not kindled His anger. (In his sins with Bathsheba and against Uriah, David, as the head of his household, was responsible, and Nathan pronounced consequences upon David and his family, not Israel. These sins had been confessed and punished. Although this punishment upon the king and his family adversely affected the nation, David's grievous sins were not hidden, festering sores; these sins did not require further retribution.)

8   God was angry with Israel, but He did not immediately punish the nation. God's choice to leave sinful man in charge on the earth means that He works within the authority He has given humanity. God does not automatically intervene and deal with injurious people or the problems they create. He does not need to. He will accomplish all of His purposes while mankind has authority over the earth. In this case, neither David as king nor Israel as a nation had committed a national sin; God did not yet punish Israel.

9   And Satan, as a condemned creature of God, is greatly restricted. Although he stood against Israel and brought up a real problem, Satan was not free to act against the nation. He is a powerful angel, but he cannot arbitrarily usurp human authority on earth and neither can he act outside of God's authority.

10 However, with God's being angry, Satan had an opening to tempt David to commit a national sin and thus cause a judgment against Israel as a nation. But it appeared as though David's heart for God and his God-honoring reign over Israel would make it impossible for Satan to tempt David into sinning in that manner. Certainly David would refuse any thought of worshipping idols or forgetting God; hence, the temptation would have to be different: a sin on a national scale, yet one not evil in David's eyes. Satan "provoked David to number Israel" (I Chronicles 21:1). God also "moved David against Israel to say, 'Go, number Israel and Judah'" (II Samuel 24:1).

11 Satan tempted David to order a census, a mandate which, on the surface, would actually seem to be a good idea. Since organizing a national government's security and services required accurate accounting, a census of the people should help the nation, not harm it. In fact, Moses counted the Israelites twice in the wilderness at God's specific direction.

12 But God's law included a warning when He instructed Israel concerning the taking of a census. He told Moses,

> When you number the people, every man must give ransom money for his soul unto the LORD so that there be no plague among the people when you count them.

A plague among the people! The government was doing the counting; the people might not even know about it. However, taking a census was a national act, and therefore a national sin with national consequences if it were not done as God had directed. A plague on the nation from taking an improper census would be a just punishment. Hence, if David were to count the people in Israel at his own discretion and not collect the ransom (atonement) money, Israel could be plagued.

13 Satan's accusing opposition to Israel and God's "Satan-induced" anger against Israel led both of them to incite David to order a census. King David was now the right man in the right position to commit a national sin and cause a judgment against Israel. Punishment for an unauthorized census ordered by the king would assuage God's anger, and it would certainly delight Satan.

14 A remarkable situation thus unfolded, raising many difficult questions. It seemed incredible that God should act in concert with, or even side with, Satan against His chosen people. Should He not always act with Israel and against Satan?

15 Additionally, God had other ways to resolve His anger; inflicting a punishment on Israel was not His only option. For instance, if God had told Nathan about His anger and then sent him to the king, David could have acted to correct the situation. Because God is merciful and wants His people to repent and do right, it is difficult to understand why He, at this time, seemed intent on sending a plague without offering Israel a way to resolve the problem that kindled His anger. God told Jeremiah that when He speaks to destroy a nation, that nation

could avoid punishment by turning away from evil. God spared even the anti-Israel, idol-worshipping Assyrian nation based in Nineveh when it repented after hearing Jonah pronounce its destruction. Here, evidently, God did not give David or Israel an opportunity to repent.

16   These events also raise questions concerning the nature of the problem that kindled God's anger against Israel? Was an error ingrained into Israel's culture or David's administration? Had the problem been observed and ignored by David or by Israel's leadership for too long? Now that the Gibeonites were restored to harmony with Israel, was there an issue with the tabernacle's location at the high place in Gibeon? The separation of the Ark of the Covenant from the tabernacle had not been God's design.

17   Whatever the reason for God's anger toward Israel, it seems unthinkable that He would not tell anyone why He was angry or even that He was angry. Even if no one could correct the problem, knowing the reason for God's anger might help Israel avoid this kind of perilous situation in the future and possibly clarify why God did not seem to guide anyone toward a solution. Did God's people lack the humility, prayer, and repentance needed in order for God to forgive and act favorably toward a nation?

18   Although many questions remain unanswered, it is clear that God was angry before David wanted to count the people. Yes, an unauthorized census would displease God, but it could not be the reason for His prior anger against Israel. The judgment required as a consequence for taking this census would give God a way to punish the nation. Quite expectedly, by this national judgment against Israel, the wise and almighty God would advance His grand purposes for the world and for His people as well. But, very unexpectedly, the merciful and gracious God would also exalt the place of an unworthy King David in those divine plans.

8-2 King David orders Joab to take a census
(I Chronicles 21:2,3; II Samuel 24:2,3)

While turning the focus to David highlights his dishonorable behavior at this time, it raises additional questions. By what means did Satan tempt David? How did God move him to take a national census? The Bible specifies neither the source nor the nature of the enticement that overcame David. A frustrated government administrator, a proud military captain, or David himself may have wanted the count.

2   If the source were within David himself, then taking a census could have been a new idea that an aging king knew must happen right away or it could have been a smoldering but forgotten desire that suddenly returned to his mind as a fresh, powerful longing. In any case, at this moment, David was not inclined to support God's plans.

3   David succumbed to Satan's provocation and to God's moving him. He
yielded to this tempting idea, this census-taking; he did not turn away from it nor
find a way to escape it. His order to his chief military captain Joab was precise,

> Count the people in all the tribes of Israel, from the southernmost city to
> the north and bring me the number.

Joab was not to count people in all of the lands under David's dominion, just
those of the tribes of Israel.

David did not seek counsel

4   His order to Joab seemed abrupt, as though he were in a rush to have the census. In the past, before he had moved the Ark of the Covenant and before he had
attempted to build a house for the Ark, David conferred with others prior to acting on ideas affecting the whole nation. Taking a census was also a significant
national event, yet apparently he did not ask anyone's opinion. He charged
ahead, ignoring the good and necessary counsel of those who might have
expressed reasonable concerns or options.

5   David knew this census-taking idea was wrong; even Joab knew it was
wrong. For him simply to consider committing such an atrocious sin, which
could bring severe punishment upon the people he loved, is unimaginable. His
self-absorbed desire here was in stark contrast to his life's pursuit of glorifying
God and blessing His people. Evidently, a maturing David was not above this
type of evil. Maybe it did not seem so evil when compared to his adultery and
murder of Uriah some twenty-five years before. At that time, he did not handle
the Bathsheba temptation well, and he would handle this current temptation no
better.

6   If he had considered the law's requirement, he could have collected the
atonement money and avoided the plague; the people would pay a price, one way
or the other. Of course, neither David nor his kingdom needed the money, but
to demand the census without the collection would jeopardize the people. His
rash and reckless decision showed that he did not realize, or even worse, that he
did not at this moment care about the cost of taking an unauthorized census in
Israel.

David did not ask God for guidance

7   Then there is God to consider. Again, the Bible gives no indication that
David, in this critical situation, physically walked over to the nearby Ark of the
Covenant to meditate in God's presence and ask the LORD about this census-taking plan. In times past, he had often enlisted the aid of Abiathar, now a priest
with Zadok, to ask God for direction. To call upon God, to hear Him, and to do
what He said was David's heart and habit. Possibly, he was afraid that God would
say no, as He did when David wanted to build God's house. God always had a
better idea. He never let David do what he wanted ... or so it may have seemed
at this moment, with this desire.

8   With this mindset, it was actually good that David did not seek God for guidance. For him to be intent on taking a census that he knew God opposed was bad enough. But, if knowing God's opposition, David still asked for wisdom and direction, he would be showing hypocrisy of heart – an evil that he did not manifest here or at any other time in his life. His motives and desires in serving God were pure. He prayed to avoid the sin of presuming upon God's abundant grace. He sincerely lamented each time he did not follow God's way; in every error, he humbly accepted his responsibility, suffered the consequences, and repented. No, David never asked God for direction out of a mere show of religion; he did not seek God with his mind determined to act in a specific way regardless of what God said. David was a "man after God's heart." He served God with integrity – not with a pretense of piety.

Joab strongly opposes the census

9   When he gave the order to Joab, David had been, at best, ignoring God's word, God's way, and God's warnings. But God would not let him claim ignorance – this selfish, willful ignorance. God required David to face his own evil intent; He required David to hear His counsel plainly from a very unlikely source.

10   Joab's response to David's order was wise beyond his maverick character. He strongly objected to taking the census, reasoning,

> *May God multiply his people in Israel a hundredfold. The number does not matter.*

Joab reminded his king,

> *Are not the people of Israel your servants?*

Even Joab knew there would be serious consequences and appealed,

> *Why do you require this, my lord?*
> *Why will you bring guilt upon the nation?*

Whether David sought any advice or not, Joab's plea made the issues clear. His entreaty should have awakened David's sense of justice, his care for the people, his responsibility as king, and God's promises for Israel.

11   But, alas, Joab's words had no effect on King David. Years before this event, Joab had marred his ability to influence David with the blatantly insubordinate act of killing David's son Absalom in order to end Absalom's coup. Because of this murder, David assigned another one of his nephews, Amasa, to replace Joab, but Joab also killed Amasa, his own cousin. Including Abner, Joab had murdered three men who were important to David. Joab's wise plea did not change the king's mind.

12   Maybe the king thought he could write Joab off as a ruthless scoundrel, a rogue servant, and an ungodly counselor, but a king ruling wisely would receive counsel from any source and then ask God if the advice had any value. After being confronted by Joab, David's taking the census became willful disobedience

to God's expressed direction. The full responsibility for this action and its consequences rested upon King David alone.

David was not fated to require the census

13   Yet, it was not fate for David to pursue taking a census. He had a clear option to withdraw his order to Joab. Suppose David had humbly received Joab's words, considered the impact his actions would have on Israel, and made the decision to cancel the census. The people would not then be punished for an unauthorized census. This reprieve, however, would not alone solve the problem of God's being angry with Israel.

14   What would alert David that a serious, unknown problem even existed? An even more humble King David could ask God, "LORD, thank you for Joab's counsel, but why did I order the census that could have caused a disaster in Israel? This is not the way I want to use my authority as king."

15   Concerned about the impact his census would have on Israel, he could have gone on to ask God, "Are we out of danger? Or do we need to correct a problem or root out some evil?" If God had chosen to tell David what angered Him, David could have gone on to learn what must be done to solve the problem, as he did when solving the famine crisis.

16   Avoiding a tragedy would have been great, but David could have gone even higher if, after God were no longer angry with Israel, he asked, "LORD, thank You for Your mercy; what can I do now to bless Your people?" Instead of giving God a way to punish Israel, David could have given God reasons to bless the people for whom he was responsible, thereby turning an impending judgment into a blessing.

17   Speculating further, if David had applied this hopeful process to the Bathsheba temptation many years before, could he have avoided sinning against Uriah, and could his family have avoided the deep and long-lasting trouble that ensued? He had the authority to bless or to curse his entire household; the Bathsheba temptation may have been his final chance to learn that a severe punishment loomed over his large family. What if a humble David had asked why he was strongly tempted? What if he had considered the impact his adultery would have upon his family and had contrasted that with God's promises for his household – might he have found a way of escape? If he had chosen not to sin in a way that might bring a curse upon them, he then could have asked God if he or his family had a problem that kindled His anger, and, if so, how to correct it. Finally, he could have behaved in ways that would bless and not curse his household. Of course, David did sin grievously, yet God continued to advance His purposes despite the corrupted circumstances and Israel's tarnished king.

8-3 Under protest, Joab obeys the King's order
(I Chronicles 21:4-6; 27:23,24; II Samuel 24:4-9)

Sadly, even after Joab's plea, King David showed no inclination to change his mind and cancel the census. He sent Joab to count all of Israel. Joab took the military captains – who also resisted the king's command – and as many people as he needed for this loathsome project. Taking almost ten months to complete the task, they went through the land of Israel counting the people. Joab's count included only those more than 20 years old and only those who were capable of drawing the sword and going to battle.

2   Actually, Joab did not complete the task. He did not count the nearby tribe of Benjamin, which included the city of Jerusalem. Neither did Joab count the tribe of Levi, which was given 48 cities scattered throughout the territories of the other tribes of Israel. Because the Levites were set apart to serve the priests of God, they were exempt from military duty.

3   Joab did not complete the census for two reasons. First, the king's word was abominable to him. Not only did he believe it was the wrong action to take, but, additionally, he was not pleased with a task which was so far from his life's calling and passion as a military man. Fighting battles is what fulfilled Joab. He was not a civil servant, and he had no desire to count hundreds of thousands of people over a vast area of land. It was ten months of frustration for the head of Israel's vaunted army. Secondly, Joab recognized that the punishment for taking an unauthorized national census had already begun. "Joab did not finish counting because wrath fell against Israel."

8-4 God punishes Israel for David's census
(I Chronicles 21:7-15; II Samuel 24:10-16)

While Joab counted the people, Israel experienced no consequences, God did not personally halt the census, and David did not repent or direct Joab to stop counting the people. The king may have been hoping that there would be no punishment, or he may have been rationalizing that since ordering the census was already a grave wrong, he may as well let Joab finish the job. David did nothing to forestall the impending judgment. Then, after Joab had taken the king-ordered, national census for ten months, God began to punish the nation of Israel.

2   As a consequence, the Israelites began to suffer, and – finally – God had the king's full attention. David recognized the punishment to be a divine judgment, but unlike with Uzza's death many years before, he immediately knew why God was judging Israel. He was convicted and openly acknowledged to God,

> I have sinned greatly in what I have done. I implore You to take away
> my iniquity because I have acted very foolishly.

In this confession and entreaty to God, David offered no excuses and blamed no one else. He saw the punishment and knew that he alone was responsible. Feeling intense guilt, he implored God to take his sin away.

3   God answered his plea by sending the prophet Gad, another one of David's advisors. God told Gad to tell the king,

Thus saith the LORD, "I offer you three options. Choose one and I will do that."

David was alarmed to learn that the punishment had barely started. Gad continued,

Thus saith the LORD, "Choose either,

(1) Three years of famine, or

(2) Three months of defeat by the sword of your enemies on the battlefield, or

(3) Three days of pestilence upon all of Israel from the sword of the LORD and the destroying angel."

Now consider the options and decide which one I take back to God.

God offered him no immediate mercy or pardon – only a choice.

David chooses the punishment to fall upon Israel

4   God required David to choose the specific method of Israel's punishment. David considered the choices. The nation had recently experienced three difficult years of famine so that was not a good choice. Losses on the battlefield also meant the probable loss of dominion and influence in the world, which was not an acceptable option for David. David answered Gad,

I am greatly troubled. Let me fall into the hand of the LORD because His mercies are very great, but let me not fall into the hand of man.

David chose the three-day plague, committing Israel and himself to their merciful God.

5   Gad returned to God with David's choice in an the interaction that was all very cold and formal. God did not negotiate with David, and David did not debate with God. In His response to David's confession, God merely allowed him to choose the type of punishment. This meant that both the cause and the manner of punishment lay with David, and he experienced even greater responsibility and deeper regret for his census decision.

6   He accepted Gad as God's messenger, but God's response was not what he had hoped for. Although David had acknowledged his great sin and foolishness in ordering the census, God did not mention his sin. God did not condemn him, reprimand him, or punish him, but neither did God pardon him or release him from his profound guilt and responsibility. If God had assigned him a task to perform or had punished him severely, thereby allowing him to reduce the punishment intended for Israel or even make restitution, he might have had some relief. God had regularly given him a part in what He was doing, but not here; for three days David had to watch Israel suffer for his sin and feel still more personal grief and pain.

7   Such formal, impersonal communication with God was unusual for David, who, from his youth, had enjoyed intimate contact with God. Staying close to God was a high priority for any king of Israel and should have been a routine activity for this king. But, he had not prayed about taking the census, and it appears the ten-month period that followed was a selfish, proud, or childish time when David lived without seeking God's direction. Fortunately, this tragedy jolted David; he was about to regain communication with God in a dramatic way.

8   After David decided how Israel was to be punished, God sent a pestilence that killed 70,000 men throughout the land of Israel. Then God sent the destroying angel to Jerusalem, but when He saw the angel doing its work near the threshing floor of Ornan the Jebusite, God told the angel,

> *That is enough. Stop.*

Israel had been punished sufficiently for David's unauthorized census. God's anger against Israel was satisfied, but He was not finished. As with Uzza's death when David moved the Ark on a cart, God's judgment here fit the situation, and it too accomplished much more than punishing sin or correcting error. God had a plan to turn this tragedy into triumph, and He had a significant role for the aging, now humbled king. The final resolution of this disaster would break out into what may be David's finest days.

8-5 David makes an offering to end the judgment

(I Chronicles 21:16-26; II Samuel 24:17-25)

David and the elders of Israel were together in Jerusalem to mourn the deaths of the previous three days. They dressed in sackcloth, humbled themselves, and acknowledged their responsibility as national leaders. They repented for their part in causing this tragedy and made themselves available to do what they could to end the plague.

2   While David was mourning, he looked up and saw the destroying angel between heaven and earth with his sword still drawn and extended over Jerusalem. Was the destruction over? The angel's sword was not sheathed. This ominous sight caused David and the elders to fall on their faces. David prayed. As he had done three days earlier, he took full responsibility and admitted to God,

> *I am the one who ordered the census. I have sinned and done evil – not*
> *the people who are dying. These sheep have done nothing wrong.*

This tragedy had awakened the king's care for Israel and its people. Having watched the plague afflict the Israelites for three days and having witnessed the dreadful means of that judgment, David passionately interceded for them. He referred to the people as innocent sheep; he was the shepherd, and he had failed them. He lamented because he had ordered the census. O, how deeply David regretted that he had any part in causing all of these deaths, much less THE part. He pleaded,

O LORD my God, punish me and my family; please do not plague the people.

This time, in his confession, David did not ask for pardon. Instead, he asked that all necessary punishment be redirected from the people to him and his family. Yet, a punishment upon David's family would not solve the problem. Both the causes and the solutions for this tragedy were rooted in his actions as King of Israel. God's judgment would loom over the nation until the king dealt with his national sin – God now graciously showed him what he had to do.

3   In response to David's prayer, the destroying angel told the prophet Gad to direct David:

Set up an altar on the threshing floor of Ornan the Jebusite.

Its location was directly below the angel, who still looked very threatening. Ornan and his sons stopped threshing wheat and hid when they saw the angel above them.

4   As soon as Gad gave David the angel's instructions, David went to Ornan's threshing floor. Ornan, also called Araunah, reverently bowed his face to the ground and inquired,

Why has my lord the king come to his servant?

The king respectfully asked Ornan,

Grant me the place of your threshing floor that I may build an altar to the LORD on it. Give it to me for the full price that the plague may be stopped.

Ornan graciously responded,

Take it, and let my lord the king do whatever he thinks is right. I also give you the oxen for burnt offerings, the threshing implements for wood, and the wheat for a meal offering. I give it all.

But David replied,

No. I will buy it for the full price. I will not take that which belongs to you and make it my offering to the LORD. I will not take that which costs me nothing and make it my offering to the LORD.

5   David purchased the threshing floor from Ornan for 600 shekels of gold (about 20 tons in weight) – a very large sum of money. In addition, David bought all of the implements used in the threshing process of separating the grain seeds from the plant stalks. He bought the oxen that trampled the harvested stalks of grain and the oxen's wooden yokes. He bought the equipment, like stone cylinders which – when pulled by oxen – rolled on the flat, hard floor, crushing the stalks and the husks to release the seeds. David's new threshing floor, with a prime location on top of Jerusalem's Mount Moriah, may have been smoothed out of the mountaintop rock itself. The winds there helped winnow (blow) the chaff and straw away from the heavier seeds of grain. Although the land and business that David had purchased were extremely valuable, he had no

interest in operating a threshing business. All that he had purchased was available to God.

6   As he was directed, David built the altar on the newly acquired threshing floor. The rocks enclosing the threshing floor or those on the nearby mountain slopes provided plenty of uncut stone needed to construct the altar. But what was David to do after building the altar? Several times Abraham built an altar to call upon God, most notably on a mountain of Moriah when he offered a ram instead of his son Isaac. Isaac and his son Jacob, whose name was changed to Israel, also built altars and called upon God.

7   David too used this altar to call upon the LORD, but first – the idea was actually Ornan's – David offered the oxen on the altar as burnt offerings and peace offerings. In the burnt offerings, he burned the whole ox and submitted himself entirely to God, being ready to receive the mercy he needed or the punishment he deserved. In the peace offerings, he burned just the fat and internal organs of the oxen as he gratefully acknowledged this stay of punishment and God's gracious direction concerning the threshing floor.

8   Now God had what He wanted. This time, when David called upon the LORD, his heart was broken; he did not merely feel guilty. This time his commitment was to God and not simply a desperate cry for better circumstances. And this time, the LORD answered him personally and very dramatically from heaven by sending fire down upon the altar David had just made. God heard David's call and accepted his offering. David's humility, repentance, trust, and gratitude satisfied God more than any amount of punishment sent upon Israel. Now God commanded the angel to sheath his sword. The plague was over … but David was not done.

Chapter 9

David Receives Mercy ... and a Revelation

9-1 David worships on the threshing floor (I Chronicles 21:26-30)

David was awestruck; he had little reference for understanding this fire from heaven. In Abraham's day, God rained fire and brimstone out of heaven, destroying the cities of the beautiful garden plain of the Jordan River, including Sodom and Gomorrah, for their grievous sins. But at other times, fire did not come down from heaven as punishment. When the new nation of Israel had come out of Egypt, God led them to Mt Sinai in a pillar of cloud during the day and in a pillar of fire at night. When He made a covenant with Israel at Mt Sinai, God came down to the mountain in a fire accompanied by a thick cloud with lightning, thunder, and an extremely loud, trumpet-like voice – sights and sounds which awed and humbled the Israelites. Then, after the tabernacle was first assembled, the pillar of cloud and the pillar of fire remained upon the tabernacle as a visible sign that God was present among the people of Israel, leading them in the wilderness. Here, the fire did not consume David in punishment. Instead, to his great relief, he saw the angel put the sword into its sheath, and knew that the plague had indeed ended.

2   When God answered David by fire from heaven, He demonstrated that He had heard David's cry and had accepted David's offering. When God answered David by fire from heaven, He turned a dark place of fearsome judgment under the sword of the destroying angel into a place ablaze with the mercy and grace of the holy God. At this point, David also realized that the fire from heaven was God's answer to him.

3   According to the biblical record, God had never answered anyone with fire from heaven – not even Abraham or Moses. Fire did not come down on any altar that Abraham had made. In fact, God would send fire down from heaven upon an altar only two more times – once upon the altar that Solomon would build at this very location, and later upon the altar that Elijah would build on Mt Carmel. All who saw those events fell down on their faces worshipping before the felt and observed presence of their holy God.

4   David too was in awe. He did not feel deserving of such great mercies or of such special treatment. When God answered David by fire from heaven, He drew near to David to comfort and stay with him there.

5   The end of the plague! The answer by fire! What was David to do but worship God! He sacrificed again upon the altar that he had built, but this time out
of an abundance of gratitude and thanksgiving. "The LORD answered me! I was
responsible for a deadly plague in Israel, but God has not abandoned me!" God
extended mercy to David and delivered him from his heavy burden of guilt for
causing this tragedy. His spirit was again free to express his praise to God, joy-
fully and extravagantly. Because God had answered his call and accepted him,
David offered to God not only the sacrifice, but also himself anew.

6   Twice David offered sacrifices on his new altar, yet the appropriate altar on
which to offer sacrifices was in Gibeon with the tabernacle. David actually
thought about going there to sacrifice, but he was afraid of the angel's sword,
which remained drawn over Ornan's threshing floor. Each step of obedience led
to the next. First, David obeyed by building the altar. Then, being afraid of further judgment upon Israel and having the oxen and other items needed to make
a proper sacrifice close at hand, David decided to remain in Jerusalem. He sacrificed burnt offerings and peace offerings upon his altar, pleading to the LORD
for mercy and forgiveness. The LORD accepted his offerings and answered him
with fire from heaven upon this altar. Then, again at this location, the destroying angel put his sword into its sheath. Therefore, on this threshing floor, David
offered additional sacrifices, this time out of a heart of worship and thanksgiving.

9-2 The temple location is revealed!
(I Chronicles 22:1; Deuteronomy 12:1-14)

This is it! What happened next was even more breathtaking. While David
worshiped and poured out his gratitude to his most merciful and gracious God,
God came down in an even more powerful way. This time the altar was David's
contrite heart. This time the offering consumed was David's broken spirit. This
time the fire was the revelation of God's purpose. David expressed his utter
amazement when he exclaimed,

This is the house of the LORD God!

This is the altar of the burnt offering for Israel!

2   His worship and praise became so much more profound. "God has chosen
to put His house right here where I have built this altar!" The ramifications of
this revelation began to fill David's heart and mind. Being now humble and
grateful before God, he was amazed that God would still include him in His
divine plans, especially at this time when he felt so undeserving. From the ending of the plague to the spectacular answer by fire to this momentous revelation,
David was overwhelmed with the grandeur of God's purposes and with the
majesty of God's thoughts.

3   With this revelation, God completely renewed and gloriously expanded
David's desire to build Him a house. Thirty years before, he could do little to act
on that desire beyond the continual storing up of building materials. By the time

he received this revelation, he knew that God had chosen Solomon to build His house, and David may have assumed that Solomon would design it and choose its location under God's direction. But God had a role for David far beyond his own diminished expectations.

4   Of utmost significance, God brought together the fulfillment of two special promises in this revelation to David. First, in the words spoken by the prophet Moses to God's people at the border of Canaan, God promised to choose the place where He would establish His name, the place where His people would worship Him. Second, during the previous revelation given to David in response to his strong desire to build God's house, God promised that David's son would build that house (Section 6-4). At this stunning moment, God revealed that He had chosen the place of David's altar to be both the place where He would establish His name and the location where David's son would build His temple.

5   David, by his amazed exclamations identifying this threshing floor as the LORD's house and Israel's altar, showed he understood that God's revelation here was highly significant. This mountaintop was far more than a parcel of land on which to build an altar or a temple; God, in His wisdom, was working out His eternal purposes and putting David right in the middle of the fulfillment of both an ancient and a recent promise.

6   Deuteronomy 12 records the ancient promise. Verses 1–14 follow, with some key phrases underlined and three key words capitalized. Moses said,

> These are the statues and judgments which you shall observe to do in the land, which the LORD God of your fathers gives you to possess.... You shall utterly destroy all the places, wherein the nations which you shall possess served their gods, upon the high mountains, upon the hills, and under every green tree: and you shall overthrow their altars, break their pillars, and burn their groves with fire; and you shall chop down the graven images of their gods, and destroy the names of them out of that place.
>
> You shall not do so unto the LORD your God.
>
> But unto the place which the LORD your God shall choose out of all your tribes to put His name there, even unto His habitation shall you seek, and you shall come: and unto that place you shall bring your burnt offerings, and your sacrifices, your tithes, heave offerings of your hand, and your vows, your freewill offerings, and the firstlings of your herds and of your flocks: and there you shall eat before the LORD your God, and you shall rejoice in all that you put your hand unto, you and your households, wherein the LORD your God has blessed you.

You shall not do after all the things that we do here this day, every man doing whatever is right in his own eyes. For you are not yet come to the rest and to the inheritance which the LORD your God gives you. But WHEN you go over Jordan and dwell in the land which the LORD your God gives you to inherit, and WHEN He gives you rest from all your enemies round about, so that you dwell in safety; THEN there shall be a place which the LORD your God shall choose to cause His name to dwell there; to that place shall you bring all that I command you: your burnt offerings, your sacrifices, your tithes, the heave offering of your hand, and all your choice vows which you vow unto the LORD; and you shall rejoice before the LORD your God, you, your sons, your daughters, your menservants, your maidservants, and the Levite that is within your gates; forasmuch as he has no part nor inheritance with you.

Take heed to yourself that you offer not your burnt offerings in every place that you see; but in the place which the LORD shall choose in one of your tribes, there you shall offer your burnt offerings, and there you shall do all that I command thee.

9-3 God reveals how He must be worshipped

Moses declared that it was unacceptable for the people of Israel to offer sacrifices wherever they desired. Additionally, the Israelites were not allowed to worship God in any way they desired or felt would be right at the time. God established rules; to follow these rules brought blessings, but to break them brought curses.

God created physical and spiritual laws

2   This Holy God created the universe with both physical laws and spiritual laws that never change. Reliable physical laws govern the natural universe and make natural life possible. God formed the earth as a special place to support life. After creating plant and animal life on this earth, God made a physical man from the earth's dust. He breathed spiritual life into that first man, Adam, who then became a living soul. Eve came from Adam, and the entire human race descended from them; every person has been born with a body and a soul like those of humanity's first parents, Adam and Eve. Specific spiritual laws, including laws on how to approach and worship God, order spiritual life as well. Even before his sin, Adam had rules to obey, including one restriction which would bring death if disobeyed. Adam could freely approach God and talk with Him only as he honored and respected God's authority and wisdom.

Difficulty in worshipping God after Adam's sin

3   Everything changed for Adam when he and his wife ate fruit from the forbidden tree. While God's rules did not change, breaking one of God's rules

caused universal corruption. Adam's sin not only put the whole earth under a curse, but the resulting corruption was also passed on to the body and soul of every human ever conceived with the seed of man. As a result, every person was doomed to die, and no one could ever enjoy God's presence or talk with Him as Adam had previously done. Furthermore, neither a sinful Adam nor any other person nor any group of people in the corrupted human race could undo or fix the problem of being separated from God. Although mankind still had its God-given dominion over all of the earth, it could not restore the relationship with God that Adam's sin had destroyed. Making the situation seem even more hopeless, God Himself could not restore the relationship until mankind made a proper atonement – an act that a corrupted humanity could never carry out. Nevertheless, God had a restoration plan.

4   On the other hand, even after Adam's sin, any person could still know and worship God. The natural, created world and the conscience of every person communicate to each person essential aspects of the nature and the moral laws of the one Almighty God. Having this common revelation of the invisible God and His eternal power, individuals still believe in the Creator God. In fact, no person has any valid excuse for not worshipping the Creator – each person is entirely free and responsible to worship God. But, since worshipping and relating to the unseen God is unnatural, most people do as they please and trust gods of their own invention. On rare occasions, God has responded to such error and unbelief by manifesting Himself in a naturally irrefutable way, as He did when He sent fire from heaven during Elijah's contest with Baal. Yet, few people are actually changed following such a demonstration. For some, it confirms either trust in or opposition to God; for most, however, it degrades from an emotional worship to a proud, ineffective memory. Hence, neither God nor His servants attempt to force a recognition of His deity or an expression of worship from any person. Such coercion cannot be successful, and it is unnecessary because God's restoration plan respects the free and responsible humanity He created.

Even before Adam, God had a solution in mind

5   Another consequence of Adam's sin was that God lost the fellowship with man that He deeply desired. It did not please God that no person in the corrupted human race, not even Moses, could see the glory in His face and live; the loving, gracious God found this barrier to be unacceptable. Yet Adam's sin did not surprise God, and God did not need to change His plan. Although He had placed a perfectly innocent man in control of a perfectly harmonious environment, there was always the possibility that some innocent man, at some unsuspecting time, would eat the God-forbidden fruit and introduce sin into the world. Sin, as well as the death that comes because of sin, was always looming to defile people and the entire earth – after just one disobedience. There appears to have been no way for Adam either to escape the potential of sinning or to turn his innocence into a holy righteousness that remains free from sin.

6   Therefore, God's eternal plan would have been necessary with or without man's disobedience. From the beginning of the world, before He created Adam and before Adam sinned, God had prepared a permanent solution to the problem posed by sin and death. He had designed a way to condemn sin and reconcile the world to Himself so that any person could be at peace with God, even with corrupting sin causing havoc in his or her world. He sent His Son Jesus to make the needed atonement on behalf of the entire human race. God was in Christ Jesus reconciling the world to Himself. Each person who trusts this reconciling God enters the covenant relationship that God desires to have with His people. This permanent solution provided in Christ was God's great, eternal plan to deal with sin and death. But, with a corrupted humanity still having authority over the corrupted earth, it took several thousand years to prepare the way for God's Son to come and bring this purpose to fruition.

God makes covenants with Noah and Abraham

7   God gradually revealed how He must be worshipped after Adam's sin. At certain times, He spoke a dramatic, life-altering word to some who trusted Him. As they believed His word and obeyed Him, God revealed more of Himself. For instance, God graciously spoke a saving, though difficult, word to Noah after his world had wickedly departed from God's ways. Noah's world did not understand God's ways because they had been ineffectively passed down to the generations following Adam. By faith, Noah obeyed God's directive to build an ark in which his family and pairs of animals floated above the global floodwaters that caused the violent death of every other breathing animal. Noah discovered that there was grace in God's eyes and learned that God showed mercy in the midst of judgment. God made a covenant with Noah and the entire human race that a flood would never again destroy the whole earth. God spoke clearly in covenant promises, allowing people born after Noah to gain a better understanding of God's ways, both of faith toward Him and of proper living on the earth.

8   God made known more of His ways when He called Abram to leave his home and family. Acting in faith, Abram learned that God must be obeyed without reservation. God spoke inconceivable promises to Abram and made a covenant to give him innumerable offspring and a vast land with specific boundaries. For more than two decades, Abram grew strong in faith, learning to trust God instead of his own limited resources and to believe God instead of his impossible circumstances. God then confirmed His promises and gave Abram the new name Abraham, meaning "father of nations." This name, bestowed upon Abraham before he and his wife Sarah had a child or owned a plot of land, represented God's promise to bless him and added hope to Abraham's faith. God kept His promises and gave Abraham and Sarah a son, Isaac, even after they had grown old and infertile. While Isaac was his God-given heir, Abraham had other children, whose families also multiplied into many nations and inhabited vast lands.

God makes a covenant with the nation of Israel

9   God revealed much more of Himself and His purposes when He chose the family-nation of Israel, Isaac's son and Abraham's grandson, to be His people. At the time God defined to Moses and Joshua the precise borders of the homeland He had promised for Israel's inheritance, the land was inhabited by the descendants of Canaan, the son of Noah's son Ham. Since Abraham's ancestor was Noah's son Shem, the Canaanites were not heirs of Abraham; they could not stay in the land given to Abraham's seed or, particularly, in the land promised to Israel.

10   Not only were the Canaanites without the special promises God had made to Abraham, they were also without the special revelation which the Israelites received when God delivered them from Egypt's power and gave them His laws at Mt. Sinai. The Canaanites had no part in the covenant relationship which God, at that time, established with the nation of Israel. In fact, the Canaanites had so extensively abandoned even the common revelation of God's ways that their wickedness, especially in various sexual abominations, caused the land which they inhabited to reject them. Beyond this, the Canaanites and their vile, sensual worship before idols would compete for the allegiance of the people of Israel, to whom God had promised this land.

11   In this context, God identifies Himself as jealous for His people. God is jealous for the free, whole-hearted worship of His people, but not for His pleasure alone. Not only is it a high honor for all people to know their glorious Creator and His wise ways, but worshipping and following Him is also the most fulfilling way of life, by God's design. His jealousy is also a warning: if His people succumb to the appeal of idols and trust man-made gods which neither see nor hear, they will provoke their gracious, merciful God to anger. God's holy jealousy shows His deep desire for His people and encourages them to stay true to Him.

Israel is susceptible to error

12   The Israelites needed every possible encouragement to serve their Creator God because they were alarmingly susceptible to the distractions of impotent idols. Just a few months after their Almighty God had freed them from slavery and had demonstrated His power over Egypt's gods and the Pharaoh's mighty cavalry, the Israelites showed an evil tendency to abandon their God in favor of gods they could see and understand. They did this even while God manifested His presence in a cloud on a nearby mountain, and honored them as His special, covenant people. As He was writing down His ways for them, just forty days after Moses had ascended that mountain to receive these laws of God, the impatient Israelites gave up on Moses and persuaded Aaron to make a god to lead them on. The people of Israel shamefully worshipped the calf, which Moses' brother Aaron sculpted from their golden earrings. They brazenly gave that "god" the credit for their astonishing deliverance from slavery in Egypt.

13   With such grave errors as this in their recent past, God instructed the Israelites on how they could remain true to their Almighty God and trust only

Him when they conquered Canaan. God, by Moses, clearly commanded Israel to destroy all of the Canaanite places of worship and to wipe out the names of their gods. These powerless gods were not God. Although the God of Israel was not threatened by these gods, He commanded the Israelites to obliterate them until there was no hint about what or how the Canaanites had worshipped. If not wiped clean, those places of worship might catch the eye of God's people and tempt them to the idolatrous worship of false gods. If God's chosen people were led astray by the Canaanites' depraved lifestyle or the shameless worship of their gods, the land could reject them as well. Such a departure from God's ways could provoke God Himself to throw His Own people out of their promised land. In Deuteronomy 12, Moses made it extremely clear that every Israelite must approach and worship God only as He had directed and only in the place He would choose for His name.

God Himself chooses the place for His name

14   Nevertheless, during all of David's reign, the tabernacle built for God's presence and Israel's worship had been at the high place in Gibeon. But God never chose Gibeon, a Canaanite city, as the place for His name. Israel's tabernacle did not belong at a Canaanite place of worship. The nation of Israel would have demolished Gibeon's sacred place had they not signed a treaty with the wily Gibeonites. That treaty, however, did not give Israel any right to set up their tabernacle at a Canaanite center of worship, a place known for the practice of rituals designated by God to be so wrong and so dangerous. The area around the tabernacle may have been cleansed somewhat, but the history of worship at that location did not change. When the Israelites traveled to the high place at Gibeon to offer their sacrifices, they risked being distracted from their intended worship of their one true God. Even worse, viewing remnants of false gods or corrupt Canaanite ceremonies might arouse the curiosity of God's people or appeal to their senses.

15   This was why God did not tell David to bring the Ark of the Covenant to the tabernacle in Gibeon or direct him to sacrifice there when the destroying angel was over Jerusalem. God did not compromise His holy name by choosing to live among His people at a place of worship that had formerly been consecrated to pagan gods. The God of Israel did not honor this location or the pagan deities that had been idolized here.

16   Furthermore, the tabernacle's location in Gibeon may have been a reason that God was angry with Israel. The fact that the Ark of the Covenant was missing from the holiest place of the tabernacle in Gibeon raised a question about God's presence during the worship rituals that Israel's priests performed at the tabernacle. Yet, there seemed to be no ambition in David or in Israel to reunite these holy items. The judgment upon Israel because of David's census ended with the destroying angel over Ornan's threshing floor and with the instruction that David build an altar at that location. The glorious result was

God's revelation that this threshing floor was the place where His house, containing all of the holy items, would be built and where He would be worshipped as present among His people.

17   God Himself chose the place for His name – not Moses, not Samuel, and not David. God fulfilled His word to Moses in His Own way and in His Own time. Now, under David, Israel lived in the land that God had promised them. In this place they experienced peace and safety from their enemies. God's people met the condition in Moses' prophetic declaration:

   When you possess the promised land ... and live there in safety.

Now, near the end of David's reign, God fulfilled the prophecy:

   Then there shall be a _place_.

This was that "then" – at this very moment when God's revelation came to a humble, repentant King David. This was that "place" – on this very spot, on the threshing floor where David built the altar and pleaded for mercy. David proclaimed,

   This is the house of the LORD _God!_

He was the right man in the right place at the right time to receive this revelation concerning the prophesied home for God's name. Wow!

9-4 The temple pattern is given!
(I Chronicles 28:11-19 with I Kings 6,7 and II Chronicles 3,4)

   This revelation exploded in David's mind and heart. God not only identified the place for His name, He also revealed the blueprints of the house to be built and of the ministries to be done at this location. David later declared,

   All this the LORD _made me understand in writing by his hand upon me,_
   even all the works of this pattern.

He received the pattern by the spirit. From the temple location to its design, from the builders and the building materials to the maintenance and his son's management, from the priestly ministry to the organization of the Levites, David's spirit was ablaze with the grandeur of both his gracious God and this glorious new revelation.

2   In his spirit, the temple became so real to David that he could almost touch it. He beheld both its glorious beauty and its precise details. The dimensions of the temple itself were 30x10x15 y/m (length x width x height in yards/meters – the cubit measure in the Bible is approximately 18 inches or ½ yard or ½ meter), over three times the floor space of the portable, 15x6x5-y/m tabernacle that Israel, also using a God-given pattern, had built in the wilderness under Moses' supervision. Like the tabernacle, this temple was divided into two rooms, the holy place where the priests ministered to God on behalf of the people and the holiest place of God's presence. The temple was a magnificent stone structure with a roof made of cedar wood. Only the highest quality stones, such as marble, were used in its construction. Some of

the foundation stones were enormous, up to 5 y/m on a side. The outer walls of the temple glistened, being garnished with a lavish array of precious gemstones. Cost was not a consideration in the design or in the materials used to build the temple. The doors into the temple were made of fir wood, and a porch 5 y/m deep was in front of the temple. Two gigantic bronze pillars, nearly 2 y/m across, stood on each side of the temple entrance; their sculpted beauty was recorded in detail.

Design of the holy rooms inside the temple

3   As David, in his vision, entered the house of God, he beheld the splendor of a spacious, 20x10x15-y/m holy place for the priests' ministry, much larger than the 10x6x5-y/m dimensions of the tabernacle's holy place. The interior floor, ceiling, and walls were paneled with artistically carved fir and cedar wood and then overlaid with gold. David was amazed to see not one, but ten, golden candlesticks and ten golden tables with all of their associated implements, also made of gold.

4   David's focus turned to the wall separating the holy place from the holiest place of God's presence. The entrance into the holiest room of the temple was an opening 2 y/m wide in the center of the wall. This opening had two matching doors made of carved olive wood overlaid with gold. The golden altar of incense stood in front of these doors. Behind the doors, a striking network of golden chains hung in front of an exquisite, elaborately woven linen veil. This network of chains was replicated seven times around the capstone upon each of the two huge pillars standing by the temple entrance.

5   Entering beyond the veil, David gazed into the place of God's presence, the holiest room, also called the oracle. This most holy room was designed to be a perfect cube, 10 y/m on each side. (These exact dimensions would be specified for the holiest room of the temple described in Ezekiel's vision many centuries later.) Inside the most holy room was the Ark of the Covenant, covered by the mercy seat and its two cherubim. In front of the back wall and new to this most holy place were two large winged cherubim, intricately carved from olive wood and overlaid with gold. These two cherubim stood side by side facing the Ark of the Covenant. The tips of their inner wings touched at the center, while their outer wings reached to the walls on opposite sides. This holiest of rooms was elaborately embellished to be a glorious place of God's presence. Some thirty years before, God had not allowed David to build a house for the Ark of the Covenant. Now, it was God's time, and this was God's design.

Blueprints of areas outside the temple

6   In his vision, David's view moved outside the temple building to the court of the priests in front of the porch. He saw a massive bronze altar, on which the priests offered sacrifices, and a huge bronze basin, in which the priests bathed. The temple altar was 10 y/m square and 5 y/m high. It covered the same area as the holiest room inside the temple and was 16 times the area of the 2.5-y/m

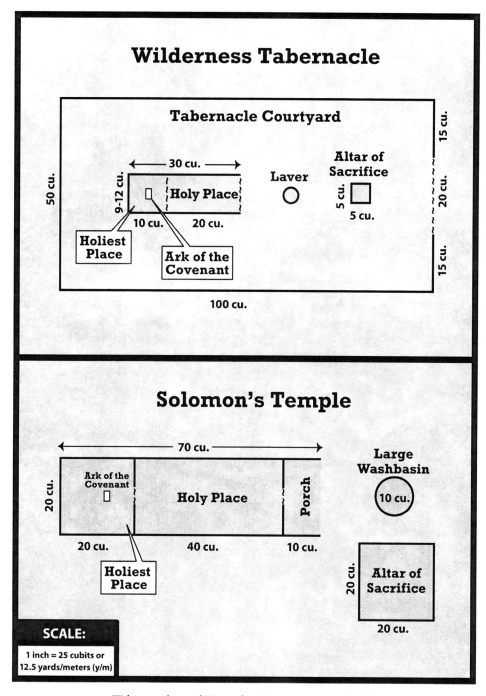

Wilderness Tabernacle

Tabernacle Courtyard

50 cu.

15 cu.

20 cu.

15 cu.

100 cu.

30 cu.

9-12 cu.

Holy Place

10 cu.

20 cu.

Laver

Altar of Sacrifice

5 cu.

5 cu.

Holiest Place

Ark of the Covenant

Solomon's Temple

70 cu.

20 cu.

Ark of the Covenant

Holy Place

Porch

20 cu.

40 cu.

10 cu.

Holiest Place

Large Washbasin

10 cu.

20 cu.

Altar of Sacrifice

20 cu.

SCALE:

1 inch = 25 cubits or
12.5 yards/meters (y/m)

Tabernacle and Temple Dimensions to Scale

square, 1.5-y/m high altar that had been built at Mt. Sinai for the tabernacle. In addition, he noted ten large washbasins, or lavers, five on each side of the temple. Under each of these ten lavers was a sophisticated 2x2-y/m rolling base; the historian detailed the specifications of the base design. The new and redesigned items for this temple were larger and more numerous in order to accommodate the growing nation.

7 The pattern that God was revealing to David was a precise blueprint for constructing every part of the temple. For another example, the large bronze basin was half of a hollow sphere. It rested on the backs of twelve bronze oxen, three facing each compass direction. The top edge of the basin was fashioned like the rim of a cup with lily flowers engraved all around. Attached below the rim were two rows of small knobs centered less than two inches apart. Each knob was molded in the shape of the large oxen supporting the basin. The outside diameter of the basin was 5 y/m from rim to rim, and its height was 2.5 y/m. The circumference of the top of the basin was 15 y/m, and it was about 3 inches thick. Because of the precision of the blueprint, the crafters knew exactly how far the top rim should curve out.

8 David, in his spirit, looked beyond the priests' courtyard to the great courtyard surrounding the temple. The design included parlors for the priests and many storage rooms to hold items and supplies needed for the priests' ministry. The great courtyard also contained treasury buildings to safeguard the valuable gifts that the people dedicated to the LORD. Gates in a wall enclosing the entire temple complex allowed entry from every compass direction. The size and majesty of this place of worship was almost beyond comprehension; every part was a choice work of art to glorify God.

Pattern of worship and ministry at the temple

9 Included in this revelation of God's house were the ceremonies of worship that would take place there. David observed the priests, descendants of Aaron, dressed in their holy, anointed garments and serving daily in the temple. Their work included lighting the ten candlesticks, burning the incense, and arranging the loaves of bread on the ten golden tables. With these services, the priests honored God and filled the holy place with light, aromas, and tastes. In the courtyard outside, the priests washed with water, offered sacrifices, and sprinkled the blood as instructed in the laws God had given to Moses, but on an expanded and more impressive scale at this location chosen by God Himself.

10 David also observed the ministry of the Levites. First, he saw them assisting the priests in their service, as written in the law. But here, God also incorporated music into the worship that was to take place at the new temple. With instrument and song, the Levites were to prophesy, thank God, and praise Him in ministry on an even wider scale than that which had been taking place at the Ark of the Covenant and at the tabernacle for thirty years. In addition, God gave the Levites responsibility over the care, operation, and maintenance of all of these

magnificent facilities of worship. Their service to God, to the priests, and to Israel would become still more highly exalted and honorable.

11 David's experience in God's presence changed dramatically from when he had first built the altar on the threshing floor. David began with a broken heart, pleading with God to show mercy and stop the plague. After God's answer by fire, David's worship became filled with gratitude and thanksgiving and then with wonder and awe when God showed him where His house was to be built. With God further revealing the design for His remarkable house, David's worship turned to astonishment at the scope of the plans filling his mind and spirit. As his overwhelming amazement quieted to a more reverent humility before God, David committed himself to God anew for this great task. His worship culminated in a faith and dependence as he called on God for His wisdom, help, and direction so that he might know and do everything possible to support God's purposes for this place where He had chosen to put His name.

9-5 Temple-building preparations begin (I Chronicles 22:2-5, 14-16)

This place of God's presence, of God's extraordinary revelation, was special to David. He remained there as long as possible, beholding the beauty of the LORD, inquiring about His temple, and writing down the pattern. The presence of his great and holy God could have completely absorbed him, but this was not a time for David to relax and selfishly enjoy his glorious time with God. The realization of the immensity of this undertaking eventually sobered him. God was giving him the monumental task to make preparations for the building of His temple, using these precise blueprints to guide his efforts.

2 When the flow of God's revelation slowed, when David's worship and praise quieted a bit, and when he had absorbed some of this information concerning the temple, he got busy. He had much work to do, and he did it with a renewed passion. Several teams of laborers were organized for the various tasks. One team of workers prepared the temple site itself. Three teams harvested stone, wood, and metal. Three production teams fashioned each of these raw materials into the items used to build the temple and its great complex. In addition, many were assigned to strengthen the transportation infrastructure with roads and transport vehicles so that the various teams could do their jobs efficiently. In order to direct the teams in doing their parts and to insure that all worked together, a management structure was established.

3 This extensive work required many laborers. Low-skilled workers would perform heavy or simple tasks, such as digging and hauling. Others having more specialized skills were found to cut and shape the metals, timber, and stone. Engineers, expert technicians, and masterful artisans were also recruited to create the finished items with all of their ornate details and then to fit each into its place in the house of the LORD God. Although foreigners living in Israel were required to work on this grand project, they too may have been honored to be involved.

Because of the prosperity of David and Israel, all of the laborers could be compensated generously.

4   With excitement and great anticipation, the work began. The team at the temple site began conditioning the threshing floor for the temple itself. They also cleared an area beyond that for the courtyards and the great plaza. In addition, the land around this large temple site needed to be prepared so that it could sustain a massive construction project. The production teams chose three nearby areas to receive, store, and work with the stone, wood, and metal raw materials harvested for the house of God. Each area was equipped to enable the teams of workers to carry out their appointed tasks as efficiently as possible.

5   While the site was being prepared, the harvesting teams began the laborious undertaking of gathering huge quantities of raw materials and hauling them to their specific areas. All over the country, laborers cut out large stones, and others brought them to the stone-working area where masons shaped them. Many miners dug up an abundance of mineral ore, while others transported it to the metalworking area where it was smelted to remove the impurities and to obtain such refined minerals as iron and copper. Some of the purified metals were combined to produce a superabundance of bronze. Those assigned to work on the infrastructure built roads, storage facilities, heavy transportation equipment, etc., to help the harvesting teams to be more productive. To acquire fir and cedar wood for the temple, David, and later Solomon, contracted with Hiram, king of the neighboring nation of Tyre. Tyre's skilled loggers harvested much timber while other workers transported the wood all the way to the woodworking area. Israel paid the wages of Hiram's laborers and annually exported grain to bolster Tyre's food supply. It was a time of peace, and Israel's neighbor to the northwest eagerly provided what it could.

6   David's temple preparation work progressed well. The harvesting and transporting of raw materials was beginning. The manufacturing facilities were ready to receive their specific raw materials. In these facilities, the production teams processed the raw materials into the various finished items detailed in the blueprints that God had given to David. In the early stages of production, workers manufactured basic building materials such as nails, door latches, and hinges from the metals and alloys. As the project continued under Solomon, every piece produced had to be fabricated precisely according to its specifications before it was taken to the site of the threshing floor. During the actual construction and assembly of the complex temple building about fifteen years later, neither hammer, axe, nor any iron tool was even heard; this amazing engineering feat generated no dust or leftover scraps at the location of the temple itself.

7   Even though David could not personally oversee the building of the temple itself, he had other good reasons for such extensive preparations. He said,

The house to be built for the LORD must be exceedingly magnificent, having fame and glory in all the nations.

Because this temple was being built for the LORD, and because of the physical grandeur that God had revealed in the plans for His house, and because this house was to be known and honored throughout the world, David pledged,

I will now make preparation for it.

He expressed another concern,

Solomon my son is young and tender.

In fact, Solomon was only about twenty years old; this project was too large and its purposes too lofty to leave it entirely in his hands. Building a house for the LORD must be done right; therefore, David prepared abundantly before his death.

8   Later, David encouraged Solomon in his task to build the temple by summarizing the extensive preparations that had already been made. He told Solomon that his teams had harvested an abundance of stone and timber and iron. In addition, David gave Solomon the tally of the vast store of gold and silver that had been set aside for use in the temple. Much of this had been accumulating for about thirty years from the time that David had extended his dominion over many nations surrounding Israel. He kept accurate accounts of the inventory of the plunder and gifts received from the conquered nations and reserved much of it to build the temple. For instance, the large wash basin and the pillars at the temple entrance were made from the specific brass David had received from nations he conquered north of Israel. He also mentioned to Solomon that he had hired many workers. But, as much as David had prepared, he still suggested that Solomon should add to these resources.

9   Surprisingly, David also told Solomon,

In my trouble, I have prepared for the house of the LORD.

It would seem that nothing would give David more pleasure than his work on God's house. Certainly, many personal and national tragedies had caused trouble for him, but the preparations themselves were not easy. Excavating the mountaintop, gathering raw materials, and preparing to build were all huge undertakings. When David acted on the revelation God had given him, much painstaking effort was required. As he committed himself and Israel to this task, the effort took its toll on him; he would not want Solomon to take any of this work lightly.

Chapter 10

David Transfers Responsibility to Solomon

10-1 Solomon is appointed to build God's house
(I Chronicles 22:6-13,16)

While the preparations progressed, David met with Solomon and officially delegated to his son the authority to build God's house precisely according to God's blueprint. Overseeing the teams of workers would provide a young Solomon with some necessary leadership experience and a sense of the magnitude of the task ahead of him.

God's prior interest in His house

2   In his meeting with Solomon, David shared essential background information related to the building of God's house. He began by telling Solomon,

> *It was in my mind to build a house unto the name of* LORD *my God.*

On that occasion, God sent Nathan to halt David's efforts to build, but David's desire to build God's house did not end. God's response to David's initial desire was an astonishing revelation that included the encouraging promise that David's son would build Him a house.

3   That promise to David reinforced Moses' earlier prophecy of God's Own intention to have a dwelling place among His people:

> *When* God gives you rest ... *then* the LORD *your God shall choose a place
> and cause His name to dwell there.*

The condition was peace in Israel; God would not even identify the location of the place for His name until Israel was secure. Additionally, in Nathan's initial word to David, God revealed His plan to make Israel secure when He promised that

> *Israel will dwell securely in the place I ordain for them.*

And again to David:

> *I will subdue all your enemies.*

At that time, King David's only national military effort had been to lead Israel's stand against the Philistines. The nation of Israel was then neither safe nor at rest from its enemies, but God had chosen His man.

God's continuing interest in His house

4   By these promises, God commissioned David, at least in part, to direct Israel's forces in battle, to defeat its enemies, and to bring peace to the entire

country. Establishing peace in Israel was a great work. God protected and preserved David while he obeyed his calling. But God planned much more than the expansion and glory of Israel; God was also preparing the way for His house to be built among His people.

5   This higher work remained on David's mind as well. In fact, at the end of his life, he told Israel's leadership that he had again desired to build God's house. Thus, David too may have had a higher motive in his military quest for dominion – a motive higher than nationalistic zeal, or selfish desires, or even divine service. If he had realized that peace in Israel fulfilled Moses' prophecy, David may have hoped that he could then build the temple.

6   But God did not change His mind. Though He had subdued all of David's enemies, God still did not want David to build His house. This time He gave David a new reason for saying no. Addressing Solomon, David explained,

God told me, "You will not build a house unto My name because you
have made great wars and shed much blood upon the earth in My sight."

While David was making Israel secure, God noted his war activities and again refused him permission to build God's house. Solomon would later say,

David, my father, could not build a house unto the name of the LORD
his God because of the wars which surrounded him, until the LORD had
subdued his enemies.

7   God did not condemn him; David did not make great wars out of a selfish ambition to conquer and kill. Shedding blood was a consequence of his military calling to lead God's people into a place of peace and safety. Still, the very actions that David performed when he obeyed God's call disqualified him from doing the work of building God's house; God chose Solomon for that task. One man could not do both of these great works.

8   (It is noteworthy that Jesus, God's son, the Prince of Peace, came to do two similar works. Not only is He reigning at God's side as conquering Lord while God subdues all His enemies, Jesus is also building a perfectly clean people to become God's temple in the Spirit. The complete subduing of God's enemies and the building of God's people for God's presence both seem far from reality in the early 21st century. Yet David and Solomon completed the securing and building tasks to which God had called them, and the Lord Jesus is even more certain to complete His greater works.)

David tells Solomon his place in God's plans

9   Although God again told David that he could not build His temple, once again, God did not end with no. God continued by telling David whom He had chosen to do this work. David now told Solomon what God had said:

A son will be born to you, a man of rest, and his name will be Solomon.
He will build a house for My name.

God did not choose any of David's living sons who may have had an aptitude for this work. David was able to assure Solomon that, even before he was born, God had named him and chosen him to build the temple of the LORD.

10   This new word containing God's second no came to David after his military campaigns but before the birth of Solomon. It was somewhat similar to the first great revelation, but it contained new promises for the yet unborn Solomon. During their meeting, David told his son what God had now promised:

- *I will give him rest from all his enemies around him.*
- *I will give peace and quietness to Israel during his reign.*

God never promised David a reign of peace and rest; these were great, new blessings for his son's reign. Solomon was not called to be a military leader; instead, he could expect peace in Israel without the wars and bloodshed his father had experienced. These new promises indicated substantial progress in Israel, and they demonstrated another way that God had advanced His purposes during the first part of David's reign. What a joy for David to be an integral part of God's plan!

11   Furthermore, in this second word, God repeated promises He had previously made concerning David's son, and this time He expressly spoke of Solomon – the named, unborn son. David listed these for Solomon:

- *He will be My son and*
- *I will be his father.*
- *I will establish the throne of his kingdom over Israel forever.*

God did more than confirm these magnificent promises; He applied them specifically to Solomon. Solomon was about twenty years old when David told him of God's amazing plans for him. This knowledge of his part in God's purposes would show Solomon that he was in a God-appointed place.

12   It was an astonishing position. Knowing that Solomon could not handle this assignment unless he trusted, confidently and whole-heartedly, in the God Who called him to this great work, David blessed and exhorted him:

Blessing: The LORD be with you and prosper you.

Exhortation: Build the house of the LORD your God as He has said you would.

Blessing: The LORD give you wisdom and understanding, and the LORD give you command of Israel.

Exhortation: Keep the law of the LORD your God.

Blessing: You will prosper.

Exhortation: Since the LORD is giving you command over Israel, make sure you work out those same statutes and judgments that the LORD gave Moses to enable him to take command of Israel in the wilderness.

Exhortation: Be strong and very courageous.

Exhortation: Do not be afraid or dismayed.

Final Exhortation: Rise up therefore and get to work.

Final Blessing: The LORD be with you.

13   David's exhortations all directed Solomon to be the kind of man and king who would be able to finish building God's house. David did not attempt to motivate Solomon by warning him about the consequences of failure; God had clearly spoken that this house would be built. David looked forward; he blessed and encouraged Solomon in God's ways in order that he might boldly perform his duty and carry out this great work.

10-2 David commands the support of Israel's leadership
(I Chronicles 22:17 – 19)

Solomon was not the only leader in Israel given duties for building God's house. David also called a meeting of the national leaders and commanded all of the princes of Israel to aid Solomon. The king commanded – his orders were not optional. He commanded all of the princes, leaving no one out. In doing so, David made it a priority for everyone in his administration to help Solomon.

2   David did not consult with his leadership as he had done when he brought the Ark of the Covenant to the City of David. He did not waste time persuading any leader who had not yet recognized the importance of this work. But, unlike his disastrous census, the source of this command was not an evil temptation, a personal whim, or a selfish agenda, and its result would not be a judgment against the nation. God was already blessing this task, which He had revealed to David. Gathering and preparing materials for the temple had already energized much of Israel. The leaders should not have been surprised that David expected them to assist in this project; in fact, many may have already joined a work team.

3   David next asked the leadership two rhetorical questions to assure them that helping Solomon would not be a burden for them. First, David asked,

> Is not the LORD your God with you?

Of course! The great God of Israel was their God. As leaders in Israel, God's plans included them, and they were responsible to serve Him. God was with them to guide and help them as they assisted Solomon in building the temple. David also asked,

> Has not the LORD given you rest on every border?

Again, yes! There was peace in Israel; the nation was secure.

4   David continued,

> God gave me the victory, and the land is subdued before the LORD and before His people.

As busy as they may have been, the leadership was not required to deal with the urgent security matters that occupy most nations. This was a time of rest, but it was not a time of leisure. This prophesied peace in Israel not only prepared the way for God to choose a place for His name, but it also provided an opportunity for the nation to focus on building the LORD's house.

5   David then told Israel's leaders,

> Set your heart and soul to seek the LORD your God.

This was a God-directed work. Normal worship times were not sufficient; neither could their communication with God be a simple matter of convenience. Each leader in Israel must carry out a clear and fixed purpose to seek God.

6   Israel's princes may have had other pressing duties and desires, but, in seeking God, they would obtain and maintain their desire to do their part in this great work commanded of them. These leaders could have many questions concerning their particular roles, but, in seeking God often, they would understand their place and be able to provide confident guidance. There would be many distractions and difficulties, but in seeking God, the leaders of Israel would find the ability to be faithful and help advance this work of building God's house. Additionally, as the national leaders sought God, their example would encourage the people to set their hearts to seek God and receive His help.

7   Finally, David told them,

Rise up and build the sanctuary of the LORD God.

There was work to be done! David named one specific objective:

Bring the Ark of the Covenant of the LORD and the holy vessels of God
into the house that is to be built to the name of the LORD.

The holy items crafted for the tabernacle in the wilderness would be gathered together in this new temple. After more than fifty years of separation, the Ark of the Covenant of the LORD's presence was to be in its proper place – in the temple built where God had chosen to put His name. This was a profound, historic occasion! God had His purpose; God had His chosen servants; and God now had His time and place.

10-3 Solomon is made king (I Chronicles 23:1; I Kings 1)

David, however, did not heed his own exhortations; he became complacent, but not without reason. For one, Solomon had taken responsibility for the building preparations. For another, David was getting old; he lacked energy, or even desire, and spent much time in bed trying to stay warm. After all, he had served God and Israel faithfully. Had he not fulfilled his calling? Was it not time for others to take up the work? Actually, no. He still had two crucial, unfinished obligations.

2   First, David did not clearly communicate to the nation as a whole who was to be their next king. David had previously assured Bathsheba that her son Solomon would be king. As head of the temple project, Solomon was the logical choice to be king, but David had not made that known. David had previously told Solomon that God had chosen him to build His house and that God had promised to establish the throne of his kingdom over Israel forever. David had also assigned the princes of Israel key roles in support of Solomon, but apparently he did not tell Israel's leadership that Solomon would be king. King David had not prepared the nation of Israel for a smooth transition of power to his successor.

3   Into this vacuum entered David's fourth son Adonijah, who exalted himself, saying,

I will be king.

Adonijah wanted to be king and acted on his desire. He prepared chariots and horsemen and fifty men to run before him. Although David knew of Adonijah's activities, he did not correct or even question Adonijah as to why he was making himself visible to the people in a royal and exalted manner. Knowing only what they could see in public, the people may have assumed that Adonijah had David's blessing.

4   David did not act to take control of this unsettled situation. Maybe he thought that Solomon was still too young or that Adonijah's actions were harmless. David was able to rule a kingdom and organize a great building project, but he did not properly communicate with his sons as a father or even as a frail king whose throne needed a successor. This unnecessary failing once again caused trouble for David and Israel.

5   Adonijah, emboldened by David's silence, enlisted the services of the commander Joab and of Abiathar, the priest who had given David faithful companionship and prayer support while David was a fugitive from King Saul. With the beginnings of an administration in place, Adonijah organized a feast to establish himself as king. At Adonijah's invitation, the servants of King David in Judah, Adonijah's half-brothers (other sons of King David), and the captains of Israel's army all came to the celebration to make Adonijah king. This was an incredibly high-ranking guest list; Adonijah had powerful, broad, and well-placed support. Some notables not invited were Adonijah's half-brother Solomon, the priest Zadok, the prophet Nathan, and the elite guard headed by security chief Benaiah. Apparently, Adonijah considered Solomon his only rival for the throne.

6   Nathan learned about the feast and acted quickly to prevent Adonijah's coronation. The situation was urgent since the lives of Solomon and his mother Bathsheba would be in danger if Adonijah became king. Nathan, knowing that Solomon should be the next king, informed Bathsheba about the distinguished assembly that had gathered to make Adonijah king and told her what to do. First, Bathsheba would ask David,

Did you not pledge to me that my son Solomon would reign next and sit on your throne? Why does Adonijah reign?

Nathan would then come in and confirm Bathsheba's words.

7   David was shivering in his bed when Bathsheba and Nathan worked their plan to expose Adonijah's intentions. Bathsheba also informed the king that

the eyes of all Israel are looking to you to tell them who shall sit on your throne after you.

David understood the urgent need. He assured his wife Bathsheba,

As the LORD lives, Who has redeemed my soul out of all distress; even as

*I swore to you by the LORD God of Israel and said, "Surely Solomon your
son will reign after me and will sit on my throne after me;" even so will
I certainly do this day.*

Not only had God spoken great promises concerning Solomon, but David had
also sworn to his wife that Solomon would be Israel's next king. Now, finally, he
resolved to keep his oath.

[8]   David called for Zadok and Benaiah to join Bathsheba and Nathan and
directed them:

- *Put my son Solomon on my mule, and*
- *bring him down to Gihon.*
- *Then Zadok the priest and Nathan the prophet are to anoint him
  with oil, and*
- *blow the trumpet, and*
- *say "God save King Solomon."*

Benaiah's security forces were to accompany a short parade ending in the public
anointing of Solomon and the public proclamation that Solomon was now king.
Lastly, David instructed,

- *Come back up with him that he may sit on my throne.*

The final step, establishing Solomon as ruler over Israel, was to happen immediately; there was no time to organize and hold a national celebration. David
clearly told these four:

*Solomon shall be king in my place, and I have appointed him to be ruler
over Israel and over Judah.*

David acted decisively to make the proper transfer of authority a reality for the
nation of Israel. Solomon was to take David's place as king.

[9]   The plan was a wise one. Benaiah, Zadok, and Nathan did exactly as David
had commanded them, and Solomon's coronation happened quickly. As Adonijah and his guests finished their meal, the city of Jerusalem reverberated with all
of the people shouting,

God save King Solomon.

Abiathar's son hurried to the coronation feast and explained why they were hearing such an uproar in Jerusalem:

*Truly our lord David has made Solomon king. Zadok the priest and
Nathan the prophet anointed him king, and the city rang out with joy.
And now, Solomon sits on the throne of the kingdom.*

These startling details halted Adonijah's celebration; the suddenly alarmed guests
scattered. Two serious consequences of Adonijah's attempt to become king were
the executions of Joab, and of Adonijah himself. Solomon would order these executions after David's death. In addition, Solomon removed Abiathar from his
office as a priest.

10　　Seeing his son Solomon on the throne of Israel delighted David. Even though the transition of power was not nearly as smooth as it should have been, the son chosen and named by God now reigned on the throne of Israel. David was able to see the fulfillment of still more of God's promises first spoken to him by Nathan so many years before and later confirmed and applied to Solomon. Although David was not properly able to groom the young Solomon to be king, he could trust in God to keep His promises to be a father unto his son and to establish his kingdom forever.

Chapter 11

David Organizes Temple Worship

11-1 God has another job for David

David still had one unfinished duty – another task needed for God's house. Much had already been accomplished in preparing for the great work of building a temple for God's presence. David had mobilized teams of workers, appointed Solomon to lead the project, and commanded the princes of Israel to help. By now, the Israelites were well aware of the activity in Jerusalem and throughout Israel.

2   Many people in Israel may have been captivated by patriotic visions regarding the temple that their great God deserved. Compared to all other temples, His house would be a magnificent physical edifice, showing the world that their God was most glorious.

3   Of course, every detail of the temple itself and every item inside was designed to give glory to God by its very appearance. It would indeed be unlike any other place of worship in its grandeur. But the Israelites were not to come this building merely to gaze upon its beauty, marvel at its amazing structure, and behold its ornate contents. This temple would not be a museum where human workmanship could be exhibited; the priests and the Levites were not tour guides.

4   Of course, the Israelites would worship their most glorious God here. Certainly, the priests and Levites would minister before the LORD with well-prepared excellence, and their ministry would be appropriately reverent and enthusiastic. This temple, however, would not be a theatre where people could be entertained; the priests and the Levites were not performers.

5   Of utmost importance was the fact that God was putting His name there. God had chosen to make this house the place of His habitation among His people. Even as God had revealed how every part of His house with its furniture was to be built to His honor, so had He revealed to David how the priests and Levites were to serve in this place. They would glorify God in the traditional worship, firmly established in Israel since Moses received God's law at Mt. Sinai. They would also glorify God in the new ways that He had revealed to David. In each facet of their ministry, new and old, the priests and the Levites were God's special servants, set apart to support and lead all of God's people in actively giving God the glory He deserved.

6   In order to give God His due honor in His house, the manner in which the Levites served could not be guesswork or impromptu decisions made by a priest or anyone else. Temple ministries had to be set up as precisely as the beams in the temple building. Even though he was very old and his body was not working well, David could not leave this task to Solomon. God had revealed the organization for worship to David, but He did not allow David to dictate the instructions so that others could implement them after he died. David was God's man to organize the priests and Levites and assign them to their temple ministries.

11-2 The authority of David's reorganization of the Levites

David's organizational work actually resulted in new commandments for the nation. Moreover, it seems surprising, even shocking, to realize that David's new rules for temple worship carried the same authority as the commandments that God had given Moses on Mt. Sinai.

2   On five separate occasions over the next six hundred years, the required service of the priests and Levites needed to be set up at the temple. Unfortunately, a queen and several kings would abandon the worship of God and even worship false gods in the temple at Jerusalem. Each time the proper services of worship were re-established, the commandments of both Moses and David were re-instituted. Of course, Solomon would obey his father's commandments when he initially installed the Levites to minister at the new temple he was soon to build. However, at four other times, God's servants implemented the commandments of David, as well as those of Moses, when they revived the proper ministries of worship at the house of God in Jerusalem. Listed below are excerpts from the Bible for those five installations of worship. Approximate dates are given and key phrases are underlined.

1005 BC – Solomon establishes worship at the new temple

3Then Solomon offered burnt offerings unto the LORD on the altar of the LORD … after a certain rate every day, offering <u>according to the commandment of Moses</u>, on the Sabbaths, and on the new moons, and on the solemn feasts, three times in the year, even in the feast of unleavened bread, and in the feast of weeks, and in the feast of tabernacles. And he appointed, <u>according to the order of David</u> his father, the courses of the priests to their service, and the Levites to their charges, to praise and minister before the priests, as the duty of every day required: the porters also by their courses at every gate: <u>for so had David the man of God commanded</u>. And they departed not from the commandment of the king unto the priests and Levites concerning any matter, or concerning the treasures (II Chronicles 8:12-15).

880 BC – Jehoiada, the priest, revives worship after Athaliah's corrupt reign

4Jehoiada appointed the offices of the house of the LORD by the hand of the priest the Levites, <u>whom David had distributed in the house of</u>

the LORD, to offer the burnt offerings of the LORD, <u>as it is written in the law of Moses</u>, with rejoicing and with singing, <u>as it was ordained by David</u>. And he set the porters at the gates of the house of the LORD, that none which was unclean in any thing should enter in (II Chronicles 23:18, 19).

725 BC – Hezekiah revives worship after the corrupt reign of his father Ahaz

[5][After Hezekiah had cleansed the temple] he set the Levites in the house of the LORD with cymbals, with psalteries, and with harps, <u>according to the commandment of David</u>, and of Gad the king's seer, and Nathan the prophet: for so was the commandment of the LORD by his prophets. And the Levites stood with the instruments of David, and the priests with the trumpets. And Hezekiah commanded to offer the burnt offering upon the altar. And when the burnt offering began, the song of the LORD began also with the trumpets, and with the instruments <u>ordained by David king of Israel</u> (II Chronicles 29:25-27).

620 BC – Josiah revives worship after Manasseh's corrupt reign

[6]And [Josiah] said unto the Levites … "Prepare yourselves by the houses of your fathers, after your courses, <u>according to the writing of David</u> king of Israel, and <u>according to the writing of Solomon</u> his son. And stand in the holy place according to the divisions of the families of the fathers of your brethren the people, and after the division of the families of the Levites. So kill the passover, and sanctify yourselves, and prepare your brethren, that they may do <u>according to the word of the LORD by the hand of Moses</u>."

And the singers, the sons of Asaph, were in their place, <u>according to the commandment of David</u>, and Asaph, and Heman, and Jeduthun the king's seer; and the porters waited at every gate; they might not depart from their service; for their brethren the Levites prepared for them (II Chronicles 35:3-6, 15).

450 BC – Nehemiah re-establishes temple worship after the Babylonian captivity when the temple and the wall of Jerusalem were rebuilt.

[7]And the chief of the Levites ... with their brethren over against them, to praise and to give thanks, <u>according to the commandment of David</u> the man of God, ward over against ward [and] porters keeping the ward at the thresholds of the gates (Nehemiah 12:24, 25). And at that time were some appointed over the chambers for the treasures, for the offerings, for the firstfruits, and for the tithes, to gather into them out of the fields of the cities the portions of the law for the priests and Levites: for Judah rejoiced for the priests and for the Levites that

waited. And both the singers and the porters kept the ward of their God, and the ward of the purification, <u>according to the commandment of David, and of Solomon</u> his son. For in the days of David and Asaph of old there were chief of the singers, and songs of praise and thanksgiving unto God (Nehemiah 12:44-46; see also Ezra 3:10,11).

8   David must have done this job really well. The prophets Gad and Nathan confirmed David's organization of temple worship and his use of the Levites. The ministry commandments of Moses and of David each carried God's authority for Israel and its kings. Furthermore, Jeremiah proclaimed God's eternal purpose for both David and the Levites, declaring,

> Thus saith the LORD, "If you can break My covenants with the day and with the night, to stop the orderly cycle of day and night, then might My covenant with the Levites, the priests, My ministers be broken and My covenant with David, My servant, be broken, to stop him from having a son to reign on his throne."

Jeremiah then proclaimed an extension of God's purposes, saying,

> "As the stars of heaven and the sand of the sea, which cannot be counted, so will I multiply the seed of David, My servant, and the Levites that minister unto Me."

11-3 David eliminates a major Levite duty (I Chronicles 23:24-27)

Major changes occurred in the nation of Israel since Moses had received God's laws at Mt. Sinai. At that time, the Israelites were a nomadic people, a group of ex-slaves traveling to a promised land. Under David, several hundred years later, they had become settled and secure in their God-given land with a capital city and a strong king. Soon they would have a temple for the Ark of the Covenant and the other items needed to worship God as He had commanded in Moses' laws. Thus, even after the changes in Israel, it might seem as though David did not need to modify Israel's worship at all.

2   Nevertheless, David declared,

> The Levites shall no longer carry the tabernacle nor any of its vessels.

With this statement, David eliminated one of the two major duties that God, by Moses, had assigned to the Levites. The book of Numbers, Chapter 4, details their responsibilities to take down and to carry the physical tabernacle and all of its holy items. When the Israelites traveled to Canaan through the wilderness for forty years, the Levites, under the priests' direction, disassembled, carried, and then reassembled the tabernacle each time they moved camp. The families of Levi's three sons, Kohath, Gershom and Merari, were each responsible for different parts of the tabernacle.

3   Presently, however, the Levites were singing at the tabernacle, not carrying it. Now that David had begun preparations for Solomon to build a temple at the location God had chosen, the Levites should never need to move the tabernacle

again. Actually, since the days of Joshua, the tabernacle had been moved just once, from Shiloh to Gibeon. Therefore, in practice, caring for the tabernacle had required much less effort for a long time. David prophesied:

> The LORD God of Israel has given rest to His people that they may dwell in Jerusalem forever.

Not only was Jerusalem to be the location for the temple of God's presence, but Jerusalem was also to be the city where God's people would dwell forever. It appeared to be the glorious fulfillment of God's covenant promise to live among His people forever. Because David expected that Jerusalem would be the permanent location for the temple and that this temple would forever replace the portable tabernacle built at Mt. Sinai, he officially terminated the Levites' duty to move the tabernacle.

⁴   The second major task given to the Levites in the wilderness at Mt Sinai was to assist the priests with their ministries in the presence of God. This was an indispensable service to God and to His people. At that time God stated,

> I have taken the Levites instead of all the firstborn, and I have given the Levites as a gift to Aaron and to his sons from among the children of Israel to do the service of the children of Israel in the tabernacle of the congregation.

David did not change this divine mandate.

11-4 Special Levite ministry is neglected prior to David

Historically, the tribe of Levi, one of the twelve sons of Israel, did not start out as God's special servants. During the plague that took the life of Egypt's firstborn sons, God accepted the sacrifice of a lamb and "passed over" Israel's firstborn. Immediately after the Israelites left Egypt, God made all of Israel's firstborn sons holy and claimed them as His special servants – but the firstborn never served God in a special way. At Mt. Sinai, the people of Israel made and worshipped an idol, which they honored as the god who delivered them from slavery in Egypt. When Moses asked, "Who is on the Lord's side?" the Levites consecrated themselves to stand with God in judgment against this idol worship and against the Israelites who were committing the idolatry. Hence, God chose the Levites to serve in His presence and to shield the Israelites from the wrath resulting from not honoring the presence of the Holy God. Because the firstborn remained holy to God, He directed a man-for-man exchange of Israel's firstborn for the Levites. (Every firstborn son born after this formal substitution had to be redeemed with money.) In addition, God mandated a special ceremony to cleanse the Levites and to set them apart as His special servants. God gave these consecrated Levites to Aaron's family in order that they might assist the priests and minister in the tabernacle on behalf of the Israelites.

²   For forty years, while the nation traveled together through the wilderness from Mt. Sinai to Canaan, the tabernacle was at the center of the Israelites, both

when they camped and when they journeyed. This extensive travel resulted in much work for the Levites to take down and then to reassemble the tabernacle. In addition, the priests often had hectic schedules at the wilderness campsites and needed much Levite support. The Levites assisted the priests in offering the ritual sacrifices every day, week, month, and year. They also helped when the people brought their tithes, voluntary offerings, and sacrifices for the atonement of sins. Since the Ark of the Covenant and the sacrificial altar were at the center of Israel's camp, it was convenient for the Israelites to offer sacrifices. While Israel journeyed to Canaan, the Levites stayed active in both of their God-given duties: serving the priests and caring for the physical tabernacle.

3   But life changed for the people of Israel. After completing a seven-year campaign to conquer Canaan, the land God had promised them, the Israelites needed to adjust to three dramatically different circumstances. The way in which they would worship their God was significantly affected by these changes, and, consequently, the ministry of the Levites came to be largely neglected. First, when Joshua and Israel's leaders assigned a large section of their new homeland to each tribe, the Israelites spread out to occupy and settle a vast land. Each Israelite family took possession of a plot of land and forged out its new life in ways that seemed best or most convenient. Because they were no longer a nomadic people traveling together, the Israelites had fewer national gatherings and felt fewer national obligations.

4   Second, the leadership structure in Israel was unsettled following Joshua's death; new leaders emerged somewhat haphazardly. Many of these rulers, called judges, were men or women sent by God to lead in defeating a nearby oppressive enemy. After such successes, the judges gained at least the tacit allegiance of some of the people. Although the people of Israel maintained their national and tribal identities, they did not have the strong national leadership mandating worship together that they had had during their forty years in the wilderness.

5   The third change that affected the worship of the Israelites was a practical one. Most families now lived a long distance from the tabernacle, which was erected in Shiloh, a city centrally located in Canaan. God had commanded national worship in His presence three times every year, but traveling to Shiloh, to the tabernacle and Ark of the Covenant located there, was not very convenient for many of the Israelites.

6   Because of the distractions and difficulties of living far from Shiloh and from families in the other tribes, obeying the commandments regarding the formal worship of God became a lesser priority for many of the Israelites. Some, like Samuel's parents, traveled to Shiloh every year to offer sacrifices and worship God, while others increasingly neglected God's way of worship. The dishonorable reputation of this era was that the people of Israel did what they thought was right, even to the point of making their own gods and holy places.

7 With such "self-rule" increasing and with fewer Israelites making the journey to the tabernacle to worship God, the people had less need for the ministry of their priests. The priests, in turn, had less need for the Levites' help. In addition, God's law required the people to offer specific portions of their produce to provide for the Levites, God's full-time servants in Israel. But, along with the decline in formal worship, fewer Israelites supported the Levites as required. Without this help, the Levites had to find ways to support their families and had less time for tabernacle ministry or any other kind of ministry, even if such service had been needed.

8 Making the situation still worse was a problem of corrupt priests at the tabernacle in Shiloh. The priests had religious power over the people, and they could make use of anyone they desired, Levite or not. Some priests would serve well, as God had instructed, while others, such as Eli's rebellious sons, took advantage of their position and defiantly disobeyed God's laws.

9 After Eli's death, Samuel, already a respected prophet of God, became Israel's main leader. Samuel led the nation of Israel to see God's majesty in dramatic ways. After he had anointed Saul as God's choice to be Israel's first king, Samuel continued as Israel's spiritual leader. Yet, even under Samuel, the Israelites had no clear national focus to worship God regularly. The situation of the Levites did not change noticeably under Samuel.

11-5 David expands the Levite duties (I Chronicles 23:28-32)

Finally, when David became king over all of Israel and moved the Ark of the Covenant, the Levites were given a long overdue place of honor. At that time, about thirty years before, David had appointed some Levites to remain at the Ark and at the tabernacle as porters, and he had appointed others to praise God with music. This, however, was only a foretaste of what God had in mind for the new temple.

2 God's extraordinary revelation of His Own house included the manner in which the priests and Levites were to serve. Now, although the temple was not yet built, David had to organize all of the Levites into the various ministry positions they would fill in God's new house. David described four Levite duties, as follows:

(1) Assist the priests in the service of the house of the LORD. As written in the law God had given Moses, the Levites were responsible to serve the priests as they ministered in the house of God. Their specific tasks included cleansing and purifying the holy items of worship. They were to bake the showbread, which the priests, on every Sabbath day, would place on the ten golden tables in the holy place of the new temple. The Levites also baked or fried the bread and cakes for the ceremonial grain offerings, which were a part of Israel's sacrifices. As the Levites performed such tasks, the priests were better able to

concentrate on their calling to minister in God's presence and make atonement for the people.

(2) <u>Thank and praise the LORD every morning and evening</u>. The Levites' praise ministry was to continue at the new temple. Such praise had not been commanded in the law, and the Bible does not record that it ever took place at the tabernacle until David had moved the Ark of the Covenant.

(3) <u>Take care of the house of God, the holy place, and the priests</u>. Being responsible for administrative duties in the house of God was another way the Levites blessed the priests. For the new temple, these duties included caring for the large courtyards and the many chambers used for storage and preparation. By cleansing the sacrificial areas, maintaining the facilities, keeping inventory, and coordinating the schedules for the ritual sacrifices, the Levites helped the priests focus on their required work.

(4) <u>Offer all the ritual sacrifices commanded in God's law</u>. To offer such sacrifices to God on behalf of Israel was a high honor for the Levites, and this work provided still more support for the priests. The ritual sacrifices took place every morning and evening, on the Sabbath, on the first day of the month, and during Israel's seven annual feasts. Many of these special times required offering multiple sacrifices. In offering a ritual sacrifice, a Levite did just what any Israelite would do when he or she brought a sacrifice.

3   Below is a step-by-step summary of what took place during the offering of a ritual sacrifice:

(1) Each Levite who offered the sacrifice brought the animal as commanded in God's law.

(2) This Levite presented the animal to a priest, a male descendant of Aaron, for approval as an acceptable sacrifice.

(3) The Levite then killed the accepted animal, shedding its life's blood in the presence of the LORD and before the priests.

(4) The priest took the blood of the slain sacrifice (only a priest – never the supporting Levite – handled the blood of the sacrifice) and sprinkled it upon and around the altar of sacrifice. The life of the sacrificial animal was in its blood. God gave Israel this blood upon the altar to make an atonement for the people's souls. For some sacrifices, the priest also put the blood of the sacrifice on the corners of the altar with his finger. Often the priest sprinkled the blood in front of the holy place of the LORD's presence. On the Day of Atonement, the high priest sprinkled blood on the mercy seat of the Ark in the tabernacle's holiest place. In special cases, he put blood on the right ear, right thumb, and right big toe of the one offering the sacrifice. The priest poured out the remainder of the blood around the bottom of the altar of sacrifice.

(5) Next, the Levite cut the sacrificial animal into pieces.

(6) The priests put wood on the altar to stoke and maintain the fire as needed. The fire on the altar must never go out.

(7) The Levite then presented the required parts of the animal to the priest.

(8) The priest received those parts of the animal being sacrificed and burned them on the altar. Different types of sacrifices required the burning of different parts of the animal.

(9) For some sacrifices, the priest who sprinkled the animal's blood ate a specific portion of the sacrifice. In order for an atoning sacrifice to be accepted in the sight of the LORD, the priest was required to eat his portion, thereby consecrating and sanctifying the atoning sacrifice.

(10) For every sacrifice, the priest had to burn all of the fat of the sacrifice and drain all of its blood; neither could ever be eaten.

(11) Along with every ritual sacrifice, the Levite gave a drink offering of wine and a grain offering of dried corn or pure flour, which could be baked, fried, or left dry. The Levite poured oil and spice on the grain offering (also referred to as a meat offering) and always seasoned it with salt. The priest burned a portion of every grain offering upon the altar; therefore, the grain offering contained no leaven or honey, neither of which can be burned on the altar. This priest ate the remainder of a cooked grain offering, but if the grain offering were dry corn or flour with oil, all of the priests were to eat equal portions.

4   In clearly laying out this Levite duty to offer sacrifices (a priest brought a sacrifice only when he was offering it for himself or on the Day of Atonement), David gave the regular, commanded worship of God a high priority and central focus for the nation of Israel. Doing so also encouraged the rest of the Israelites to bring their required and voluntary offerings to the place where God had chosen to put His name; they could offer their sacrifices only at this place, as God had commanded.

11-6 David organizes the priests and Levites for their work
(I Chronicles 23:2-23 and Chapters 24 – 26; also 6: 1-49 and 9:10-34)

After identifying all of the necessary Levite functions and duties, David assigned each Levite to a specific task. It was a long, tedious process involving much detail work.

Counting the Levites
2   First, David counted the Levites. The last census David had ordered caused a plague in which 70,000 men died, and Joab did not then count the Levites. Yet, even an aged David, having this regret, took another step of faith forward as God's servant and did what was necessary to organize the Levites for their work. The princes of Israel assisted David as he gathered all of the priests and Levites and counted 38,000 Levite males who were at least 30 years old. By comparison, Israel counted 8580 Levite males between the ages of 30 and 50 when they were given their work assignments at Mt. Sinai. (At that time, Israel also numbered

22,000 Levites males older than one month who were exchanged with Israel's firstborn males to become God's special servants.) David's counting mentioned no retirement age, possibly because the Levites' work would require much less physical labor now that the tabernacle would never again be relocated.

Allocating Levites to job categories

3   Acting on God's revelation, David divided the service of the priests and Levites into four job categories with many specific tasks. David, with the priests and princes of Israel, specified job descriptions and determined how much work would be required. Then they allocated Levites to each of the four categories.

24,000 for assisting the priests and setting forward the work of the house of the LORD

6000 for work as officers and judges

4000 for work as porters

4000 for praising the LORD and prophesying with instruments that David had made

Levite family groups

4   While counting the Levites, David and Israel's leaders divided them into family groups according to Levi's three sons, Kohath, Gershom, and Merari. They grouped the families of Levi's grandsons and great-grandsons as well. Where possible, David assigned families to work together. Special mention is made of Aaron, one of Kohath's grandsons. The priests of Israel were male descendants of Aaron, just one small family out of the tribe of Levi. Moses, Aaron's brother, was a special servant of God to Israel, but no one in Moses' family could be a priest. God chose only those in Aaron's family to minister to Him as priests in Israel.

Supervising the 24,000

5   At Mt. Sinai, God instructed Aaron's sons, Eleazar and Ithamar, to oversee the work of the Levites. Here, too, David put the priests of the family of Aaron in charge of the Levites who were allocated to help them in the work of the house of God. David himself, with the priest Zadok, representing Eleazar's family, and a priest named Ahimelech, representing Ithamar's family, selected 24 priests to supervise these 24,000 Levites. They chose 16 priests who were descendants of Eleazar and 8 priests who were descendants of Ithamar.

Assigning the 24,000

6   A lot was held to select which Levites served under which priest, as well as what the order of ministry would be for the 24 groups. The lot was a holy selection process done in the presence of David, Zadok, and Ahimelech, plus a Levite scribe and the leaders of the Levite tribe. They chose 1000 Levites to serve under each of the 24 priests. I Chronicles 24:7-19 lists the names and order of ministry for the priests who supervised the 24,000 Levites.

Assignment of Levite praise teams

7   Next, David and his captains chose Asaph, Heman, and Jeduthun to direct the 4000 Levites allocated to praise and prophecy. These three men had been

leading the music at the Ark of the Covenant and the tabernacle continuously for about thirty years. They then selected 24 group leaders – four sons of Asaph, fourteen sons of Heman, and six sons of Jeduthun. Including these 24 group leaders, 288 trained and skilled musicians were chosen to be music leaders. Again using the lot, they assigned 11 other music leaders to each of the 24 group leaders and determined an order for the groups. Finally, the remainder of the Levite musicians were placed in one of the 24 groups. I Chronicles 25:9-31 lists the leaders of the 24 groups in the chosen order.

Three family praise ministries

8   Significantly, Asaph, Heman, and Jeduthun each represented one of the three sons of Levi. Heman descended from Kohath, Asaph descended from Gershom, and Jeduthun descended from Merari. I Chronicles 6:33-48 lists their genealogies. (Although 6:44 and 15:17 named Ethan under Merari, Ethan was immediately identified as Jeduthun in 16:41 and thereafter.)

9   At Mt. Sinai, God had directed Moses to divide the tabernacle-moving tasks among Levi's three sons. Gershom's family had been responsible for the outer coverings and wall curtains of the tabernacle; Kohath's family for its furniture, the holy items of ministry; and Merari's family for the boards and bars of the wall, along with their heavy metal foundation sockets. Gershom and Merari were given ox-drawn carts to carry their loads, but Kohath and his family always carried the holy furniture on their shoulders when the tabernacle was moved. (David had eliminated these transporting jobs earlier in this organization process.) Now, for the new temple, the groups descending from Levi's three sons received three separate functions in the new praise and prophecy ministries. Asaph was to direct the groups under his sons in prophecy, according to the order of the king. Jeduthun was to direct the groups under his sons to prophesy with a harp, to give thanks, and to praise the LORD. Heman was to direct the groups under his sons in song with cymbals and other instruments for the service of the house of God.

Assigning the porters

10   David then organized the 4000 Levites allocated to be porters. Leaders from the Levite families of Gershom and Merari were chosen. Listed with the family of Gershom were the sons of Obededom, who had been a porter at the Ark of the Covenant for the prior thirty years. His sons were described as "able men of strength for the service." In fact, the porters of two other families were specifically noted to be "strong men," indicating that the physical presence of many of the porters was intimidating, a characteristic which supported the work of controlling access to the temple. The duties of the porters included more than crowd control; they were responsible for keeping anything unclean from entering the temple area – a vital task. The porters were selected by lot to one of seven locations: the east gate, the north gate, the south gate, the house of Asuppim toward the south, the west gate, the road going up from the west, and the area at Parbar toward the west.

Assigning officers and judges

11   Lastly, David assigned a place of service for the 6000 Levites allocated to be officers and judges. Levites from the families of Gershom and Kohath were responsible for the safekeeping and accounting of the vast accumulation of wealth. Moses' family served in this capacity. Shelomith, a Gershomite, is twice credited with having oversight over all of the treasures dedicated to the LORD, including both gifts and spoils of battle. Many of these Levites worked at the temple or in the capital of Jerusalem. In addition, 2700 officers and judges served among the tribes of Israel located east of the Jordan River, while 1700 served in Canaan, west of the Jordan River.

12   Although he was already very old when he installed Solomon as king, David then carried out this task of setting the Levites in their places of ministry. It is not surprising that he did not finish counting and placing all of the Levites in their jobs until the fortieth and last year of his reign. David was God's man in the right place to complete this assignment, so essential for Israel at that time and for many centuries to come. The God Who descended upon Mt. Sinai in fire to meet with Moses was the same God Who graciously answered David by fire from heaven and revealed His plans for His house. These rules may not have been written in tablets of stone, but Israel was required to keep the commandments of David, as well as the commandments of Moses, in order to honor and worship its God properly.

Chapter 12

David Inspires Public Support for God's Temple

12-1 David calls Israel's leadership to a national celebration

(I Chronicles 28:1,2)

David finished strong. After organizing the Levites, he called for a national celebration. Here, just before his death, David assembled many thousands of Israel's
leaders in Jerusalem. They included

* the national princes of Israel,
* the princes of the tribes of Israel,
* the captain of each of the 12 regiments which served the king month by month,
* those under these captains having authority over 1000 or 100 servants (264
  leaders from each of these 12 regiments of 24,000 servants),
* those who had oversight of all of the possessions of the king and his family,
* the Levite officers whom David had just appointed, and
* David's special mighty men with all of the valiant men.

2   Although his body was already weak prior to making Solomon king, David
stood to his feet. His presence commanded the attention of this host of leaders.
With his storied and stormy life, his military successes, his humble reign, and his
future in God's plans, King David was revered in Israel – and in the world.

3   David spoke to the assembly:

Hear me, my brethren and my people.

He humbly considered them as family and asked for their attention. No matter
how weak or frail his body, his words carried the authority and wisdom of one
who had reigned over God's chosen people for forty years and had served God
from the time of his youth.

4   Of course, David's being king was God's grand idea, not his own. He put
that in perspective for these leaders by listing several choices that God had made
in order for him to be king:

*The LORD God of Israel had **chosen** the tribe of Judah to rule, and then
He **chose** my father Jesse's family, and finally, out of all of Jesse's sons, He
chose me to be king over Israel.*

Chosen by God! As the youngest son in Jesse's ordinary family, David was an
unlikely prospect to be king. His selection was the fulfillment of plans that God
had been working out for many centuries. David was God's man.

12-2　King David: you have been the man (I Chronicles 28:3,4)

　　When Nathan confronted David, declaring, "Thou art **the man**," the words came with conviction and condemnation concerning his sins against Uriah. But in many other remarkable ways, David was **the man**, specially chosen and graced by God; David's place in God's eternal purposes was truly unimaginable.

2　　David was **the young man** who alone was ready to stand with God for His glory against the defiance of Goliath (Section 1-2). He also became **the man** who, as a fugitive from King Saul, set and enforced a high standard of respect toward the king God had chosen and anointed (Sections 1-6 through 2-2). And, after Saul's death in battle, David was **the man** who was anointed as king over Israel (Sections 2-3 through 2-6).

3　　Yet David's being king over God's people was an opportunity for him to feature even more significantly in God's plans. As king, he was **the man** whom God exalted to be internationally famous and even feared (Chapter 3). King David was **the man** whose early priority was to exalt God before His people by bringing the Ark of God's presence into Jerusalem. In doing so, David energized the nation of Israel to seek God (Sections 4-4 through 5-2).

4　　King David was **the man** who appointed the Levites to lead in daily worship and praise to God at the Tabernacle in Gibeon and at the Ark of the Covenant in Jerusalem (Section 5-3). Not only did this new ministry advance God's higher purposes for the Levites, but their music, greatly and consistently exalting God, was also in harmony with God's declaration that the whole earth would be filled with His glory.

5　　After moving the Ark, King David was **the man** who expressed his desire, his grand idea, to build God a house (Section 6-1). He told this gathering of Israel's leaders,

> *In my heart, I desired to build a house of rest for the Ark of the Covenant of the LORD and for the footstool of our God.*

The tabernacle built by Moses in the wilderness was not only a sacred place of worship for the nation, it was also the God-ordained home for the Ark of His presence. The suggestion that the Ark of the Covenant be housed in a different, permanent structure was a bold one.

6　　While even God said that this desire of his heart was a good one, David was **not the man** God had chosen to build His house (Section 6-2). Now, at the end of his life, David disclosed to this large assembly,

> *God told me, "You will not build a house for My name because you have been a man of war and have shed blood."*

Briefly and honestly, David explained why God had not allowed him to build the temple.

7　　But King David was **the man** to whom God revealed astounding new, eternal purposes (Sections 6-3 through 6-8). God promised to build David's house and kingdom and to establish both forever. This word from God stunned David, yet he joined his heart with God and His purposes, embracing them in faith and acting on them where he could.

8   Instead of building God's house, King David was **the man** called by God to make war and to bring security to the land of Israel (Section 10-1). He obeyed his calling to lead Israel's military in subduing the surrounding nations, thus becoming **the man** to bring peace to Israel (Section 7-1).

9   King David followed this important mission as **the man** who distinguished himself and honored his God by ruling his kingdom well, using God's standards of judgment and justice (Section 7-2). As a result, David's earthly reign provided the world with a glimpse of God's purposes for the rule of His Own eternal kingdom and for the manner in which His Own Son would reign on the throne of David forever.

10   Regrettably, David was also **the man** responsible for a massive, deadly plague on the people of Israel. When he offered sacrifices on an altar he built on Mt. Moriah in Jerusalem, he greatly mourned both his decision to take a census and the grave consequences that resulted (Chapter 8).

11   A humble and grateful King David was then **the man** to whom God revealed the location of the temple to be built for His name. This second, extraordinary revelation was an astonishing act of God's mercy. God also revealed to David the blueprints for the magnificent temple itself and the organization for the worship ministries that were to take place there (Sections 9-1 through 9-4). The nomadic days of God's people had ended long ago. With the nation of Israel secure and at peace, God could specify a permanent location for His name, the place where He Himself would dwell among His people.

12   Although nearing the end of his life, David was **the man** to accomplish several crucial God-given tasks (Sections 9-5, 10-3, & 11-6). The preparation to build the temple, the transfer of royal authority to Solomon, and the tedious organizing of the Levites all made the final years of David's reign quite eventful.

13   David had begun his life well and had matured as God's servant. Now, at 70 years of age, despite enduring long detours and making serious errors, he had fulfilled his God-given calling and finished his life well.

12-3 David informs and exhorts Israel's leadership
(I Chronicles 28:1,2,5-8)

Without a doubt, David was leaving a tremendous legacy. He and his royal family had also been granted a glorious future in God's plans. But David had not brought Israel's leadership together in order to exalt himself or his place in history, and he had more in mind than a simple disclosure of details or delegation of duties. He was about to die, and in his final actions, he once again displayed his heart to bless Israel and to honor God. During this national celebration, David

• publicly informed the nation's leadership of God's plans and directed them to obey God,

- publicly charged Solomon to build God's house,
- inspired personal giving toward building the temple,
- gave God His due honor in the presence of His people, and
- hosted a public coronation of Solomon as the King of Israel.

2   Because there had been no ceremony for the hasty, need-of-the-moment crowning of Solomon as king, David informed Israel's leaders of three of God's purposes for his son Solomon.

(1) God chose Solomon to succeed David as Israel's king:

> The LORD has given me many sons, and from among them, He has chosen
> Solomon to sit upon the throne of the kingdom of the LORD over Israel.

David did not choose Solomon as his favorite over Adonijah; he assured these leaders that God had chosen Solomon.

(2) God selected Solomon to build His house:

> Your son Solomon shall build My house and My courts.

Neither did David choose the builder of God's house. He would have built it himself, but God, actively working out His plan, chose his son.

(3) God applied the astonishing promises for David's son, specifically to Solomon. David told this leadership assembly what God said.

> I have chosen your son Solomon to be My son and I will be his father.
> Moreover, I will establish his kingdom forever if he be constant to do My
> commandments and My judgments.

3   Such promises concerning "God's son" and "forever" had stunned David thirty years before, but having found God to be completely faithful to His revealed word, he spoke to the leaders with confidence. He believed that God, Who had showered blessings upon Israel during his reign, would grant the nation and its new king an even more blessed future.

4   The question now was, "Which of God's people would be a part of it?" In the light of God's sure promises and eternal purposes, David elevated the significance of this moment:

> In the sight of the people of God, and in the audience of our God.

The king urged this entire assembly:

> Keep and seek all of the commandments of the LORD your God in order
> to possess this good land and leave it to your children forever.

5   These leaders, with the Israelites, had seen God fulfill many of His promises, including their dwelling securely in the land He had promised to give them. David expected that their experience of having God's abundant blessings would encourage them to seek and obey God because doing so was the only way to be sure that they and their families would stay in their good land – and stay in it forever.

6   In the light of God's great work of bringing the nation so far, these leaders could lead with greater determination. Knowing that God had still more

promises and purposes to fulfill, Israel's leadership could heartily embrace their obligations to serve and strengthen the nation along with its new, God-chosen king. Exemplifying this commitment, they could then direct their constituents or servants throughout the land to add their enthusiastic support.

12-4 David commissions and exhorts Solomon publicly
(I Chronicles 28:9 – 21)

Without waiting for the leadership gathered in Jerusalem to respond to his exhortation, David turned his focus to his son Solomon. Wasting no words, he began with the most important need – Solomon's relation to his God. He instructed his son:

- *Know the God of your father.*
- *Serve God with a perfect heart.*
- *Serve God with a willing mind.*

2   Serving God was more than a father's desire, it was a wise way to live. David explained,

> *God sees into the heart and understands every imagination considered in the mind.*

Unlike other gods, this God cannot be fooled. Knowing every allegiance and hatred, understanding every plan and motive, this all-wise God is never surprised and is able to direct His servants in the best way.

3   As he had just done with the leaders, David made it clear that Solomon could not properly serve God if he did not personally seek Him.

> *If you seek God, you will find Him; but if you do not seek God and His ways, He will cast you aside forever.*

The consequences of forsaking God would be severe.

4   David charged Solomon with a high calling:

> *Pay attention to this: God has chosen you to build a house for the sanctuary.*

This house was not merely for the Ark of the Covenant; it was for the sanctuary – the sanctuary of God's presence. In fact, David had just described the Ark as God's footstool on the earth. God chose Solomon to build a very special house.

5   A few years earlier, in a private meeting, David had put Solomon in charge of building the temple. Ideally, in supervising the work, Solomon would gain leadership skills, wisdom, and confidence. And, since he had been officially reigning on Israel's throne, Solomon was ready with the authority he needed. David's son was fully prepared to press the project forward.

6   Now, prior to his death, David publicly commissioned his son to build God's house:

> *Be strong, and do it.*

Being strong was an attitude: Solomon must confront every obstacle and lift it out of the way. Being strong was also a purpose: he must focus on his God-given work, advancing through every discouragement and avoiding the difficult distractions that had obstructed his father. Even further, being strong was a power: this son of David needed to take charge of each situation and bring it under control in order to complete his building work fully and properly. Though David's commission to his son was short, direct, and uncomplicated, Solomon's task was not simple.

7   Next, David gave his son the blueprints. Israel's leaders witnessed David as he released this priceless temple pattern to Solomon. They would know clearly that building God's house was not a haphazard build-as-you-go religious project and that Solomon could not build in his own way. Every part of the temple was God's design. While God's pattern allowed for artistic freedom, each item must be built according to its precise specifications.

8   David publicly reviewed the contents of the blueprints. They described the physical temple, the surrounding complex of structures, and the organization of worship activities to take place at the temple (Sections 9-4 and 11-6). He also gave an account of the gold and silver that had been set aside and then listed many specific items that Solomon was to make from this supply of gold and silver.

9   In front of this great assembly of leaders, David told how God had revealed the pattern for His temple:

> *All this, the LORD made me understand in writing by His hand upon*
> *me, even all the works of this pattern.*

This knowledge of God's direct help with David's understanding and writing down of the vision may have reminded the assembly of leaders of the significant time when God Himself wrote the pattern for the wilderness tabernacle. God gave that pattern to Moses with the command,

> *See that you make everything exactly as it is laid out in the pattern I*
> *showed you.*

10   David now encouraged his son to the task before him:

- *Be strong and courageous in building this house.*
- *Let nothing make you afraid or discourage you.*

He spoke to relax Solomon. Although the great work before his son was not trivial, and although it would require much diligent effort, Solomon did need not to fear.

11   David continued,

> *The LORD God, even my God, will be with you. He will not fail you;*
> *He will not leave you until you have finished all the work for the service*
> *of the house of the LORD.*

Solomon was young, and it was critical that Solomon's confidence and hope be in the ever-present, never-failing God Who had remained with David through many years of blessing and hardship.

12   And Solomon had good reason to trust his father's God.

- David's gracious God, Who had anointed and called David as a young shepherd, had also chosen and called Solomon before he was born.
- David's faithful God, Who had established him as king and had secured his reign for forty years, had established Solomon as Israel's king and would secure his reign as well.
- David's merciful God, Who had so often answered David's cry in times of failure, would provide mercy for a humble Solomon as well.
- David's wise God, Who had guided him in so many difficult circumstances, would do the same for Solomon.
- David's eternal God, Who had already begun to fulfill some of His purposes, would continue His eternal work with Solomon as Israel's king.

¹³   David concluded his commissioning word to Solomon by pointing out that many others were ready to assist him.

- *The priests and the Levites, whom I have organized, will be with you to help in the service of the house of God.*
- *Skilled workmen will be with you for the building and for the crafting of all of the detailed items that are required.*
- *The princes and the people will do whatever you command them to do.*

All authority for building the house of God belonged to his son. In the presence of Israel's leaders, David proclaimed that those who led worship and those who constructed the temple, as well as any other leader or citizen, were entirely available to Solomon as he needed them.

12-5 David and leaders make offerings to build God's house
(I Chronicles 29:1-9)

Having commissioned Solomon and exhorted both Solomon and Israel's leaders to their tasks, David told this large gathering,

Though chosen by God, Solomon is yet young and tender, and this work is great. The palace is not for man but for the LORD God.

David had spoken similar words immediately after receiving the vision of God's house.

Solomon my son is young and tender, and the house of God must be exceedingly magnificent . . . .

At that time, he pledged,

I will make preparation for it.

²   Now, several years later, David announced to this assembly,

I have prepared with all my might for the house of my God.

David did not hold back; he spearheaded the massive undertaking. Resources were harvested from across the land, and the huge inventory of tribute and plunder was released for use in this building project. He listed some of the materials already gathered:

*Gold ... silver ... brass ... wood ... colorful, sparkling stones ... pre-
cious gems ... and marble stones in abundance.*

3   In addition, David made tangible, personal sacrifices, but he did not call
them sacrifices:

*Because I have set my affection to the house of my God, I have given, of
my own proper store of gold and silver, to the house of my God, over and
above all that I have prepared for the holy house.*

David specified his heart's motivation, three times uttering the phrase: "the house
of my God." This underscored his earlier mention of the purpose of his heart to
build a house of rest for the Ark. His longing for God's house appeared now to
be stronger and more personal than ever.

4   Making a huge offering from his own possessions, David designated specific
amounts of gold (3000 talents or about 100 tons) and silver (7000 talents or
about 235 tons) to overlay the walls of God's house. And he gave additional gold
and silver to make other precious items specified in the blueprints. Yes, David
was rich, but he held nothing back from the house of his God.

5   David gave this assembly of leaders the same opportunity to give, asking,

And who, today, is willing to consecrate his service unto the LORD?

David did not extend this offer to Israel's leaders until they knew that he had
made ready to build and that he had freely invested himself and his own resources
to build God's house.

6   But he did not attempt to coerce their sacrifice nor to obligate them by his
extravagant personal gifts. His genuine example was that of a man whose deep
desire was to give to God's house. King David did not pledge to release resources
on the condition that the leaders also give. Neither did he set up a giving contest. No one could outgive the king, and no one competed with any other to see
who would give most.

7   Importantly, David asked for their willing service; their sacrifice for God's
house was not a duty. Even more, their gifts were not simply a general donation
added to a common fund, nor were they a contribution to an undefined project.
In the blueprints God had given to David, the architecture, materials, and service
required in order for this building to function as God's house were all precisely
defined. The leaders could give to areas that matched their own gifts, abilities,
and interests. And this project had a clear leader in David's son, who had been
chosen by God and had now been publicly commissioned to complete the task.

8   Being thus properly prepared and motivated to contribute, the response was
staggering. Israel's leaders, from the nation's top officials to those having much
smaller responsibilities, gave abundantly for the service of the house of God ...
and they offered willingly. The total gifts offered by Israel's leaders exceeded the
amount David had given and included

Gold: more than 5000 talents
Silver: 10,000 talents

Brass: 18,000 talents
Iron: 100,000 talents
Precious stones from those who had them.

⁹   Joy was the immediate effect of this giving. The people rejoiced because they had given with perfect, undivided hearts; because they had made willing, unco-erced contributions; and because they had directed their offerings to the LORD, not to David, nor to Solomon, nor simply to a worthy project. Predictably, David rejoiced as well. The great joy produced by their sacrifice substantially outshone any personal or material loss they may have experienced in giving so generously toward the building of God's house.

12-6 David blesses God (I Chronicles 29:10-21)

God had abundantly blessed David, Solomon, the nation, the leaders, and the people of Israel. David now blessed the LORD before the entire assembly.

²   First, he extolled God, saying,

> *Blessed are You, LORD God of Israel our Father, forever and ever. Thine, O LORD, is the greatness, and the power, and the glory, and the victory, and the majesty.*

³   As David proclaimed next, God owns all, and every power exists only because it was given by Him.

> *For all that is in the heaven and in the earth is Yours; Thine is the king-dom, O LORD, and You are exalted as head above all.*

> *Both riches and honor come from You, and You reign over all; and in Your hand is power and might; and in Your hand is the power to make great, and to give strength unto all.*

All! All glory to their Almighty God and King, Who is the source and giver of all riches, honor, and strength.

⁴   David then blessed Israel's great God with thanksgiving and praise.

> *Now, therefore, our God, we thank You and praise Your glorious name.*

He could have thanked the generous leaders, individually and collectively, or he could have thanked God for specific blessings so clearly seen, but he did not. He thanked God alone. David could have praised God for all He had done to make this national gathering a huge success, but he did not. He praised God's glorious name. Being struck anew by the grace needed simply to give willingly, David continued,

> *But who am I, and what is my people, that we should be able to offer so willingly after this sort? For all things come from You, and of Your Own have we given to You.*

> *For we are strangers before You, and sojourners, as were all of our fathers: our days on the earth are as a shadow, and there is none abid-ing.*

5   "All comes from God." David repeated that theme yet again as he blessed
God further:

> O LORD our God, all of this store that we have prepared to build You a
> house for Your holy name comes from Your hand and is all Your Own.

He had not mentioned the temple until now. It had been the focus of their giving, but God Himself was the focus of his praise. Such was the king's perspective
at the close of a life wholeheartedly given to God and His glory. David testified,

> I know also, my God, that You test the heart and have pleasure in
> uprightness. As for me, in the uprightness of my heart I have willingly
> offered all of these things.

6   David closed his prayer of blessing to God by requesting that Solomon and
the people of Israel always have willing and obedient hearts toward God and His
ways:

> And now have I seen with joy Your people, which are present here, offer
> willingly unto You O LORD God of Abraham, Isaac, and of Israel, our
> fathers.
>
> Keep this forever in the imagination of the thoughts of the heart of Your
> people and prepare their heart unto You:
>
> and give unto Solomon, my son, a perfect heart
> - to keep Your commandments, Your testimonies, and Your statutes, and
> - to do all these things, and
> - to build the palace, for which I have made provision.

7   During this gathering, David had publicly challenged the leaders, commissioned Solomon, inspired willing offerings, and worshipped God. With his last
act, he led the people into the presence of their God and exhorted those assembled here,

> Now bless the LORD your God.

In response, all of the congregation blessed their LORD God and respectfully
bowed down their heads; they worshipped the LORD and the king.

8   Following David's example, this great and extended assembly set their focus
upon God. The Israelites' worship led them immediately to make burnt offerings
to the LORD, thereby giving themselves entirely to God. The next day they continued their worship of God by offering thousands of sacrifices.

9   It was an occasion of joyful praise and thankful acknowledgement of God's
supply. The assembly also sacrificed in recognition of their great need. They
looked ahead to a young king leading the monumental task of building a temple;
the purposes of God before them were boundless and inconceivable. Yet, having
God's sure promises brought a unity and sense of destiny to the people of Israel;
these promises gave them the confidence and direction to walk together in the
light of His purposes.

12-7 The coronation of Solomon (I Chronicles 29:22-25 & I Kings 2:1-9)

The atmosphere of worship grew into the celebration of Solomon's coronation. The sacrifices with which they honored their God provided the meat and drink for every person present.

2   On this day of adoration and joyful expressions, the nation of Israel anointed Solomon king for the second time. This time no one else sought to be king; this son of David became the center of attention. Neither was there an urgency; the people could take their time to worship God and rejoice that Solomon was now king over Israel. The vast assembly united to celebrate the crowning of David's son.

3   During Solomon's coronation festivities, the nation also anointed Zadok to be priest. (Abiathar had lost his privilege to serve as priest when he followed Adonijah.) Then Solomon took his place on the throne of Israel. His reign began well; he prospered as king, and all of Israel obeyed him. In addition, the leaders in Israel, along with David's other sons, submitted themselves to Solomon.

4   Before his death, David gave some final instructions to Solomon:

I am about to die: therefore, be strong and show yourself a man.

Keep the charge of the LORD thy God,

to walk in His ways,

to keep His statutes,

> *His commandments,*

> *His judgments, and*

> *His testimonies,*

as it is written in the law of Moses,

that you may prosper in all that you do and wherever you go.

David's advice: you must be strong, courageous, and obedient in order to prosper in every work and in every place.

5   David remained positive as he exhorted his son,

Do this, in order that the LORD may continue His word concerning me, saying, "If your children take heed to their way, to walk before Me in truth with all their heart and with all their soul, you will not be without a man on the throne of Israel."

The Scriptures do not record when God spoke these conditional words about David and his family. God, in His first extraordinary revelation, did not make a conditional promise. Although God had cautioned that, as a Father, He would chasten David's son for disobedience, He assured David that his son would always have mercy and that he would sit on the throne of David forever.

6   David then instructed Solomon to deal appropriately with Joab for his shifty peacetime murders of two rival captains in Israel's army, Abner and Amasa. David did not cite Joab's defiant murder of the treasonous Absalom, even though

it had caused him deep grief. Finally, he advised Solomon to bless Barzillai, who had blessed David, but to curse Shimei, who had cursed David when he fled from his son Absalom.

7 And the son of David sat on the throne of David, reigning over all of God's people and leading the monumental enterprise of building God's house. His kingdom was established greatly. Moreover,

> the LORD magnified Solomon exceedingly in the sight of all of Israel
> and bestowed on him such royal majesty as had not been on any king
> before him in Israel.

12-8 The end is not the end ...
(II Samuel 23:1-7; I Chronicles 29:26-30; Psalm 132)

David reigned over Israel for forty years – seven in Hebron, and thirty-three in Jerusalem. The biblical historian introduced the last words of David in II Samuel 23:

> David the son of Jesse said,
> and the man who was raised up on high,
> the anointed of the God of Jacob,
> and the sweet psalmist of Israel, said,

2 After this gracious and descriptive introduction, the historian recorded David's own introductory comments:

> *The Spirit of the LORD spoke by me,*
> *and his word was in my tongue.*
> *The God of Israel said,*
> *the Rock of Israel spoke to me,*

3 David's words here were God's words. After forty years as king, David declared with his last breaths a few essential, God-inspired conclusions:

> *He who rules over men must be just,*
> *ruling in the fear of God.*

At the end of his life, David was concerned with leaders who had authority to make decisions affecting others.

4 With grand poetic language, he declared that those leaders who fear God and rule with justice would bring fresh light and life to their world:

> *And he shall be as the light of the morning,*
> *when the sun rises,*
> *even a morning without clouds;*
> *as the tender grass springing out of the earth*
> *by clear shining after rain.*

He continued,

Although my house be not so with God;

yet He has made with me an everlasting covenant,

ordered in all things, and sure:

for this is all my salvation, and all my desire,

although He make it not to grow.

David was not confident in his own house or family and expressed its unworthiness. Yet, he maintained a sure hope in God's everlasting covenant and salvation. His God had acted and spoken, and it would stand – whether his house grew or not.

5   David closed his final words by declaring a grim future for proud, selfish rulers:

But all the sons of Belial shall be as thorns thrust away,

because they cannot be taken with hands:

But the man that shall touch them must be fenced with iron and the staff of a spear;

and they shall be utterly burned with fire in the same place.

6   I Chronicles 29:26-30 gives the following eulogy for King David:

And King David died in a good old age, full of days, riches, and honor.

Now the acts of David the king, first and last, are written in the books of Samuel the seer, of Nathan the prophet, and of Gad the seer. These men wrote of all of his reign, of his might, of the history of his life, of Israel, and of all kingdoms in surrounding lands.

7   But David's life and impact are not wrapped up in the chronicles of the kings and the history books – his royal family and kingdom had a God-revealed, God-ordained future. In addition, David's longing for the presence of God, as well as the honor he gave it, has not been lost; this desire has steadily grown in the hearts of God's people for 3000 years. The best days are ahead as God continues to fulfill all of His promises and to accomplish all of His purposes.

8   Psalm 132, for example, speaks glowingly of the presence of God and exalts His covenant with David. The psalmist first recalled David's intense desire to find a place for God to dwell:

LORD, remember David, and all his afflictions:

How he swore unto the LORD,

and vowed unto the mighty God of Jacob:

Surely I will not come into the tabernacle of my house,
nor go up into my bed;
I will not give sleep to mine eyes,
or slumber to mine eyelids,
Until I find out a place for the LORD,
a habitation for the mighty God of Jacob.

9   Next, the psalmist expressed the corporate desire to worship in God's presence:

Lo, we heard of it at Ephratah:
we found it in the fields of the wood.
We will go into His tabernacles:
we will worship at His footstool.
Arise, O LORD, into Thy rest;
Thou, and the ark of Thy strength.
Let Thy priests be clothed with righteousness;
and let Thy saints shout for joy.

10   The psalmist continued by recalling God's promise and oath to David and His choice of Jerusalem, of Zion, as the place of His presence forever. Embracing these truths in song could give God's people a confidence that they would enjoy His actual presence among them.

For Thy servant David 's sake
turn not away the face of Thine anointed.
The LORD has sworn in truth unto David;
He will not turn from it;
Of the fruit of your body will I set upon thy throne.
If your children will keep My covenant and My testimony that I shall teach them,
their children shall also sit upon thy throne forevermore.
For the LORD has chosen Zion;
He has desired it for His habitation.
This is My rest forever: here will I dwell;
for I have desired it.

11   The psalmist closed with the assurance that God abundantly blesses the place of His presence.

I will abundantly bless her provision:
I will satisfy her poor with bread.
I will also clothe her priests with salvation:
and her saints shall shout aloud for joy.

There will I make the horn of David to bud:

    I have ordained a lamp for Mine anointed.

His enemies will I clothe with shame:

    but upon himself shall his crown flourish.

Author's Epilogue

1 – Honesty about David's sins

I have been asked how I could write a book on the life of David and not cover the details of his sin with Bathsheba and the consequences of that atrocity. How could such a book provide an accurate picture of David? It is a fair question, especially since the title of this book comes from the confrontation during which Nathan exposed David's guilt by declaring to the king, "You are the man!" According to David's own judgment, he himself deserved to be put to death for his horrible sins against Uriah.

While the narration of this book did not walk with David through some of his errors, it did not ignore those sins either. A detailed exposé of those events would not require any change in this telling of David's story. The Bible is candid about its characters' sins, and this book is written with a purposeful effort to show honestly the errant actions of David recorded in the Bible.

2 – The reality of David's repentant heart

Yet, it is clear that David's heart remained perfect toward God. With David's great responsibilities, there were serious consequences for each sin, but he always trusted God in troubling times, including those hard times not described in this book. David did not lower his view of God or of His holy standards because he sinned often. He always acknowledged his sin, repented, and became more humble and responsive to God than before. As a result, David came out of both good and bad experiences more committed and more thankful to God.

The Bible justly condemns Cain, Esau, and Balaam for the selfish or evil motives that controlled their hearts, but it never condemns the motives of David's heart. Israel's kings, the prophets, Jesus Himself, and the apostles always praise David's perfect heart toward God and honor his established place in God's purposes – always, without exception. As would be expected, his disobedience in the matter of Uriah is chronicled later in the Bible's history. Nevertheless, David's early heart for God and impressive reputation did not change after he was anointed King of Israel. He continued to grow as a man after God's heart and remained fully God's servant. David's heart was perfect toward his God until his death.

Certainly, on occasion, there was a large contrast between David's heart on the inside and his life on the outside. He is such a clear example that what is on the inside matters most. As God told Samuel, "Man looks on the outside appearance, but the LORD looks on the heart." God indeed gives grace to avoid sin, and we wish that David had drawn more upon that grace.

However, David
- never defended his sin or stubbornly held on to it as Cain had done,
- never despised God's correction or lashed out in greater sin as Cain had also done,
- never despised God's call on his life as Esau had done, and
- never abandoned his commitment to serve God at all times, as Balaam had done.

David is also an example that God gives individuals the grace to confess sin, to be cleansed from sin, and to continue to live ever closer to the heart of God. Even more, God's dealings with David provide a clear picture and a certain promise of God's sure mercies.

3 – The astonishing fact that David was so special to God

It truly is amazing that David was so special to God. Summarizing David's life, he began merely as a good shepherd and then a good servant to the king. He learned to trust God no matter what the obstacles when he was running from King Saul. However, after he became king, he sinned horribly and publicly. He did not seem to be a good father. Two different sons of David each attempted to take over the kingdom for themselves while David was still alive. He was far from perfect, and he always seemed to need mercy.

Nevertheless, on two highly significant occasions, God showed parts of His universal, eternal, and Messianic purposes to David. Knowing that he was working in harmony with what God was saying and doing, David responded to these extraordinary revelations with passionate obedience. As a result, David accomplished significant works toward the fulfillment of God's purposes.

Nathan delivered the first revelation after David moved the Ark of the Covenant. As a part of its fulfillment, Jesus is called the Son of David and is destined to sit on the throne of David as Lord over all of heaven and earth forever. This revelation was given before his sin with the wife of Uriah. Following this sin, David's entire life seemed to go downhill. He endured many years of family and kingdom troubles; he even ordered a census that caused tens of thousands of God's people to die in a plague.

Yet, even after these miserable years and horrible failings, he was God's chosen vessel for another eternal work. Remarkably, God dramatically and graciously revealed to David the specific place He had chosen to put His name, as prophesied by Moses – the place where His house was to be built. God also revealed to David detailed specifications for the temple and the worship there. David was even the one to start the building preparations and to organize the Levites to minister properly in the presence of God. The fact that David's son was the one who actually built God's house and implemented the worship there again shouts the Messianic, saving purposes of God.

The magnitude of these two revelations of God's eternal purposes is staggering. It seems almost impossible that both could be given to just one man. If so, such a man would surely bring honor and glory to God his entire life. God did have his Daniel, who lived without blame and received glorious prophetic visions, but in David God had chosen a man with major public failures on his resumé. David was a man who did not deserve special blessings from God, yet God called him a man after His own heart. Do we find it difficult to accept – 3000 years later – that these magnificent, eternal revelations were given to a man who sinned so greatly in his life? Should we – 3000 years later – believe in a God Who judged David's character "poorly" and "foolishly" selected him as His special servant?

4 – Trust God: His choices and His purposes

How this David could be this special to God is a mystery for which I do not have an explanation. However, there is an exhortation: Let God be God. Whether He reveals great truths to a Daniel or to a David, He is God. God knows what He is doing, and He does everything exactly right.

God? Who is God? Which god is God? By definition, if there is a Supreme Creator God, there is just one God. This God, I believe, exists and is the same God Who was an anchor for David's heart from shepherd, to fugitive, to king, and all the way to his death. Therefore, as David made clear which God the young King Solomon must trust, so I will attempt to be clear about the God Whom we must honor and trust as God.

The God we must trust is the one God Who created the universe, along with everything in it. Again by definition, there can be only one Creator, even though that claim is made about many gods. How can we know which, if any, of these gods created us with our world?

The God we must trust is the God Who has clearly revealed Himself. David's God has revealed Himself as the one true God in creation, in our conscience, in Jesus, and in the Bible.

In creation, God has revealed His wisdom, power, and even His divine nature if we will but look closely. God has also revealed Himself in the Bible. It is a great mystery how God could reveal Himself in a human book with human authors, who did not know that they were actually writing Scripture. And the mystery became greater as God preserved His Bible revelation throughout several millennia of editing, copying, and translating the manuscripts. The Bible is a great gift to humanity; we can and we must trust all of it.

In the conscience, this Creator God put inside every human a personal judge. God created Adam as a free moral being with the ability to make choices – often the choice is between doing right and doing wrong. God also put in Adam the ability to judge the moral correctness of his actions. Each one of us has that same conscience. In our conscience, we not only judge the morality of our deeds, but we also bear the sole responsibility for each of our free moral choices and their consequences.

And we all have a moral problem. As free moral beings, we all judge ourselves not only for choosing to do what we know to be wrong, but also for being unable to live up to our individual principles. Not one of us has done everything we desired to do in the past and, in the future, not one of us will be able to do everything we know we should do. For these failures, we judge ourselves guilty. This fact goes to the essence of who we are; it is a reality we must face and not attempt to explain away.

And our moral problem actually goes deeper. The Holy God Who created us knows how we should live and has revealed that path; it is this revelation that makes our problem even more serious. Not only do we fail to meet the standards we set for our own life, but all of us also fall short of God's holy, unchangeable standard. Only the one true Almighty and Holy Creator can solve – and has solved – these deeply personal moral problems.

5 – Trust the God Who has solved our moral problem

So, more specifically,

The God we must trust is this Holy Creator, Who revealed Himself in Jesus, His Son and David's son, by Whom He has solved our universal, personal moral problem. (See Section 6-5 for other details and references.)

The God we must trust is the God of Love, Who sent His Own Son, Jesus Christ, to earth in the flesh to live a human life.

The God we must trust is the Holy God, Whose law is completely met and fulfilled by the righteous obedience of Jesus.

The God we must trust is the Merciful God, Who laid the sin of the whole world on His perfect, sinless Son.

The God we must trust is the Just God, Who made the final judgment against the world's sin, which Jesus carried to His cross, and condemned that sin in Jesus' flesh.

The God we must trust is the Gracious God, Who is entirely pleased with Jesus' willing offering and sacrifice of Himself to God.

The God we must trust is the Righteous God, Who is forever satisfied with the blood of Jesus – the blood which Jesus Himself brought into the holiest place of God's presence. God's holy justice demands nothing more.

The God we must trust is the Saving God, Who, having dealt with human sin on Jesus and having accepted human righteousness in Jesus Christ, made it possible for any of us to experience peace with God by faith. Believing sinners are made righteous in Christ and reconciled to this Holy God through the death of His Son, Jesus Christ.

The God we must trust is the Almighty God, Who raised Jesus Christ from the dead.

The God we must trust is the Eternal God, Who received Jesus Christ into heaven, made Him Lord of heaven and earth, and purposed that everyone and everything will submit to Him forever.

6 – Believing in this God of purpose and power

This is no mere religious dogma. Faith in God is not a simplistic response to the challenges of mysteries yet unexplained or unknown. To trust God is not blind faith. This holy and loving God has acted decisively in human history to solve our deepest problem. Christ's almighty work on the cross is essential for the present and eternal well-being of every person. We believe this God and call upon Him; out of our faith, we declare Jesus to be our Lord. We who believe in Christ Jesus meet God's holy standard because Christ's righteousness is ours. While we grow in our experience of that righteousness, God answers our heart's innermost cry for help, and in response, He supplies supernatural love, power, and peace.

We are free to believe or not to believe in this God; this Most Powerful God neither prevents our tragic choices nor forces us to accept the solution. If we choose not to trust the God Who created us as free beings or if we do not personally make this God our God, we are adrift. Many who are adrift yield to some religious or scientific authority which might help explain our existence or define a deity to trust and serve. Others are able to trust only in themselves and find answers only in their own mind and heart. But if we do not personally trust the Creator God, we miss the One Who made us; we miss the God Who knows us. As a result, we are unable to know Him or learn how He works in our lives and in our world.

7 – Committing to this God of purpose and power

Even when we choose to trust Him, we will not understand or like all that this God does. Yes, we will pour out our hearts to God and ask Him to change the troublesome events happening in our lives and in our world. We argue, but we do not rebel; we struggle, but we do not cast off our God. We trust Him; we realize that He is wise and that there is so much we do not know. In every struggle, in every cry for help, we willingly commit our situation to God, being absolutely certain that God knows us, loves us, and always does what is good and right. It is often an intense battle for the allegiance of our heart. Will we choose God's way and trust Him to provide what we need, or will we choose our own way and trust another resource? Every time we resolve to trust this God, we confirm and strengthen our commitment to him. As we trust this God, we increasingly understand God's ways with us and marvel at His wisdom. We find our personal fulfillment in obeying God and trusting Him with our lives and everything that concerns us. Nothing is held back. As David instructed Solomon, we "serve God with a perfect heart and a willing mind." Life may be cruel, but we are at peace. No trouble can shake us. We are secure in God, and from the depths of our trusting hearts, we exclaim, "O the depth of the riches both of the wisdom and knowledge of God! How unsearchable are His judgments and His ways past finding out! For who has known the mind of the LORD? Or who has become His counselor? Or who has given something to God that must be paid back again? For of Him, and to Him, and through Him, are all things; to Whom be glory forever. Amen."

Author, Sources, and Acknowledgments

Writing the Manuscript

Author The inspiration for this book came to me during a regular devotional time; for decades I have intentionally read through the Old Testament each year. One morning in October 2006, as I was enjoying grandeur of God's second revelation to David in I Chronicles 22, I knew in my heart that I must share it with God's people. An outline for this book came together within days and has remained largely unchanged.

Though educated to be a math teacher, I worked mostly as a computer programmer, building applications for smaller businesses. My actual writing experience consisted mainly of school assignments, help manuals, and letters; nonetheless, I forged ahead and completed a draft of nearly all of the manuscript in about four months. Authoring a book had never been a personal dream or goal for me; in writing – and righting – this book, I have sought only to obey God. Step by step, He has guided me, brought assistance, and sent resources to make this book something I could never have envisioned (Luke 17:10).

Personally, I had the privilege of being raised in a Christian home, gaining, by the grace of God, early and efficacious exposure to the gospel of Jesus Christ crucified. As a lay Christian, I love the Bible and its Holy Spirit taught truths. Memorizing and re-memorizing portions of the New Testament throughout the years has anchored me while I sought to expand my knowledge of the truth. I continue to attend church each Sunday, enjoy the discussion and study of biblical themes, and listen to various ministers on radio, TV, and the internet. Though my reading of Christian literature has been somewhat sporadic, authors who have impacted me are Oswald Chambers, C.H. Spurgeon, Watchman Nee, C.S. Lewis, Francis Schaffer, and P.T. Forsyth. Teachings from these authors and from many other sources aided the development of my biblical understanding in the decades prior to the writing of this book.

Main Sources By design, I have written this book out of a careful, prayerful study of just one translation of the Bible. Paragraph by paragraph, I have done what any believer might do during times of personal meditation or in preparation for a Bible lesson. My belief is that the entire Bible is inspired by God and literally true, while recognizing that, in many passages, the truth is pictured in figurative language or allegories. God has provided an interpreter: His Holy Spirit. Each believer depends upon God's Spirit; we need Him to grant us distinctive, personalized insights from the Bible, and we also need Him to guide us into all truth, including the truth which is universal and unchanging.

In addition, I have used Bible helps available in the public domain. Containing details and ideas, these sources aided me in understanding some difficult words and texts. My deep desire was to be faithful to each biblical context and to the spirit of every passage used, while remaining true and accurate to the Bible as a whole and to the Bible's portrayal of King David in particular.

Listed below are some of those Bible reference materials in the public domain that I have used. These are available in inexpensive Bible software or online:
Geneva Study Bible
John Wesley's notes
Jamieson-Fausset-Brown Bible commentary
Matthew Henry's commentary
John Gill's commentary
Strong's Hebrew and Greek dictionaries
Easton's Bible Dictionary
Nave's Topical Bible
International Standard Bible Encyclopedia

Two Bible software products with broad functionality and features that, as of 2011, can be downloaded and used free of charge, are:
1. Esword: www.e-sword.net
2. Bible Explorer: www.bible-explorer.com
Both products enable the user to download and integrate the above and additional public domain resources without charge as well as newer works that can be purchased.

During the early years of writing, I made use of the search tool in the Bible Database software downloadable at www.bibledatabase.org and the convenient Hebrew/Greek word usage Bible, which can be run or downloaded at http://dynamicbible.com/ . Also helpful on occasion was an online site, http://bible.cc/ , that shows many parallel translations for a selected Scripture verse and displays many public domain resources that have comments on the verse being viewed.

For further information on this book, please visit www.kingdavidbook.com.

Righting the Manuscript

Several of my family, friends, and even two gracious pastors encouraged me by saying that they liked that first draft. One good friend, however, unsettled me by explaining why many of my specific written expressions would dissuade him from buying my book. Initially defensive, I accepted the fact that some may not like my book. It was a necessary, though faltering first impression that the manuscript needed more work. (Much later, when the manuscript was closer to completion, his comments highlighted a stylistic flaw that hindered reading flow.) I am grateful for his honest criticism.

Three Technical Sources: With that draft manuscript nearly complete, I checked out some technical books on King David. My interest in David made these works compelling for me. Many details about the historical context, the cultural environment, the general behavior of Middle Eastern rulers, and many ancient archaeological finds were fascinating. The critical analysis of Bible texts, sometimes digging into the origins and meanings of words and phrases in their original languages, was informative. Nearly all of this information was beyond the scope of my book.

Challenging, but very helpful to me in some of these works, were interpretations of David's experiences and character that I had never encountered. The analysis of various passages of Scripture in the light of their research led to some unflattering or even negative characterizations of David. While such interpretations have apparently been a widely accepted scholarly view of David for over a century, not only were many of these ideas new to me, some were also contrary to what I understood. Thus, even with their fresh approach and stated objective to make this technical information accessible to the lay mind, I often found it difficult to assimilate the ideas and data in these books.

Because I am not qualified to address any specific scholarly interpretation, my response to this challenging material was to dig deeper into the Bible texts and contexts. I desired to portray David exactly as the Bible depicts him, both the good and the bad – neither whitewashing nor blackening him. Additionally, I believe that the Bible, when interpreted literally, is historically accurate; this ancient book is well documented to be factually true in history and culture. It is no leap of faith to believe the Bible just as it is written. Having this confidence, I am truly thankful that these technical works alerted me to questions about many specific Bible passages. They drove me to identify the Biblical details that were needed to clarify the parts of my narration which are based in those passages. This process helped to make this story of David more accurate, honest, complete, and clear.

Halpern, Baruch. <u>David's Secret Demons</u>. Grand Rapids, MI:
   Wm. B. Eerdmans Publishing Company, 2004.

Halpern provided helpful information on David's military conquests and his relation to the surrounding nations. Especially helpful were his discussions of Ammon and the Philistines. He made use of obscure Bible verses that I had missed in drafting the manuscript. I cited him in Section 7-1.

McKenzie, Steven L. <u>King David: A Biography</u> New York, NY:
   Oxford University Press, Inc., 1999.

McKenzie offered insights into the behavior of Middle Eastern rulers during the era of David's reign. While McKenzie generally applied these behaviors to King David, I used this information as a contrast to the higher standard by which David learned to rule. I cited him in Sections 1-6, 1-7, 7-1, and 7-3.

Steussy, Marti J. <u>David: Biblical Portraits of Power</u>
Columbia, SC: The University of South Carolina Press, 1999.

Steussy interpreted many events found in the Bible's history of David's life in ways which were unfamiliar to me. I appreciated her perspectives and was grateful for the motivation to study the biblical contexts for details to enhance the narration of this book. In Section 1-7, I cite her for an important insight.

Some would desire my biblical history of King David to include additional extra-biblical citations. Certainly I, and likely the text of book, would have benefited from the further insights of others far more knowledgeable than I. Yet, the Bible itself had much information, some of it largely overlooked, that almost begged to be included. I desired to fill this version of David's story with rich biblical truths that are accessible to any believer with a Bible and the Holy Spirit. It is my hope that many readers will search out further details to broaden and deepen the information and ideas contained in this book.

Grateful Acknowledgments Even after expanding the biblical account of many events in David's life, the manuscript remained the rough draft of an untrained writer. Improvement began as many, many people graciously reviewed parts or all of my ever-changing manuscript. I am extremely thankful for their investment of time and effort; every comment was valuable to me. Nearly all kindly pointed out mistakes they saw or asked questions, which usually indicated that I needed to rework and clarify a sentence or paragraph. As I think back, I feel humbled and consider each one to have been sent by God to help make this book more of what it needed to be. A few need special mention.

The first person to go the extra mile with focused effort was Claire, a bright young lady then in high school – I wanted this book to be accessible to young people. She agreed to review the manuscript carefully and to note any errors she saw or any wording that was not clear to her. By highlighting "good passages" that I should not change, she encouraged me as well. Her review and the resulting changes took many months. Thanks so much, Claire, for your outstanding contribution to the righting of this book!

In the meantime, I began a reference table to document Scripture references, removing them from the narration in order to improve the book's readability.

Both the references and an index are linked to paragraph numbers instead of page numbers, which could change as the book format changes. During this ongoing, detailed, documentation process, I rewrote many sentences and paragraphs in order to make them accurate to the text of the Bible.

Additionally, a good friend, Kathy, along with her perceptive children, read a large portion of the manuscript and offered many helpful comments leading to improvements in context and clarity. Four important changes stemming directly from their comments were (1) the inclusion of more tables and listings, (2) the move of detailed background information to an appendix and preparing a short, to-the-point introduction, (3) the addition of a pronunciation guide, and (4) an extensive rework of the three important sections at the end of Chapter 6. Because I believe those sections to be crucial to David's story, I determined that no one else would experience the great struggles my friend had experienced with those sections. My deepest thanks, Kathy! Your efforts have been invaluable!

With continued input, the manuscript had improved by mid-2008, but not nearly as much as I had assumed, and certainly not as much as needed. Enter an incredible grammar technician, Pat, and a five-hour review of Chapter 1. She pointed out errors, made suggestions, and offered comments in what was an intense and practical grammar lesson for me. That session, reinforced by her subsequent reviews of the manuscript, increasingly affects every sentence I write. Pat left it up to me to decide if and how to make the corrections and adjustments she suggested. She also proofread a late version of the manuscript, and then commented on many of the changes made over the following months. Words cannot express my thanks to you, Pat, for the time and effort you have so graciously given. You have been an immeasurable blessing to me and to the quality of this work.

In making the content as accurate as possible, I needed to be alert to input from many sources. Errors found during the process of documenting Scripture references confirmed, yet again for me, how easy it is to assume that I know what a passage says only to find out that I am wrong or imprecise. Among those named below are many well-read, biblically knowledgeable people who offered helpful content suggestions and comments for which I am grateful. Additionally, over these years, the valuable teaching and preaching heard at church or on various media often spurred me to consider corrections, clarifications, or enhancements that could be made to the book.

But this book needed more focused help with content. It was ably provided by Doug, a highly regarded lay minister. He noticed, for instance, that I had described an eminently mature faith in a young David, even while highlighting his stumbling growth as God's servant. This glaring inconsistency existed despite my key objective and strong desire to be scripturally accurate,

especially in my portrayal of David. Doug also pointed out where my manuscript communicated unintended or unbiblical impressions of many specific
events. Helpful, too, was his honesty in telling me where and why his reading
flow was broken. His input led to many reworked paragraphs. I thank you,
Doug, and honor you for your honest and most excellent contribution to this
book.

(For three years, this book had been transforming into more of what it
needed to be, yet the necessary changes in the author did not keep pace. As
may be common in a project such as this, many people in various capacities
helped me grow personally, but I knew that much more work needed to be
done in me. I did not know what changes were needed and called upon God
for help. He answered by sending a special person (I will call her Jacy) to me.
Jacy's impact on my life cannot be overstated. She jolted me with her strong
and beautiful heart. God first dealt with me to remove a powerful desire that
had deceived me into thinking it was a ministry. Next, responding to Jacy's
integrity and strength, God dealt with me to remove persistent, deep-seated
engrossments. Astonishing changes to my inner thought patterns and outer
habits took place in just three intense months. These changes resulted in more
focus and fewer distractions and made the next step, an enormous step, possible. As Jacy continued to be herself, I then had to face the deceitful lusts
behind my old habits and passions. "The heart is deceitful above all things and
desperately wicked. Who can know it?" (Jeremiah 17:9). Facing heart disease
is a fierce, humbling battle, but I am so grateful that some of this desperate
wickedness is no longer hidden. Over many years, my disease led to actions
that produced wreckage in me and around me. With meekness and humility,
I must face each regrettable memory that surfaces in my thinking and act
appropriately. Thankfully, God gives grace to deal with the plague of my own
heart and to go on to put on the new man with its righteousness and true holiness (Ephesians 4:22-24). Providentially helping to solidify these remarkable
transformations was a wonderful discipleship class, which began meeting at the
same time I met Jacy. The people in this class along with much Scripture reading and memory provided rich support and necessary food for my spirit. Since
these changes in me were highly significant and encouraging, I assumed that
my personal growth would consist of working to ingrain them into all parts of
my life. Thus, it was beyond imagination how God suddenly deepened and
expanded His transformative work in me. Such grace. I have been humbled to
confront that obvious truth that I know neither my great need when facing
imposing obstacles and powerful oppositions within and without nor the abundant blessings and resources available to me as God's servant. Jesus Christ has
great goals for me and for all of His disciples; goals for our cleansing, renewal,
and life as His servants.)

In building the maps, I received great assistance from my brother Paul and his family and Tim Field. Jeff Flynn – God providentially sent me to Jeff – added the attractive, authentic appearance to the maps. Thank you all for your excellent work. I must especially thank Mike Gafa for writing the Foreword. A committed servant of God who is always learning, Mike has great wisdom and vision. He is a gracious man who effectively uses his administrative gifts to facilitate God's work among His people.

The quotes on the back page are from personal communication with those quoted. Each one gave me their permission to quote them in November 2010. I give special thanks to each of them for their encouraging and helpful feedback.

Most, hopefully all, of those who gave their time to a read portion of the manuscript and offer comments, ask questions, or make suggestions are listed below – some have provided pseudonyms. Once again, I consider each one of you to be God-sent and extend my heart-felt gratitude to each one. I pray that God's good fruit may abound to all of your accounts. John, Mary*, Tom, Carol, Tim, Paul, Shari, and Christopher Kaiser, Shirley England, Dave McNeeley, Steve Karafa, Pastor Dean Parrott*, Pastor Mark Mayou, Jim Schwartz, Mel Harju, Norm* and Marge Burkhart, Laurie Dawley, Claire Gronevelt, Pastor Michael Ferris, Tom Dunkelberger, Fred Lubben, Kathy, Emery, and Jordan Fall, Linda Burdett, Jack Murray, Sandra Jones, Jackie Riley, Bill and Linda Eubank, Jeff Karowich, Greg Elliott, Bettye Porter, Dave Axeberg, Pastor Jack Richard, Lynda Mary, Doug Hentschel, Ken and Ken Wiley, Pat Seif, Pastor Mike Green, Tim and Leah Field, Monica Walters, Mike Gafa, Pastor Tim Murdoch, and Jeff Flynn.

* So very sadly, as I complete the manuscript, these are deceased.

Background Information

Bg-1 Overview of the development of the nation of Israel

God chose the family of Jacob, son of Isaac, son of Abraham, and set them apart to be His special people. Jacob, whose name was changed to Israel, moved his family of 66 people from the land of Canaan to Egypt in a time of famine. Over time, because Israel's family grew into a huge throng of people, the nation of Egypt exercised their control over the Israelites by making them slaves. Egypt's leaders oppressed Israel's descendants until they cried out to God for deliverance. God heard them and plagued Egypt repeatedly until Pharaoh thrust the people of Israel out of Egypt. However, Pharaoh soon changed his mind and pursued Israel to get his slaves back. The people of Israel were not completely free from Egypt until Pharaoh's powerful cavalry and chariot forces were completely destroyed in the deep arm of the Red Sea, which the Israelites had just miraculously crossed.

2   Once God had redeemed the Israelites from slavery, He prepared to bring them back into Canaan, the land He had promised to give them. They camped at Mt. Sinai for almost a year while God established the ground rules for His relationship with this new nation. God spoke His laws for Israel, then wrote them down, and gave them to Moses. To receive God and His law was a priceless gift and extreme honor for the nation of Israel. These Israelites, agreeing to a blood-dedicated covenant with God, promised to obey His laws, to be His people, and to make Him their God. God also gave Moses a precise pattern, which directed Israel on how to worship Him. Israel built the tabernacle as God had designed and ordained priests to lead the people to worship God exactly as He had prescribed. God was visibly present among the Israelites, and He personally led them in a pillar of cloud or fire above the tabernacle. By the hand of Moses, God led the nation of Israel from Mt. Sinai to Canaan through a vast, desolate wilderness. Because of their repeated rebellion against God's leadership, the Israelites took forty years to complete this journey. The nomadic life of the nation of Israel ended when Joshua led the people across the Jordan River into the land of Canaan. This was their destination, but the country needed to be conquered and possessed – a task they never completely finished.

3   After Joshua led the Israelites in victory over the major powers in Canaan, they set up the tabernacle in the centrally located city of Shiloh. Joshua and tribal leaders gathered at Shiloh to partition the conquered land and assign portions to Israel's family units, called tribes. Individual Israelite families chose their homesteads in the area of land assigned to their tribe. While they traveled to their

promised land, the people had united in regular worship of God at the tabernacle in their midst. After they settled in the land, the Israelites made family decisions whether or not to travel to Shiloh for national holy days. Immediately before Samuel began to lead Israel, Shiloh's appeal was diminished because the Ark of the Covenant, representing God's presence, had been taken to battle and became separated from the tabernacle at Shiloh. The Ark remained in Kirjath-jearim during the years that the prophet Samuel and King Saul led Israel. (Chapter 4 of this book contains a more complete summary of the history of the Ark.)

4   After Joshua died, the nation of Israel did not select a national leader. Instead, mainly regional judges ruled in Israel. These judges often gained support by leading the people to defeat their current enemy. The Israelites, who were spread out over a large area, finally had enough of this somewhat haphazard rule after the prophet Samuel installed his own greedy sons as leaders. When his sons proved to be corrupt judges, the people of Israel demanded that Samuel give them a king to rule them, similar to the monarchs of other nations. Samuel resisted, but, at God's direction, he anointed Saul to be the first king of Israel. Under King Saul, the tribes came together to battle their enemies, most notably the Philistines to the west. Israel did not have a capital city to help unite the tribes. Neither did Israel have a palace for a king; King Saul led the nation from his hometown of Gibeah. Israel's monarchy had begun but it would develop and improve under Israel's second king, David. This book describes David's part in shaping Israel's monarchy, especially its worship.

Bg-2 Contents of I Chronicles

The Bible records David's story in I and II Samuel and in I Chronicles. The books of Samuel have a more complete version of his life. Chapters 10 – 21 in I Chronicles contain events described in the Samuel history. With the exception of the extensive details given about David's moving the Ark of the Covenant in I Chronicles, the event descriptions in Samuel and I Chronicles are similar. Notably, the I Chronicles historians did not retell the episodes of David's early years or his later, serious family troubles; they let those events stand as recorded in I and II Samuel. But Samuel's history contains nothing about David's extremely important preparations to build the temple. The book of I Chronicles fills this critical gap by including many events, event details, and names associated with the new temple to be built.

2   Yet, I Chronicles was written at least 500 years after David lived. This is evident from I Chronicles 9, which lists names of Levites who lived from the time of David forward to a time just after Nehemiah rebuilt the wall of Jerusalem. This information begs the question: how could the writers of I Chronicles know and record so many specific details about events that took place when David reigned many centuries earlier?

3   The Bible answers that question. First, I Chronicles chapter 9 also refers to the books of the kings of Israel and Judah. The genealogies of Levites from the time of David forward to Nehemiah's time were found in those books. These source documents were still available to those who wrote I Chronicles. Additionally, the book of Nehemiah records that such national chronicles containing key genealogies were accessible and even maintained through the destruction and rebuilding of Jerusalem. Nehemiah himself refers to and follows David's detailed instructions for Israel's worship.

4   The chronicles of a king's reign documented a nation's history, often with meticulous records of events and decrees. In addition to the books of the kings of Israel and Judah, many prophets kept their own record of the deeds of kings. I Chronicles specifically refers to books about the life and reign of David written by Samuel, Nathan, and Gad. The chronicles of the kings of Persia mentioned in the book of Esther illustrate not only that incidents were recorded with a high level of detail, but also that the journal entries were kept current; they were not summaries of events written from memories and notes years after they had occurred.

5   Furthermore, the Bible's historical books of Kings and Chronicles often refer to the books or chronicles of the kings of Israel and of Judah as external sources available to the historians who penned the Bible's historical record. These references to outside material also show that the historical books of the Bible are not themselves the detailed chronicles kept of a king's reign. The Bible's history is not a simple transcription of the minutiae recorded during the reigns of the kings of Israel or Judah, nor is it meant to be.

6   These facts are very significant. Biblical evidence makes clear that many historical documents which detailed the names, events and decrees pertaining to David's reign, were preserved and assembled as source material for writing I Chronicles. Many centuries after David's life, these historians used facts written in David's day and included much information left out of the books of Samuel. Thus, the Bible itself throws light upon how and why I Chronicles was written; it is not an out-of-date rewrite of David's life fabricated by erstwhile reporters who had a religious agenda for their age, as some might suggest.

7   Additionally, in II Chronicles, the historians who wrote about the kings reigning after David offered a fresh perspective on the history in I and II Kings. The book of II Chronicles underscores the qualities that make a king good or bad, and it includes more of the actual prayers and prophecies, which also may have been found in the minutiae recorded by contemporary chroniclers of those kings.

8   The following short overview divides I Chronicles into four sections and compares them with the contents of the corresponding chapters in the Samuel history.

⁹ **I Chronicles , Chapters 1 – 9:** These chapters have genealogies for Adam to Israel and then most of Israel's sons. The books of Samuel do not contain any family genealogies. Section 3 of this background identifies some nuggets of valuable information found in these nine chapters.

¹⁰ **I Chronicles, Chapters 10 – 12:** David is crowned King of Israel here. Those who had come to support David as a fugitive are acknowledged in these chapters by tribe, and his trusted mighty men are listed here by name. These three chapters, however, do not contain much history. I Samuel 16 – 31 and II Samuel 1 – 5 provide much more information about David's life prior to his coronation as king. It is an eventful period of David's life that is reviewed in first two and a half chapters of this book.

¹¹ **I Chronicles, Chapters 13 – 21:** These nine chapters contain the history of David's reign over all of Israel. They correspond to the twenty chapters of II Samuel 5 – 24, which cover David's reign. As mentioned above, I Chronicles 13 – 16 provides many more details about David's project to move the Ark of the Covenant to Jerusalem. Later on during his reign, David sinned with the wife of Uriah and watched his family endure one serious consequence after another – events which only II Samuel records. Chapters 3 through 8 of this book tell the story of this period of King David's reign, using primarily the I Chronicles account.

¹² **I Chronicles, Chapters 22 – 29:** Here David prepared for the building of the temple of the LORD. This preparation included readying the physical site, gathering and processing raw materials, the specific organization of the Levites for ministry and worship, and choosing people to oversee and perform the work of building the temple. I Kings Chapter 1 tells how David made Solomon king, but the detailed building preparations are not mentioned in the history of Samuel or Kings. Only I Chronicles 22 – 29 brings to light this exceptional part of David's work and of God's ways in working out His purposes. Chapters 9 through 12 of this book describe these events, which occur late in David's life.

¹³ The following table lists events from the four sections described above with their Bible chapter locations.

Event Description	Chapters in Samuel – Kings	Chapters in I Chronicles
I Chronicles 1 – 9: Genealogies (Last section of this Background Information)		
Genealogies	None	I Chronicles 1 – 9
I Chronicles 10 – 12: From shepherd to king (Chapter 1 through Chapter 3, Section 2, in this book)		
Saul becomes King of Israel	I Samuel 9 – 15	None
David's life while Saul reigns	I Samuel 16 – 30	I Chronicles 12:1-22
Saul dies and David becomes king	I Samuel 31 – II Samuel 5	I Chronicles 10 and 12
David's thirty captains	II Samuel 23:8-39	I Chronicles 11:10-47
I Chronicles 13 – 21: David's reign over Israel (Chapter 3, Section 3, through Chapter 8 in this book)		
David established as king	II Samuel 5	I Chronicles 11:1-9; 14
David moves the Ark of the Covenant	II Samuel 6	I Chronicles 13, 15, 16
David wants to build God's house	II Samuel 7	I Chronicles 17
David expands his kingdom	II Samuel 8, 10	I Chronicles 18, 19
David's administration	II Samuel 8:16-18; 20:23-26	I Chronicles 18:15-17; 27
David blesses Jonathan's son	II Samuel 9	None
David's sins against Uriah	II Samuel 11, 12	None
Family and kingdom troubles	II Samuel 13 – 20	None
Gibeonite reconciliation	II Samuel 21:1-14	None
Israel fights Goliath's relatives	II Samuel 21:15-22	I Chronicles 20
A Psalm of deliverance	II Samuel 22	None
David's orders a census	II Samuel 24	I Chronicles 21
I Chronicles 22 – 29: David's reign over Israel (Chapters 9 through 12 in this book)		
David prepares to build the temple	None	I Chronicles 22 – 26, 28, 29
David makes Solomon king	I Kings 1	I Chronicles 23:1
David's Last Words	II Samuel 23:1-7	None
David's death	I Kings 2:1-10	I Chronicles 29:26-30

Bg-3 Brief summaries of the genealogies in I Chronicles chapters 1 – 9

This section is included because only chapters 1-9 of I Chronicles were not a part of the book's narration. While they contain mainly name-filled genealogies, some important background nuggets can be found in these chapters.

2   **Chapter 1** covers the genealogy from Adam to Noah and the line of Noah's three sons. It follows Shem's line through Abraham's son Ishmael and grandson Esau.

3   **Chapters 2 – 4** cover the genealogy of Israel's son Judah. Chapter 3 has details on King David's royal line extending beyond the Babylonian captivity. It is worth noting that David's second son Daniel, who was born to the wise Abigail, never appears in David's family drama and tragedies. Chapter 4 contains the well-known and widely used prayer of Jabez. In addition, Chapter 4 has some of Simeon's genealogy and a listing of cities given to the tribe of Simeon from among the extremely large territory allocated to the southern tribe of Judah. Ziklag, where David took asylum to be safe from King Saul, was one of the cities given to Simeon.

4   **Chapter 5** has the genealogies of the Reuben, Gad, as well as half of the tribe of Manasseh. These tribes asked for and received the land that Israel had conquered east of the Jordan River. This chapter begins with important information about Israel's firstborn son Reuben. Because of his sexual misconduct, Reuben lost his firstborn rights, privileges, and blessings. The responsibility to rule the family-nation of Israel (5:1, 2, with Genesis 49:3, 4) went to Judah. King David and Jesus are descendants of Judah. Reuben's birthright and blessing went to Joseph, who received a double portion in the family and in the nation when his dying father Israel claimed Joseph's two sons as his own. Each of Israel's twelve sons was the father of a tribe in the nation, except Joseph. Instead of Joseph's having his own tribe, his sons, Ephraim and Manasseh, each became the father of a tribe in Israel. This actually made thirteen tribes. The family of Levi did not receive an inheritance of land like the other twelve tribes. The Levites held a special place in Israel to minister to God. Aaron's descendants were priests, while all of the other Levites ministered to these priests and took care of the tabernacle. The ministry of the Levites changed greatly after Jerusalem became the nation's capital and the temple was built. This book describes many of these changes.

5   **Chapter 6** includes information about the tribe of Levi, beginning with a list of the high priests who descended from Aaron until the time of the Babylonian captivity. Following this list are three additional lists – descendants of Levi's three sons, Kohath, Gershom, and Merari. These lists end with the key Levites ministers named Heman, Asaph, and Jeduthun (here named Ethan), who descended from Kohath, Gershom, and Merari respectively, as detailed in Verses 33 - 48. David appointed these three men to lead a ministry of praising God after he moved the Ark of the Covenant to Jerusalem. (Chapter 5 of this book describes those initial appointments.) At the end of his reign, David reappointed Heman,

Asaph, and Jeduthun, along with their sons, to lead in giving praise to God at the new temple Solomon would build. (Chapter 11 of this book describes these reappointments.) I Chronicles 6 closes with the list of the 48 cities given to the Levites from among the other 12 tribes of Israel, which had received an inheritance of land.

6   **Chapter 7** lists genealogies from the Israelite tribes of Issachar, Benjamin, Naphtali, the other half of Manasseh, Ephraim, and Asher. It also gives the reputation of the type of soldiers in some of these tribes. None of these genealogies are complete, and the families of the two of tribes, Zebulun and Dan, are not listed at all.

7   **Chapter 8** lists Benjamin's genealogy up through the family of Saul, Israel's first king.

8   **Chapter 9** has many names in common with Nehemiah Chapters 11 and 12. People in this chapter were selected or chose to live in Jerusalem after the city wall was rebuilt under Nehemiah's leadership. (The temple had already been rebuilt under Ezra.) They were among those released after 70 years of captivity under the Babylonians, who had conquered and destroyed Jerusalem. At the time Jerusalem was rebuilt, God's people were few, scattered, and disgraced. Not enough of them lived inside Jerusalem to take care of the city and protect it.

9   Most of those listed in I Chronicles, Chapter 9, were Levites appointed to various tasks and ministry related to the temple and the worship of God reestablished under Nehemiah. As noted in Chapter 11 of this book, Nehemiah followed the rules for worship and ministry initially set up by King David. Chapter 9 also contains a detailed listing of the duties of the porters in Nehemiah's day. That list is followed by a description of the cooking tasks of the Levites, who assisted the priests with the sacrifices. Chapter 9 closes with another list of King Saul's family.

Bible References

These Bible references are ordered by Chapter – Section as they occur in the book.

The P# identifies the paragraph number within each section to which the reference applies. There is at least one entry for every paragraph of the narrative, although some paragraphs elaborate on David's story or its context and have no specific Bible reference.

Chapter 1 - David: King in Waiting	
Chapter 1, Section 1 - Saul is Israel's first king; David is prepared	
P1– God told Samuel to anoint Jesse's son	I Samuel 16: 1-3
P1– After Saul rejected God's ways, God rejected Saul as king	I Samuel 15:26
P2– God chose Saul as Israel's first King and gave him a new heart	I Samuel 9:15-10:16
P3– Ages of Shem's family tree unto Abraham	Genesis 11:10-26
P3– Ages of Abraham, Isaac, and Jacob (Israel)	Genesis 21:25; 25:20,26
P3– God chose the Israelites to be His people	Deuteronomy 7: 6-8; Ezekiel 20: 5
P3– Condition of family of Israel when God chose them to be His people	Deuteronomy 32: 9,10; Ezekiel 16: 3-14
P3– Israel was organized into family units called tribes	Numbers 1: 2-19
P3– Samuel was the ruler in Israel prior to Saul's anointing	I Samuel 7: 6,15
P4– Samuel presented Saul to the people of Israel	I Samuel 10:17-25
P4– The Israelites demanded that Samuel give them a king	I Samuel 8: 6
P5– Saul was a very tall, good-looking man from the tribe of Benjamin	I Samuel 9: 1-5
P5– Saul had four honorable sons and two daughters by his one wife	I Samuel 14:49;50; 31: 2; II Samuel 2:8; I Chronicles 8:33
P5– Saul had two sons with his concubine Rizpah	II Samuel 3:7; 21:8
P5– The tribe of Benjamin was centrally located in Israel	Joshua 18:11-12
P6– King Saul began humbly, living & working with his family in Gibeah	I Samuel 9:21; 10:20-27

P6– King Saul ruled Israel from his home in Gibeah	I Samuel 10:26; 11: 4; 15:34
P6– Saul's early military success against the Ammonites	I Samuel 10:26-11:13
P7– David's three oldest brothers were soldiers with King Saul	I Samuel 17:12-14
P7– David, Jesse's youngest son, was a responsible shepherd	I Samuel 16:11,12,18
P7– David's family belonged to the tribe of Judah	Ruth 4:12,17-22; I Chronicles 28:4
P7– The tribe of Judah assigned the south part of the land of Israel	Joshua 15: 1-12
P8– David's was prepared for threats to his father's sheep	I Samuel 17:34-37
P9– David developed music and battle skills	I Samuel 16:16-18; 17:40
P9– David made musical instruments	I Chronicles 23:5; II Chronicles 7:6
P10– Samuel proclaimed that he and God had always led Israel well	I Samuel 11:14,15-12:11
P11– Samuel reminded the people that they insisted on having a king	I Samuel 12:12
P11– Israel's desire to have a king was a rejection of God's rule	I Samuel 8: 5-22
P12– Samuel admonished the people and king to obey their God	I Samuel 12:13-15
P13– Samuel's dramatic storm made the people afraid and receptive	I Samuel 12:16-19
P13– God sent a thunderstorm to confuse and defeat the Philistines	I Samuel 7: 8-11
P14– Samuel's exhortation that the people and King Saul serve God	I Samuel 12:20-25
P15– God was behind all of Samuel's words	I Samuel 3:19, 20; 9: 6
P15– Saul desired blessings from Samuel	I Samuel 15:25-31; 28:14-16
P16– Samuel rebuked a desperate Saul for sacrificing on his own	I Samuel 13: 1-14
P17– Saul did not heed Samuel's rebuke	
P18– Jonathan killed a guard unit and the Philistines retaliate	I Samuel 13: 3-5
P19– Jonathan's faith and courage resulted in victory	I Samuel 13:15-23; 14
P20– Saul battled Israel's enemies	I Samuel 14:47,48
P20– Abner, Saul's cousin, was the commander of Israel's army	I Samuel 14:50-52

Chapter 1, Section 2 - David vs. Goliath

P1– David delivered food to his brothers in the army	I Samuel 17:12-22
P2– Philistine champion Goliath defiantly challenged Israel's army	I Samuel 17: 1-11
P3– Goliath set terms for battle with Israel	I Samuel 17: 8-11,24
P4– Goliath challenged Israel every day for 40 days	I Samuel 17:16
P5– Goliath also defied the God of Israel's armies	I Samuel 17:10,11,16
P5– Israel kept the evening sacrifice ritual	II Kings 16:15; II Chronicles 13:11

P5– The time of the evening sacrifice was important to Israel	I Kings 18:29-36; Psalms 141:2; Ezra 9:4,5; Numbers 28:3,4
P6– God heard Goliath's defiance	
P7– David heard Goliath and challenges Israel's soldiers	I Samuel 17:23-27,31
P8– David's passion for God's glory	I Samuel 17:28-37
P9– David volunteered to kill Goliath	I Samuel 17:32-37
P10– David's faith for killing Goliath	I Samuel 17:36,37,46,47
P10– Circumcision: Abraham's part in the covenant of blessing	Genesis 17: 4-14
P10– Abraham believed God and circumcises all males in his house	Genesis 17:15-27; Romans 4:12-22
P10– God's covenant with Israel after delivering them from Egypt	Exodus 19: 1-8
P10– Israel knew that being circumcised set them apart	Judges 14: 3; I Samuel 14: 6
P11– David was face to face with Goliath, declaring his faith	I Samuel 17:40-47
P12– David killed Goliath	I Samuel 17:38-40, 48-53
P13– David's zeal for God's glory	I Samuel 17:26-30
P13– Example of an unbelieving king hoping for miracle deliverance	Jeremiah 21: 2
P13– Example: Israel faced/defeated enemies without physical weapons	II Chronicles 20: 1-29

Chapter 1, Section 3 - King Saul disobeys and God rejects his kingdom

P1– Saul asked who David's father is	I Samuel 17:55-58
P2– Saul's responsibility as king	I Samuel 15: 1
P3– God remembered Amalek's attack	I Samuel 15: 2
P3– Historical account of Amalek's attack on Israel	Exodus 17: 8-16
P3– Moses recalled Amalek's attack just before Israel enters Canaan	Deuteronomy 25:17-19
P4– Saul was commanded to defeat and utterly destroy Amalek	I Samuel 15: 3
P5– An historically important mission was an opportunity for Saul	
P6– Victory over the Amalekites, but Saul disobeyed	I Samuel 15: 4-9
P7– Saul asserted his obedience	I Samuel 15:10-13
P8– Saul blamed the people	I Samuel 15: 9,14,15
P9– Saul reasserted his obedience	I Samuel 15:16-21
P10– God rejected Saul	I Samuel 15:22-31

Chapter 1, Section 4 - David's anointing

P1– Samuel mourned over God's rejection of Saul as king	I Samuel 15:35
P2– Samuel anointed David	I Samuel 16: 1-13
P3– Meaning of David's anointing	

P4– Spirit of the LORD left King Saul and came on David	I Samuel 16:13
P5– An evil spirit from God troubled King Saul	I Samuel 16:14
P6– David was chosen to play the harp to refresh Saul	I Samuel 16:15-23
P7– David's service pleased King Saul	I Samuel 16:21-23
P7– Jonathan loved David and Saul brought David to live in the palace	I Samuel 18: 1,2; 16:22
P8– David and Jonathan established a binding friendship	I Samuel 18: 3,4
P9– Saul promoted David over men of war	I Samuel 18: 5

Chapter 1, Section 5 - Saul is threatened by David's success

P1– Saul was infuriated when David receives praise	I Samuel 18: 6-8
P1– Saul's kingdom had been given to someone better	I Samuel 15:28
P2– Saul suspicious of David	I Samuel 18: 9
P2– God had ripped the kingdom from Saul	I Samuel 15:27,28
P3– Saul attempted to kill David while he played the harp	I Samuel 18:10-12
P3– Elisha needed music therapy	II Kings 3:11-15
P3– Saul previously had God's Spirit on him	I Samuel 10: 6; 11: 6
P4– Saul reassigned David to a field command where he served well	I Samuel 18:13-16
P5– Saul plotted against David	I Samuel 18:17-27
P6– Saul ordered his servants to kill David – Jonathan intervened	I Samuel 18:28– 19: 7
P7– David escaped Saul three more times	I Samuel 19: 8-24
P8– David asked Jonathan why Saul wanted to kill him	I Samuel 20: 1-4
P9– David & Jonathan plan to expose Saul's intentions toward David	I Samuel 20: 5-23
P10– Saul made clear his obsession to kill David	I Samuel 20:24-42
P11– Saul's motive for wanting David dead	I Samuel 20:27-34

Chapter 1, Section 6 - David runs from King Saul

P1– David's life turned upside down	
P2– David uncertain what to do	
P3– David lied to obtain help from the priest Ahimelech	I Samuel 21:1-9
P4– David fled to Gath (Achish) and then to the cave Adullam	I Samuel 21:10-15; 22: 1
P5– David regrouped with family and friends in a cave	I Samuel 22: 1-4
P5– David had been privately anointed among his brothers	I Samuel 16:13
P6– Saul incentivised his servants to help against David	I Samuel 22: 6-8
P7– Saul ordered the murder of the priests and citizens of Nob	I Samuel 22: 9-19
P8– Abiathar escaped to David when priests are executed	I Samuel 22: 5,20-23
P9– Reinforcements came to David	I Chronicles 12: 8-17
P10– David's men noticed that God helped David	I Chronicles 12:18

P11– David and his men rescued Keilah from Philistine raiders	I Samuel 23: 1-5
P12– David asked God about his precarious situation in Keilah	I Samuel 23: 6-13
P13– Jonathan found David and encouraged him	I Samuel 23:14-18
P14– The Ziphites informed Saul of David's hiding places	I Samuel 23: 19-28
P15– David had questions about his future	
P16– David had questions about his current situation	

Chapter 1, Section 7 - David encounters Saul twice

P1– David's band fled to a stronghold at Engedi	I Samuel 23:29
P2– David had chance to kill Saul at Engedi	I Samuel 24: 1-5
P3– David must respect the life of the anointed King Saul	I Samuel 24: 6,7
P4– David set high standard: respect God's anointed leader	
P5– David faced Saul	I Samuel 24: 7-22
P5– The families of three corrupt, future kings of Israel were executed	I Kings 15:28-30; I Kings 16:11,12; II Kings 10:10,11,17
P5– Judah's King Jehoram executed his brothers and other leaders	II Chronicles 21: 1-4
P5– God had sought a king after His heart	I Samuel 13:14
P6– Samuel's death	I Samuel 24:22; 25: 1
P7– David's band bartered services for food	I Samuel 25: 1-8
P8– Nabal refused to help David	I Samuel 25: 9-12
P8– David planned a harsh reprisal against Nabal	I Samuel 25:13,21,22
P9– Abigail's risky intervention to give David food	I Samuel 25:14-20
P10– The pacifying power of a gift	Proverbs 16:14; 21:14; Genesis 32:13-21;33: 8
P10– Abigail spoke to David with great wisdom, insight, and effect	I Samuel 25:23-34
P11– David learning to act like God's anointed	
P11– Moses described the king God chooses	Deuteronomy 17:14-20
P12– Nabal died and David married Abigail	I Samuel 25:35-44
P13– David refused another opportunity to kill King Saul	I Samuel 26:1-11
P14–King Saul again humbled by David's plea for mercy	I Samuel 26:12-25

Chapter 2 - David Becomes King

Chapter 2, Section 1 - The Philistines give David asylum in Ziklag

P1– David's hopelessness as a fugitive	I Samuel 27: 1
P1– Saul offered rewards for David's life	I Samuel 22: 7
P1– Ziphites had helped Saul find David	I Samuel 23:19-23; 26: 1
P2– David requested asylum from Achish, a Philistine ruler	I Samuel 27: 1-3
P2– Philistines had previously refused David asylum early in his escape	I Samuel 21:10-15

P2– Philistine incursions into Israel	I Samuel 23: 1,27
P3– Philistine ruler gave David asylum in Ziklag	I Samuel 27: 5,6
P3– Ziklag had been given to tribe of Judah, then to tribe of Simeon	Joshua 15:31; 19: 5; I Chronicles 4:24,30
P4– Saul did not chase David but feared the Philistine threat	I Samuel 27: 4; 28: 3-6
P4– The Philistine army gathered at Shunem, deep inside Israel	I Samuel 28: 4
P5– Desiring direction, King Saul requested a séance	I Samuel 28: 7,9
P5– God had forbidden getting counsel from a psychic or wizard	Deuteronomy 18: 9-14; Leviticus 19:31; 20: 6,27
P6– Saul communicated with the deceased Samuel	I Samuel 28: 7-25
P6– Saul died for disobeying God and for seeking medium	I Chronicles 10:13
P7– David's exploits in Ziklag	I Samuel 27: 7-12
P8– Achish called David's band to join the battle against Israel	I Samuel 28: 1,2
P9– How could David fight with the Philistines against Israel?	
P10– David's tentative compliance with Achish's request	
P11– Philistine leaders refused to allow David to fight with them	I Samuel 29: 1-5
P11– Israelites fighting with Philistines had defected during a battle	I Samuel 14:21
P11– Philistine lords concerned about David betraying them	I Chronicles 12:19
P12– Achish sent David back	I Samuel 29: 6-11

Chapter 2, Section 2 - Drama for David at Ziklag. Saul Dies.

P1– Ziklag sacked; families of all of David's men were missing	I Samuel 30:1-3
P2– Men grieved, David prayed, God directed, all recovered	I Samuel 30:4-25
P3– David sent gifts to Judah	I Samuel 30:26-31
P4– Saul and Jonathan die in battle; David's grieving response	I Samuel 31: 1-7; II Samuel 1: 1-16
P5–David's lamentation over the deaths of Saul and Jonathan	II Samuel 1:17-27
P6– David blessed men who show kindness and bury Saul & his sons	I Samuel 31: 8-13; II Samuel 2: 4-7
P7– David's gracious respect for Saul	
P7– God is David's refuge	Psalm 62: 7,8; 18: 1,2; 91: 2
P8– Israel's soldiers joined David in Ziklag	I Chronicles 12:1-7, 19-22

Chapter 2, Section 3 - David is crowned King of Judah

P1– David's new options	
P2– David had no selfish agenda	
P3– God directs a move to Hebron	II Samuel 2: 1-3
P4– David anointed king over Judah	II Samuel 2: 4
P5– Should the next king come from Saul's royal family?	
P6– Israel wanted David to succeed Saul	II Samuel 3:17-19; 5: 1,2

P7– David's service had been loved by Israel when Saul fired him	I Samuel 18:13-16, 29, 30
P6– Three of Saul's sons had died with Saul in battle	I Samuel 31: 2
P8– God had chosen David to succeed Saul and Samuel anointed him	I Samuel 15:28; 16: 1, 12-14
P8– God had given the kingdom to Saul's neighbor	I Samuel 15:23
P9– Saul had opposed David being king	I Samuel 20:30, 31
P9– God turned the kingdom from a rebellious King Saul to David	I Chronicles 10:13,14

Chapter 2, Section 4 - Northern tribes crown Saul's son king

P1– Abner made Ishbosheth King of Israel	II Samuel 2: 8-10
P2– Ishbosheth depended upon Abner	II Samuel 2: 8
P2– Ishbosheth afraid of Abner	II Samuel 3:11
P3– Philistines were strong and possess Israelite cities	I Chronicles 10: 7; I Samuel 31: 7
P4– Israel and Judah were separate nations	II Samuel 2:10
P5– Judah and Israel battle each other	II Samuel 2:12-17,24-30
P5– Abner killed Asahel, brother of Joab and Abishai	II Samuel 2:18-23,30-32
P6– Abner defected to David	II Samuel 3: 1-11
P7– Abner agreed to terms of surrender with David	II Samuel 3:12-21
P8– Joab and Abishai murdered Abner	II Samuel 3:22-30,
P9– Joab, Abishai, and Asahel were sons of Zeruiah	II Samuel 2:18; I Chronicles 2:16
P9– Examples of Joab and Abishai retaliations	I Samuel 26: 6-8; II Samuel 16:10; 19:33
P9– David expressed frustration with Joab and Abishai	II Samuel 3:39
P10– David mourned for Abner	II Samuel 3:31-38
P11– Saul's son Ishbosheth was assassinated	II Samuel 4

Chapter 2, Section 5 - Northern Israel temporarily without a king

P1– Israel's leaders had approved Abner's treaty with David	II Samuel 3:17-19
P2– Israel did not submit to David	
P2– David unable to punish Joab for murdering Abner	II Samuel 3:39
P3– Israel should have pursued re-union	
P4– David reigned 7.5 years over Judah before reigning in Israel	II Samuel 2:10, 11; 5: 5
P5– Judah gained strength for 2 years	II Samuel 3: 1
P5– David was not ambitious to rule all Israel	
P6– David did not fight the Philistines	
P6– Philistine occupation and control in Israel	I Samuel 31: 7; I Chronicles 10: 7
P6– David and the Philistines respected each other	I Samuel 29: 6-9

P7– Philistine oppression of the Israelites	I Chronicles 11:13,14
P7– Philistine harvest time raid in Keilah	I Samuel 23: 1-5
P8– Israel waited to seek union under David	
P9– David waited for national reunion	

Chapter 2, Section 6 - All of Israel crowns David king

P1– All Israel was ready to make David king	I Chronicles 12:38
P2– Israel's soldiers came to support David	I Chronicles 12:23-38
P3– Israel asked David to rule them	II Samuel 5: 1,2; I Chronicles 11: 1,2
P4– David agreed to be king over Israel	II Samuel 5: 3-5
P5– David's coronation: Israel's leaders anointed him king of all Israel	I Chronicles 11: 3; 12:38-40

Chapter 3 - David Confirmed King in Jerusalem

Chapter 3, Section 1 - Jerusalem becomes Israel's capital

P1– Reflection on David's path to king of all of Israel	
P2– How did David change after his time as a fugitive?	
P3– David patiently trusted God and humbly obeyed Him	
P4– David's troops captured Jerusalem	II Samuel 5: 6-8; I Chronicles 11: 4-6
P4– Tribes Judah & Benjamin did not expel Jebusites from Jerusalem	Joshua 15:63; Judges 1:21
P4– Jebusites were direct descendents of Noah's grandson Canaan	Genesis 10:15,16
P5– David called the citadel of Zion, the City of David	II Samuel 5: 9,10; I Chronicles 11: 5,7
P5– David built up Jerusalem, Israel's new capital	II Samuel 5: 9,10; I Chronicles 11: 8,9

Chapter 3, Section 2 - David's finest fighters

P1– David's top three mighty men	I Chronicles 11:10-14; II Samuel 23: 8-12
P1– Joab earned the position of David's chief captain	I Chronicles 11: 6
P2– Defending crops from the Philistines	I Chronicles 11:13; II Samuel 23:11
P3– David personally opposed Philistine raids	I Chronicles 11:12-14
P3– Philistines possessed Israelite cities since Saul's death	I Chronicles 10: 7; I Samuel 31: 7
P4– David had hid in the Adullam cave when running from Saul	I Samuel 22: 1
P4– Three warriors risked their lives to get David special water	I Chronicles 11:15-19; II Samuel 23:13-17

P5– David poured the water out	I Chronicles 11:18,19; II Samuel 23:16,17
P6– By pouring out the water, David honored his men	
P7– Other notable captains under David	I Chronicles 11:22-47; II Samuel 23:20-39
P7– Solomon made Benaiah commander of Israel's forces	I Kings 2:35
P7– The extraordinary loyalty of Uriah the Hittite	II Samuel 11: 9-15
P7– Ahithophel, David's counselor, joined Absalom's coup	II Samuel 15:12; 16:23
P7– Eliam was Bathsheba's father	II Samuel 11: 3

Chapter 3, Section 3 - King of Tyre builds a palace for David

P1– David reigned in Jerusalem	
P2– Hiram, King of Tyre, received David graciously	II Samuel 5:11; I Chronicles 3: 1-9; 14: 1,3-7
P3– King of Tyre built David a palace	II Samuel 5:11, 13-16; I Chronicles 3: 1-9; 14: 1,3-7
P4– David realized God made him King of Israel	I Chronicles 14: 2; II Samuel 5:12
P5– David was the man to be king	

Chapter 3, Section 4 - Victories over the Philistines

P1– Philistines were unhappy with David in Jerusalem	I Chronicles 14: 8; II Samuel 5:17
P2– The Philistine army came after David	I Chronicles 14: 8,9; II Samuel 5:17 18
P3– David hesitated fighting the Philistines preferring peace	
P4– David hesitated fighting the Philistines because they were strong	
P5– David asked God about fighting and defeating the Philistines	I Chronicles 14:10; II Samuel 5:19
P5– During the judges, God had said, 'Fight' – and yet Israel lost	Judges 20
P5– God told David, 'Fight the Philistines. You will win'	I Chronicles 14:10; II Samuel 5:19
P5– God gave David victory in first battle	I Chronicles 14:11-12; II Samuel 5:20,21
P6– God gave new direction for second battle	I Chronicles 14:13,14; II Samuel 5:22, 23
P7– Israel routed the Philistines in the second battle	I Chronicles 14:15, 16; II Samuel 5:24, 25
P8– David received international fame	I Chronicles 14:17
P9– How would David handle his new fame	

Chapter 4 - David Attempts to Move the Ark of the Covenant	
Chapter 4, Section 1 - David's first priority: the Ark of the Covenant	
P1– David had military and political options	
P2– David desired to exalted God among the nations	Psalm 2; 108
P2– Assyria & Babylon administered God's justice w/o honoring Him	Isaiah 10: 5-15; 47: 5-15
P3– David wanted to bring the Ark to Jerusalem	I Chronicles 13: 3; II Samuel 6: 1,2
Chapter 4, Section 2 - Summary of the movements of the Ark of the Covenant	
P1– Table of the Ark's movements – holy places in Israel	II Chronicles 8:11
P2– Israel's enthusiasm for the Ark of the Covenant	I Samuel 4: 3-5
Chapter 4, Section 3 - Israel's history with the Ark of the Covenant	
P1– The pattern for the Ark of the Covenant that God had given to Moses	Exodus 25: 8-21
P1– God dwells between the cherubim of the Ark's mercy seat cover	Exodus 25:20-22; II Samuel 6: 2
P1– Moses put the tables of the law into the Ark of the Covenant	Exodus 40:20; 25:21
P1– God's law was the basis for His covenant with Israel	Exodus 34:27; 19: 5-8; 24: 3-8; Deuteronomy 26:16-19; I Chronicles 16:15-17
P1– Israel promised to obey God and be His people	Exodus 19: 3-8; 24: 3-7
P1– God promised to make Israel His people and to be their God	Exodus 19: 4-6; 6: 4-8; Deuteronomy 29:12,13
P1– God wrote the 10 commandments on tablets with his finger	Exodus 31:18; 32:15,16; 34: 1,28; Deuteronomy 4:13; 5:22; 9: 9-11; 10: 4
P1– God told Moses to write out a copy of the law	Exodus 34:27,28; 24: 4
P1– God told Moses to put the tablets He wrote in the Ark	Exodus 25:21; Deuteronomy 10: 1,2
P2– Israel completed the tabernacle one year after leaving Egypt	Exodus 40: 1,17; 12: 2
P2– God told Moses to setup the tabernacle with its holy items	Exodus 40: 1-11
P2– Moses verified that all of the tabernacle is built to specification	Exodus 39:42, 43; Hebrews 8: 5
P2– The Ark was put in the most holy place behind the inner veil	Exodus 26:31-34; 40:20, 21; Hebrews 9: 3-5
P2– Only the high priest could enter the holiest place & one day a year	Leviticus 16: 1,2,17,29,34; Hebrews 9: 7
P2– High priest took blood & incense into the holiest place each year	Leviticus 16:2-19; Hebrews 9:25
P2– Aaron and his four sons chosen to minister to God as priests	Exodus 28: 1; 40:12-15

P2– Two priests, Aaron's sons, died in the presence of the Holy God	Leviticus 10: 1-3
P3– God brought Israel out of Egypt to give them the land of Canaan	Leviticus 25:38; Joshua 24:11-13
P3– God's glory filled the tabernacle; the cloud & fire remain connected	Exodus 40:34-38
P3– God directed Israel in the wilderness by the pillars of cloud & fire	Numbers 9:15-23; Nehemiah 9:19-21
P3– In wilderness, cloud covered them and fire for light at night	Exodus 13:21,22; Deuteronomy 1:33; Psalm 105:39
P4– Ark and tabernacle in center area of Israel's wilderness camps	Numbers 2:17; Numbers 1:50–2:34
P4– When traveling, Ark was positioned in the midst of the Israelites	Numbers 10:13-28
P4– God's provision in the wilderness and Israel's unbelief	Nehemiah 9:12-26; Psalm 78:11-32
P4– Israel scouted a great land of promise, but 10 spies were intimidated	Numbers 13
P4– After two years, Israelites did not believe to enter their promised land	Deuteronomy 1:25-35; Numbers 14: 1-10
P4– Israel wandered 38 more years; all unbelievers died in the wilderness	Deuteronomy 2:14-16; Numbers 14:28-37
P5– Ark central as God stopped the Jordan River for Israel to cross	Joshua 3: 1–4:13
P5– When Israel entered Canaan, God exalted Joshua as their leader	Joshua 4:14
P5– The Canaanites knew that God had promised their land to Israel	Joshua 9:24
P5– God had shamed Egypt's gods	Exodus 12:12; Numbers 33: 4
P5– The Canaanites knew what God had done for Israel in Egypt	Joshua 9: 9,10
P5– Canaanites awed at Red Sea crossing and the Amorites defeat	Joshua 2:10,11
P5– Canaanites noticed the Jordan crossing and fear the Israelites	Joshua 5: 1; 9:24
P5– Only Israel's God acts powerfully & purposefully for His people	I Kings 8:56; Isaiah 64: 4
P6– The ark traveled with Israel during the conquest of Canaan	Joshua 4:11; 6: 4
P6– Caleb's age shows seven years were needed to conquer Canaan	Deuteronomy 2:14; Joshua 14: 7,10
P6– Pockets of strong Canaanites left to be conquered	Joshua 13: 1-6; Judges 1: 1; 2: 1-9
P6– The tabernacle and ark set up in Shiloh after conquering Canaan	Joshua 18: 1

P6– Solomon built temple for the Ark 480 years after Israel left Egypt	I Kings 6: 1
P6– Israel gathered in Shiloh	Joshua 18: 1-10; 19:51; Judges 18:31; I Samuel 1: 3
P7– Corrupt activities of the sons of Eli, the high priest	I Samuel 2:11-17
P7– The Ark taken to battle and captured	I Samuel 4
P7– Eli's death; Samuel became the spiritual leader of Israel	I Samuel 7: 3-17
P8– The captured Ark plagued the Philistines	I Samuel 5
P9– The Ark returned to Israel on a driverless cart	I Samuel 6: 1-12
P9– Bethshemesh, a city in the tribe of Judah, was given to the Levites	Joshua 21:16
P10– Bethshemites receiving Ark looked inside and were punished	I Samuel 6:13-19
P10– The Ark was sent to the home of Abinadab in Kirjathjearim	I Samuel 6:20 – 7:2
P11– The Ark in Kirjathjearim was separated from the tabernacle	
P11– A priest ministered at Shiloh early in Saul's reign	I Samuel 14: 3
P11– Saul had asked for the Ark to be brought to battle	I Samuel 14:18,19
P11– Tabernacle was at a high place in Gibeon early in David's reign	I Chronicles 16:39
P11– Gibeonites tricked Israel's leaders into making peace with them	Joshua 9
P11– Gibeon was located in the tribe of Benjamin	Joshua 18:11,25,28
P11– Gibeon was one of the forty-eight cities given to the Levites	Joshua 21:17
P12– The tabernacle was moved from Shiloh to Gibeon	
P12– Tabernacle in Shiloh from the time of the judges to King Saul	Judges 18:31; I Samuel 14: 3
P12– Jeremiah said that God had set His name in Shiloh	Jeremiah 7:12-14
P12– Jeremiah said Shiloh's desolation is an example to avoid	Jeremiah 26: 6,9; Psalm 78:59-61
P13– Ark of the Covenant was not used publicly during Saul's reign	I Chronicles 13: 3
P13– Presence of God was with the Ark of the Covenant	Numbers 7:89; 10:33-35; Exodus 25:21, 22
P13– Regular sacrifices continue at Israel's tabernacle in Gibeon	I Chronicles 16:39,40
P14– Day of Atonement blood sprinkled on Ark's mercy seat	Leviticus 16
P15– Importance of the Day of Atonement	Leviticus 23:27-32; 16:17,33,34
P15– Sin separated God and Israel and hid His face from them	Isaiah 59: 1,2

Chapter 4, Section 4 - David prepares to move the Ark	
P1– David wanted to move Ark of God's presence to the City of David	I Chronicles 15: 1
P2– David did not move the Ark privately	I Chronicles 13: 3
P3– David wanted to restore public use of the Ark	I Chronicles 13: 3
P3– God is the LORD Who dwells between the cherubim of the Ark	I Chronicles 13: 6; II Samuel 6: 1
P4– David discussed Ark move with leaders	I Chronicles 13: 1; I Samuel 6: 1
P5– David asked the leadership if moving the Ark was a good idea	I Chronicles 13: 2
P6– David suggested inviting all citizens to join in moving the Ark	I Chronicles 13: 3
P7– David included all since Israel did not use the Ark in Saul's reign	I Chronicles 13: 3
P8– Israel's assembly of leaders agreed to move the Ark	I Chronicles 13: 4
P9– David's respect for the Ark of the Covenant	I Chronicles 13: 1-4
P10– David did not seek God or God's direction for the relocation	I Chronicles 15:13

Chapter 4, Section 5 - The procession of the Ark of the Covenant begins	
P1– David called all Israel together to move the Ark	I Chronicles 13: 5,6
P2– David's expectation for God to be present among His people	
P3– The Israelites came together at Kirjathjearim to help move Ark	I Chronicles 13: 5,6; II Samuel 6: 1,2
P4– The processional to Jerusalem began with the Ark riding on cart	I Chronicles 13: 7; II Samuel 6: 3,4
P4– God's instructions for carrying the holy items	Numbers 4: 4-15
P4– The Philistines had sent the Ark back to Israel on a cart	I Samuel 6: 7-11
P4– Some Levites had used carts, but Ark must be carried on shoulders	Numbers 7: 1-9
P5– Israel celebrated the Ark of the Covenant	I Chronicles 13: 8; II Samuel 6: 5

Chapter 4, Section 6 - God interrupts the Ark's procession	
P1– The Ark of the Covenant approached a threshing floor	I Chronicles 13:9; II Samuel 6: 6
P2– God struck Uzza dead for touching the Ark of the Covenant	I Chronicles 13: 9,10; II Samuel 6: 6,7
P3– David was upset about Uzza's death	I Chronicles 13:11; II Samuel 6:8
P4– David's hopes for the Ark were dashed	
P5– David wondered how the Ark of the Covenant would come to him?	I Chronicles 13:12; II Samuel 6: 9

P6– The Ark of the Covenant was taken to the house of Obededom	I Chronicles 13:13; II Samuel 6:10
P6– Second move would begin where first one ended – in Jerusalem	I Chronicles 15: 3

Chapter 5 - David Completes the Move of the Ark of the Covenant

Chapter 5, Section 1 - David prepares to move the Ark ... again

P1– David was perplexed about why God struck Uzza dead	
P2– God blessed the household of Obededom because of the Ark	I Chronicles 13:14; II Samuel 6:11
P3– Blessing on Obededom spurred David to complete Ark's relocation	II Samuel 6:12
P4– David must humbly seek God to correct his previous errors	
P4– David had learned to trust God and pour out his heart to Him	Psalm 62:8
P5– David prepared a specific location at his palace for the Ark	I Chronicles 15: 1; II Chronicles 8:11
P6– David wanted the Levites to have their God-honored place	I Chronicles 15: 2
P6– God had warned that Levites would die for touching holy items	Numbers 4:15-20
P7– God had set Levites apart to minister to Him & bless in His name	Deuteronomy 10: 8; 18: 7
P8– David gathered Israel to Jerusalem and counted the Levites	I Chronicles 15: 3-10
P9– David called 8 Levites leaders for special duties during this move	I Chronicles 15:11
P9– Importance of being ceremonially clean	Numbers 19:17-22
P9– Priest and Levite leaders sanctified themselves to carry the Ark	I Chronicles 15:12-15
P9– Wooden poles through rings in the Ark used to carry it	Exodus 25:13-15
P10– David instructed Levite leaders to appoint singers and musicians	I Chronicles 15:16
P10– Reasons the priests were to blow the trumpets in Israel	Numbers 10: 1-10
P10– Instruments of music used during ministry of prophets	I Samuel 10:5
P10– Israel singing in times of celebration	Exodus 15:1-21; Judges 5; I Samuel 18: 6
P11– Leaders appointed Levites singers & musicians for processional	I Chronicles 15:17-22
P11– Levite leaders named priests with trumpets and porters	I Chronicles 15:23,24

P12– David did not bring the Ark back inside the tabernacle	
P12– High priest sprinkled blood on mercy seat on Day of Atonement	Leviticus 16:14-16
P13– Israel's tabernacle was at the high place in Gibeon	II Chronicles 1: 3; I Chronicles 16:39,40
P13– God did not forbid David to bring the Ark to Jerusalem	

Chapter 5, Section 2 - The Ark of the Covenant is carried to the City of David

P1– David & Israel's leaders went to Obededom's house to get the Ark	I Chronicles 15:25; II Samuel 6:12
P2– The Ark was carried six steps then David offers sacrifice to God	I Chronicles 15:26; II Samuel 6:13
P3– The Levite choir wore special linen robes for the processional	I Chronicles 15:27
P4– King David wore a linen robe and an ephod	I Chronicles 15:27
P4– The ephod was worn over the high priest's robe	Leviticus 8: 6,7
P4– Design of the elaborate ephod worn by Israel's high priest	Exodus 28: 6-30
P4– All Israel moved the Ark - singing, shouting, playing, & dancing	I Chronicles 15:28; II Samuel 6:14,15
P5– David defended his expressive praise to his wife Michal	I Chronicles 15:29; II Samuel 6:16,20-23
P6– The Ark of the Covenant placed in the tent David prepared for it	I Chronicles 16: 1; II Samuel 6:17
P7– Celebration continued with offerings to God & a meal together	I Chronicles 16: 1-3; II Samuel 6:17-19
P8– Listing of the differences between David's two moves of Ark	

Chapter 5, Section 3 - David appoints Levites to praise God daily

P1– David appointed Levite musicians to minister daily before the Ark	I Chronicles 16: 4-6,37
P2– David appointed Levite porters at the Ark	I Chronicles 16:38
P3– David appointed priests & Levites to minister daily at tabernacle	I Chronicles 16:39-42; 6:48,49
P3– Levite task of supporting the priests	Numbers 3: 6-9
P3– Genealogy of the Levites leading praise at the Ark & tabernacle	I Chronicles 6:31-49
P4– David thrilled to set up and assist the daily Levite music ministry	
P5– At key times, God judged others harshly, not only Uzza	
P5– Israel punished for idolatry while God & Moses were on Mt Sinai	Exodus 32:19-35
P5– God showed His glory twice in the new tabernacle	Exodus 40:33-38; Leviticus 9:23,24
P5– Two priests judged for entering holy place in their own way	Leviticus 10: 1-3

P5– Achan stoned for not respecting God's command at Jericho	Joshua 6:17 – 7:26
P5– Two members judged for dishonesty in giving to the church	Acts 5: 1-11
P6– God's judgments are true and entirely right	Psalm 19:9; 119: 75
P6– Jesus judged when he carried the world's sin	Isaiah 53:4
P7– God's judgments are righteous and forever	Psalm 119:160
P7– God saw potential in daily Levite ministry	
P7– God's purpose to make His people a praise in the earth	Isaiah 62: 7
P8– Daily Levite praise aligned with God's universal, eternal purposes	
P8– God raised up Pharaoh to declare His name in all the earth	Exodus 9:16; Romans 9:17
P8– God made His own name glorious in leading Israel out of Egypt	Isaiah 63:12-14
P8– God told rebellious Israel that His glory will fill the earth	Numbers 14:21
P8– Angels proclaimed that the earth is full of the glory of the holy God	Isaiah 6: 1-3
P9– God is forming a people to declare His praise	Isaiah 43:21

Chapter 5, Section 4 - David's psalm of thanksgiving to God

P1– David's celebration & praise psalm for Asaph to sing at the Ark	I Chronicles 16: 8-36; Psalm 105: 1-15; 96; 106:47,48

Chapter 6 - David's Heart for God and God's Heart for David

Chapter 6, Section 1 - David wants to build a house for God

P1– Political and spiritual progress in Israel	II Samuel 7:1
P2– God's opportunity to speak a word of revelation in the earth	
P3– David wanted to build a house for God	I Chronicles 17: 1; II Samuel 7:2
P3– The Ark of the Covenant located near David's house	II Chronicles 8:11
P4– Nathan the prophet appeared abruptly here	I Chronicles 17: 1
P4– Nathan wrote a book about David's reign	I Chronicles 29:29
P4– Nathan wrote a book about Solomon's reign	II Chronicles 9:29
P4– Nathan confronted David about his sins against Uriah	II Samuel 12: 1-15
P4– Nathan aided in the transfer of the throne from David to Solomon	I Kings 1:10-46
P4– Two of Nathan's sons were in Solomon's court	I Kings 4: 5
P5– God's spirit came on David after Samuel had anointed him	I Samuel 16:13
P5– Nathan noticed that God was with David	I Chronicles 17: 2; II Samuel 7:3
P6– Nathan encouraged David in his desire to build a house for the Ark	I Chronicles 17: 2; II Samuel 7:3

Chapter 6, Section 2 - God says that David cannot do it

P1– Nathan sent to tell David NOT to build a house for God	I Chronicles 17: 3,4

P1– God seemed to question David thinking he could build God's house	II Samuel 7:4,5
P2– God had never lived in a house – only tents	I Chronicles 17: 5; II Samuel 7:6
P2– Solomon said that heaven cannot contain God, much less a house	II Chronicles 6:18
P3– The prophet Amos declares a future rebuilding of David's tabernacle	Amos 9:11
P3– James expounds on Amos' prophecy; God's plans for David's tent	Acts 15:16,17; Revelation 21: 3
P3– Solomon sacrifices before the Ark in the tabernacle at Jerusalem	I Kings 3:15
P4– God never commanded anyone to build him a house	I Chronicles 17: 6; II Samuel 7:7
P5– God said that David's desire to build Him a house was a good one	II Chronicles 6: 8; I Kings 8:17,18

Chapter 6, Section 3 - God reminds David what He has already done

P1– The Lord of Hosts prefaces His revelation to His servant David	I Chronicles 17: 7; II Samuel 7: 8
P2– God reminded David of his exaltation from shepherd to king	I Chronicles 17: 7; II Samuel 7: 8
P2– God reminded David of his deliverances and of his fame	I Chronicles 17: 8; II Samuel 7: 9
P3– God addressed David as His servant	I Chronicles 17: 4,7; II Samuel 7:5,8
P3– God makes vessels of mercy on whom to show His glory	Ephesians 2: 7; Romans 9:23
P4– David needed to remember to avoid pitfalls of success and power	
P5– David needed to remember to avoid pitfalls of great fame	
P6– David needed to remember to avoid pitfalls of having promises	

Chapter 6, Section 4 - God says that He will do more for David

P1– God promised a secure place for His people Israel	I Chronicles 17: 9; II Samuel 7:10
P2– God promised to subdue David's enemies	I Chronicles 17:10
P3– God promised blessings for David's family and kingdom	I Chronicles 17:10-12; II Samuel 7:11-13
P4– God promised to build a house for David	I Chronicles 17:10; II Samuel 7:11
P5– God promised to build David's house with David's offspring	I Chronicles 17:11; II Samuel 7:12
P5– God promised to set David's seed on the throne	Psalm 132:11,12

P6– God promised to establish the kingdom of David's son	I Chronicles 17:11,12; II Samuel 7:12,13
P7– God said David's son will build a house for God	I Chronicles 17:12; II Samuel 7:13
P7– Later David prepared to build and God refused for a new reason	I Chronicles 28: 2, 3
P8– More promised blessings for David's family and kingdom	I Chronicles 17: 13,14; II Samuel 7:14-16
P9– God promised to be a father to David's son	I Chronicles 17:13; II Samuel 7:14
P9– God is a great king above all gods	Psalm 95:3
P10– God promised never to take His mercy from David's son	I Chronicles 17:13; II Samuel 7:15
P10– Jesus never needed mercy because he did not sin	Hebrews 4:14-16
P11– God repeated promise to establish throne of David's son forever	Psalm 89:33-37
P11– God promised to settle David's son in His house	I Chronicles 17:14; II Samuel 7:16
P12– Three times God said His purposes for David's son were forever	I Chronicles 17:12,14; II Samuel 7:13,16

Chapter 6, Section 5 - Scope and gospel fulfillment of God's promises to David

P1– God's promises were beyond David's comprehension	
P2– David was a man to whom God can make eternal promises	Psalm 89:19-29
P3– God spoke in the earth and made a covenant with Noah and all life	Genesis 9: 1-17
P3– God spoke in the earth and made a covenant with Abraham	Genesis 12: 1-3; 13:14-17; 15: 4-6; 17: 1-22
P3– God spoke in the earth to Moses and made a covenant with Israel	Numbers 12: 5-9; Deuteronomy 9: 9-11
P3– God blessed Israel by Balaam	Numbers 23; 24: 1-24
P3– God spoke to Daniel of His everlasting kingdom	Daniel 7
P3– God spoke His eternal word by His Son – Jesus	John 1: 1; Hebrews 1: 2
P3– God speaks with power	Psalm 29: 3-9; Jeremiah 23:29
P3– God's word creates	Psalm 33:9; 148: 5
P3– God's word prospers and accomplishes its purposes	Isaiah 55:11; 46: 9-11
P3– God, by His word, created the ordered universe	Hebrews 11: 3; Genesis 1: 3,9,24
P3– God fulfills His word – when the time is right	Ephesians 1: 9-11
P4– Blessings promised to all nations in Abraham & his seed – singular	Genesis 22:18; 12: 3; Galatians 3:16
P4– God promised Abraham would be the father of many nations	Genesis 17: 5,6; Romans 4:17

P4– Abraham was a model of faith	Galatians 3: 6,7,9,29; Romans 4:12,16
P4– Abraham was the father of all of those who believe	Romans 4: 9-17
P4– God's promise to Abraham included all who believe like Abraham	Galatians 3: 6-9
P5– Peace and security in the land of Israel was part of God's plan	Jeremiah 33:14-26; Ezekiel 34:22-31
P5– Prophesied peace for God's people related to the house of God	Micah 4: 1-7; Haggai 2: 7-9
P6– Aspects of Jesus' life and calling in God's word to David	
P6– God's promise to be a father to David's son was applied to Jesus	Hebrews 1: 4,5; 5: 5-8
P6– Jesus was born of David's seed twenty-eight generations later	Matthew 1:17
P6– Jesus was physically born into David's royal family	Romans 1: 3; Luke 1:27,32; 2: 4
P6– Jesus was called the son of David	Matthew 1: 1; 12:23; 21: 9; 22:42
P6– Jesus declared Himself the offspring of David	Revelation 22:16
P7– God sent His son to be born when the time was right	Galatians 4: 4
P7– Jesus is declared to be the Son of God	Luke 1:35; Romans 1: 4; Hebrews 4:14; John 1:34
P7– Jesus conceived in Mary by God's Spirit before her marriage union	Luke 1:31,35; Matthew 1:20-23
P7– Jesus was born Saviour, Lord and King	Luke 2:11; Matthew 2: 2
P7– Jesus revealed to be the Christ, the Son of the living God	Matthew 16:16,17
P7– Jesus' purpose to save God's people from their sins	Matthew 1:21
P8– God loved the world and sent Jesus to save the world	John 3:16,17; I John 2: 2; 4: 9,10
P8– God created Adam as the first human	Genesis 2: 7; 1:26-28
P8– Adam broke God's rule, resulting in decay and death reigning	Genesis 3: 1-19; Romans 5:15-17
P8– Adam sin affected all of the physical creation as well	Romans 8:19-22
P8– Since Adam sinned, everyone born of Adam's seed is a sinner	Romans 5:12
P8– Everyone has failed, none are perfect	Romans 3: 9-12
P9– Two universal problems: sin and imperfection	Romans 3:23
P9– Day of Atonement offering in God's presence was needed annually	Hebrews 9: 7,8; 10: 3,4
P9– No ceremony or sacrifice makes anyone perfect for God's presence	Hebrews 10: 1,2; 9: 9,10
P9– God sent Jesus to solve the sin and imperfection problems	Romans 3:24-26
P9– God did not send Jesus to condemn the world, but to save it	John 3:17,18

P10– Jesus came to earth & lived a human life in a natural human body	Philippians 2: 7,8; I John 4:2
P10– Jesus began life without corruption	John 1: 1,14; I Peter 1:23
P10– Jesus lived without sinning	I Peter 2:21,22; Hebrews 4:15; Isaiah 53: 9
P10– Jesus convicted of blasphemy by Jewish leaders & sentenced to die	Matthew 26:63-66; Mark 14:61-64
P10– Jesus did not defend himself or appeal his conviction	John 18:29-19:11; Luke 23: 1-24
P10– Jewish leaders unwittingly aided God's plan by ensuing Jesus' death	I Corinthians 2: 6-8; Acts 2:23; 3:13-17
P10– The shame & suffering of Jesus was part of his great saving work	Hebrews 5: 8,9; 2:10; 12: 2
P10– Jesus allowed injustice to be done to him	I Peter 2:23; Hebrews 12:2; Isaiah 50: 6,7
P10- The faith of Jesus to endure the cross	Hebrews 12:2; John 6:38; Matthew; 26:39; Luke 23:46; Galatians 2:16
P10- The meekness and lowliness of Jesus	Matthew 11:28-30; Philippians 2:3-7; Ephesians 4:1,2
P10– Jesus humble and obedient all the way to his death on the cross	Philippians 2: 5-8
P11– Jesus bore our sins in his own body on the cross	I Peter 2:24; Isaiah 53:12
P11– Jesus willingly gave his life for his saving work	John 10:11,17,18; Matthew 20:28
P11– His enemies thought they had defeated Jesus and mocked him	Matthew 27:38-44 ; Mark 8:31; Psalm 22: 6-16
P11– Jesus is the Lamb of God sacrificed for the sin of the world	John 1:29; Isaiah 53: 6,7,11
P12– In Jesus' death, God condemned the sin that Jesus bore	Romans 8:3; 6:6; Hebrews 2:14,15
P12– Sin's misuse of God's holy law proves its guilt	Romans 7: 7-24
P12– Jesus carried our sin	Isaiah 53: 4-6,8,11,12
P12– Jesus put away sin forever by his one sacrifice	Hebrews 9:24-26; 10:10-14
P12– No further sacrifice for sin is needed	Hebrews 10:10,16-18,25
P12– The devil and his works are destroyed by Jesus' death	Hebrews 2:14,15; I John 3: 8
P13– Jesus poured out his soul unto death	Isaiah 53: 10-12
P13– As our high priest, Jesus brought his own blood into God's presence	Hebrews 7:26,27; 9:11,12,14,24
P13– Jesus represented humanity	Hebrews 2:16-18; Philippians 2: 7; Romans 5:15-19
P13– Jesus' blood satisfied the Just God and His justice	Romans 3:24-26; I John 2: 2

P13– Judgment on sin allows freedom from sin's guilt & condemnation	Romans 8: 1-4
P13– Those believing in Christ are justified by God's grace	Galatians 2:16; Romans 3:22-24
P13– Redemption, cleansing, and forgiveness through Jesus' blood	Ephesians 1: 7; I John 1: 7; Colossians 1:14; I Peter 1:17,18
P13– Grace reigns unto eternal life	Romans 5:17,21; 6:23; 8:2
P13– God shows off the riches of His grace toward believers	Ephesians 2: 5-16
P14– Jesus offered himself without spot, acceptable to the Holy God	Hebrews 9:14; Ephesians 5: 2
P14– God can justify believing sinners and make them righteous	Romans 3:21-26; 5:18,19; Philippians 3: 9
P14– God put human sin on Jesus & His perfection on believing sinners	II Corinthians 5: 17-21; Isaiah 53: 6,10
P15– Jesus, the Son of God, gives eternal life to believers	John 17: 2,3; 5:21-29
P15– Jesus sends the Holy Spirit from the Father to believers	John 16: 7; 7:39; 15:26; Luke 24:49
P15– The Holy Spirit of Christ dwells in believers	John 14:16,17; Romans 8: 9-11; Colossians 1:27
P15– The Holy Spirit empowers believers	Acts 1: 8; Romans 15:13; II Timothy 1: 7
P15– Believers are united in Christ Jesus	Galatians 3:28; Romans 12: 5
P15– Believers are sealed in Christ Jesus – a permanent union	Ephesians 1:13,14
P15– Jesus opened a way for believers to enter God's holy presence	Hebrews 10:19,20
P15– In Christ Jesus, believers are accepted in God's presence	Ephesians 1: 4-6
P15– Jesus made a way for God to relate to His people	Ephesians 2:13-17; Colossians 1:18-22
P15– God's covenant relation with His people established permanently	Hebrews 10:12-18; 8:10-12
P16– Jesus offered one sacrifice for sins forever	Hebrews 10:12-14
P16– God resurrected Jesus, who can never die again	Romans 6:4,9
P16– God gave Jesus a seat in heaven and authority over all creation	Ephesians 1:20-23; Philippians 2: 9-11
P16– Believers both die and are raised in Christ Jesus	Romans 6: 4,5; Colossians 3:12-15
P16– In Christ, by God's grace, believers are free from sin to live anew	Romans 6: 6-14; 8: 1-3; Ephesians 1:20 - 2: 10
P16– The ever-living Jesus prays for believers' complete salvation	Hebrews 7:25; Romans 8:34

P16– Jesus works to make God's people look like Jesus	Romans 8:29; Ephesians 4:13-16
P16– Jesus builds God's people into a temple for God's presence	Ephesians 2:19-22
P16– Jesus is cleansing, uniting, and building up God's people	Ephesians 2:21,22; 5:26
P16– Believers receive gifts and grace for mutual growth	Romans 12:2-8; Ephesians 4:1-13; Hebrews 10:24,25
P16– The continuing power of Jesus' sacrifice perfecting His bride	Ephesians 5:25-27
P17– God promises to give His Son the throne of David	Luke 1:31-35
P17– God's Son to reign on the throne of David forever	Isaiah 9: 6,7; Luke 1:31-35; Revelation 11:15
P17– Every other authority will be subdued under Jesus	I Corinthians 15:24-28; Ephesians 1:10
P17– Jesus is man who takes the responsibility to rule over all creation	Hebrews 2: 5-9; Psalm 8
P17– Jeremiah proclaimed the permanence of God's covenant with David	Jeremiah 33:20,21

Chapter 6, Section 6 - David says "Wow!"

P1– The scope and effect of God's promises are unimaginable	
P2– After hearing the revelation, David sat in God's presence & replied	I Chronicles 17:15, 16; II Samuel 7:17,18
P3– God had sent Nathan with consequences of David sins against Uriah	II Samuel 12
P3– David had confessed his sins and repented	Psalm 51
P4– David expressed amazement at God's blessings upon his family	I Chronicles 17:16,17; II Samuel 7:18,19
P5– Almost speechless, David rested in God's knowledge of him	I Chronicles 17:18,19; II Samuel 7:20,21
P6– David glorified God above all	I Chronicles 17:20; II Samuel 7:22
P7– David marveled at God's redemption of Israel	I Chronicles 17:21,22; II Samuel 7:23,24
P7– Moses had expressed how God exalted Israel above other nations	Deuteronomy 4: 6-8
P8– David's pure heart & humble response accepting God's great word	

Chapter 6, Section 7 - God includes David in His plans

P1– David was the right man to receive God's glorious revelation	
P2– David's actions supported God's plans	
P3– God gave all of His people a calling, a part in His plans	I Corinthians 7:17-24; Ephesians 4: 1

P3– God gives His people gifts and grace to fulfill their calling	Ephesians 4: 7-13; Romans 12:2-8; II Peter 1:3,4
P3– All things to work together for good to those who love God	Romans 8:28,29; John 11: 4
P4– God sees all of history clearly. He understands and guides.	Job 28:20-28; Psalm 139:1-5,23,24; I Chronicles 28: 9
P4– God, in His wisdom, personally and specifically leads His people	Isaiah 48:16,17
P4– God provides for His people who trust Him and do His will	Isaiah 41: 17-20; 43: 1-21
P5– God made Adam & humanity the responsible to care for the earth	Genesis 1:26; 2:15
P5– God gave humanity the ability & authority to care for all of creation	Psalm 8; Heb 2: 8; Genesis 9: 1,2
P5– God and Adam communicated directly	Genesis 2:16-20; 3: 8,9
P5– God told Abraham His plans knowing he will act in line with them	Genesis 18:17-19
P5– God told Noah of His plans to preserve humanity and Noah obeys	Genesis 6: 8,13-22
P5– God reveals secrets to His servants before He acts on earth	Amos 3: 7
P6– Adam sinned and caring for the earth became more difficult	Genesis 3
P6– Adam's sin and its consequences have been passed to all humanity	Genesis 2:16,17; Romans 5:12
P7– Actions opposing God's purposes of salvation and peace	Isaiah 59: 4-14
P7– God receives glory in judging those opposing His purposes	Romans 9:17-22; Ezekiel 28:22
P7– Some do not work for God's purposes of salvation, justice & truth	Isaiah 59: 1-4
P8– God does not intervene but seeks those pleading for His salvation	Isaiah 59:15,16
P8– God planned to establish Saul's kingdom & then chose David	I Samuel 13:13,14
P9– God honored the Israelite plea for deliverance from slavery in Egypt	Exodus 2:23-25
P9– Jehoshaphat prayed, believed answer, ordered praise, and was blessed	II Chronicles 20: 1-30
P9– God accepted Moses' plea for Israelites	Numbers 14:13-24
P9– God is always looking for faith on earth	Luke 18: 1-8; Hebrews 11: 6; II Chronicles 16: 9
P9– God's covenants encourage the faith His servant	Psalm 104: 4-10
P10– Israel ignored God's prophesied direction and was destroyed	Jeremiah 38:17 – 39:10; 42:19-43:13
P10– God's is forming a people to declare His praise	I Peter 2:9; Isaiah 43:21

P10– God works everything for good to those called after His purpose	Isaiah 46: 9-13; Romans 8:27-30
P11– God patiently waits to show mercy to His people	Isaiah 30:18; Ezekiel 12:26-28
P11– God guides His people in the way they should walk	Isaiah 30:21; Psalm 32: 8,9
P11– God's people pray for His kingdom & will on earth	Matthew 6: 9,10
P12– God's oath to establish David's seed and throne forever	Psalm 89: 3,4
P13– David to play an important role in God's plan and purposes	
P13– God personally confirmed and blessed David's kingdom	I Chronicles 14: 2; 18:13,14; Isaiah 9: 7

Chapter 6, Section 8 - David says "Let it happen"

P1– Examples of David seeking and obeying God's counsel	I Samuel 23: 2-4; 30: 8; II Samuel 2: 1; 5:19
P1– God, here, gave David nothing to do; He expressed His purposes	I Chronicles 17: 3-14
P2– With no task, David's unrehearsed response showed his heart	I Chronicles 17:15-27
P3– David asked God to do what He had spoken by Nathan	I Chronicles 17:23-27; II Samuel 7:25-29
P4– David's request displayed his heart for God	I Chronicles 17:23-27; II Samuel 7:25-29
P5– David acknowledged that God Himself had promised	I Chronicles 17:26; II Samuel 7:28
P6– David's response showed he is not selfish, manipulative, or greedy	I Chronicles 17:16,17,26,27; II Samuel 7:18,19,28,29
P7– David exhibited a heart after God's Own heart	I Chronicles 17:23-27; II Samuel 7:25-29
P8– God's overwhelming word made it difficult for David to respond	I Chronicles 17:25
P9– David believed that God would do what He said	I Chronicles 17:23-27; II Samuel 7:25-29
P9– Abraham's example of not staggering at God's amazing promise	Romans 4:20,21
P10– David wanted God to be glorified in doing what He said	I Chronicles 17:24; II Samuel 7:26
P11– David wanted God to bless his house as He said	I Chronicles 17:27; II Samuel 7:29
P12– By his faith, David prayed for all God's people	
P12– Did David realize that he also prayed for God's eternal purposes?	
P13– Believers also pray for God's unseen eternal purposes	
P14– David's heart to receive this revelation of promise and purpose	
P15– David was prepared to serve God	

Chapter 7 - David's Military Conquests and Administration	
Chapter 7, Section 1 - David conquers and subdues the surrounding nations	
P1– In the light of God's glorious revelation, David moved forward	
P2– David to advance the growth and security of Israel	
P3– David and the Philistines were a threat to each other	
P4– David subdued the Philistines and backed them into their own land	I Chronicles 18:1; II Samuel 8:1
P5– David did not require Philistines to show subservience	I Chronicles 18: 1
P5– Ittai, a Philistine captain, helped David during Absalom's revolt	II Samuel 15:18-22
P6– David attacked and punished Moab	I Chronicles 18:2; II Samuel 8:2
P6– David had brought his parents to Moab when running from King Saul	I Samuel 22:3, 4
P7– David conquered the nations north of Israel	I Chronicles 18:3-6; II Samuel 8:3-6
P8– The LORD preserved David in his battle campaigns	I Chronicles 18:6; II Samuel 8:6
P9– David conquered the nations south and east of Israel	I Chronicles 18:11-13; II Samuel 8:12-14
P9– David's respect for Ammon, the nation east of Israel	I Chronicles 19:1, 2
P9– David punished Edom harshly and created an adversary	I Kings 11:14-17
P10– The extent of David's kingdom	I Chronicles 18: 3,11
P11– God had specified the borders of Israel to both Moses and Joshua	Deuteronomy 1: 6-8; 11:24; Joshua 1: 4
P11– David purposely extended his kingdom to the Euphrates River	I Chronicles 18: 3; II Samuel 8: 3
P12– The LORD preserved David in the extension of his dominion	I Chronicles 18:13; II Samuel 8:14
P13– God remained with David in battles far from the Ark in Jerusalem	II Chronicles 15:2
P14– David & Israel received many riches & gifts from subdued nations	I Chronicles 18:7-11; II Samuel 8:7-11
P14– Examples of tributes paid to ruling nations	Ezra 4:12-20; II Chronicles 17:11; 27:5
P14– More examples of tributes paid to ruling nations	I Kings 10:25; II Kings 3: 4-7; 17: 3,4; 23:33
P15– David kept inventory – brass used to build specific temple items	I Chronicles 18:8
P15– David's administrator over Israel's national wealth	II Samuel 20:24
P15– Levites managed the wealth dedicated to the LORD	I Chronicles 26:20-28
P15– Managers of David's personal wealth	I Chronicles 27:25

Chapter 7, Section 2 - David's leadership and administration	
P1– David reigned with judgment and justice – Solomon too	I Chronicles 18:14; II Samuel 8:15; II Chronicles 9: 8
P1– God's king and kingdom are established with judgment and justice	Jeremiah 23:5; Isaiah 9:7
P2– David ruled his people with judgment	I Chronicles 18:14; II Samuel 8:15
P2– Treatment of the anointed Saul showed David's proper judgment	II Samuel 1:14-16; 2:4-6
P2– Proper judgment establishes a nation in righteousness	Isaiah 16: 5; 26: 9; Proverbs 29: 4
P2– Without proper judgment, the wicked are emboldened	Habakkuk 1: 4; Proverbs 20: 8
P3– David ruled his people with justice	I Chronicles 18:14; II Samuel 8:15
P3– David had shared loot with those who were weak	I Samuel 30:22-25
P3– David justly preserves family of Jonathan, Saul's son and his friend	II Samuel 9: 1-10; 21: 7
P4– A Psalm describing the blessed rule of judgment and justice	Psalm 72
P4– Acting with judgment and justice is better than sacrifice	Proverbs 21: 3
P4– David's administrative team	I Chronicles 18:15-17; II Samuel 8:16-18
P5– David's sons born after he became king	I Chronicles 3: 1-9; II Samuel 3: 2-5
P5– David's sons: Chief rulers about the king	I Chronicles 18:17; II Samuel 8:18
P5– Jehiel was with King David's sons	I Chronicles 27:32
P6– Amnon raped Absalom's sister and Absalom had Amnon killed	II Samuel 13
P6– Absalom's coup of his father's kingdom	II Samuel 15: 6-11
P6– Adonijah attempted to be king over Israel	I Kings 1: 4-9
P6– Nathan pronounced family consequences because of David sins	II Samuel 12: 7-12
P6– David's sins against Uriah the Hittite	II Samuel 11
P6– Ira became a chief ruler about the king	II Samuel 20:26
P7– Joab had captured Jebusite fortress and becomes chief captain	I Chronicles 11: 6; II Samuel 5: 8
P7– Joab had killed Abner	II Samuel 3:27
P7– Joab killed his replacement, Amasa, after Absalom's rebellion	II Samuel 20: 4-10; 17:25; 19:11-13
P7– Joab killed Absalom	II Samuel 18:10-15
P7– Examples of Joab's good advice	II Samuel 14:19-22; 19: 1-8; 24: 1-4

P7– Joab, unfaithful at the end of David's reign, supported Adonijah	I Kings 1: 5-7; 2:28,29
P8– Benaiah: David's security chief	I Chronicles 18:17; II Samuel 8:18; 20:23
P8– Benaiah: Solomon's military chief	I Kings 2:34,35; 4:4
P9– Priests in Israel during David's reign	I Chronicles 18:16; II Samuel 8:17; 20:25
P9– Abiathar had supported David, but supported Adonijah at the end	I Kings 1: 5-7; 2:26,27
P9– Zadok took Abiathar's priestly position under Solomon	I Kings 2:35; 4: 4
P9– Descendents of Zadok to be priests in the temple Ezekiel described	Ezekiel 44:15,16
P10– Shavsha: David's scribe	I Chronicles 18:16; II Samuel 8:17; 20:25
P11– Jehoshaphat: David's recorder	I Chronicles 18:15; II Samuel 8:16; 20:24
P11– Jehoshaphat: Solomon's recorder	I Kings 4: 3
P12– David's monthly servants	I Chronicles 27: 1-15
P12– Each monthly leader was one of David's captains	I Chronicles 11:10-47
P12– Abner had killed Asahel	II Samuel 2:23
P13– Princes over the tribes of Israel	I Chronicles 27:16-22
P14– Responsibilities of David's eleven caretakers	I Chronicles 27:25-31
P14– David's counselors	I Chronicles 27:32-34
P15– Ahithophel's counsel as though from the oracle of God	II Samuel 16:23
P15– Ahithophel hanged himself after Absalom did not follow his advice	II Samuel 17:23
P16– Hushai: David's companion	I Chronicles 27:33
P16– Hushai remained behind to counter Ahithophel's good counsel	II Samuel 15:31-34
P17– Adoram, or Adoniram, given responsibility over the tribute	II Samuel 20:24; I Kings 4: 6
P17– Adoniram over the labor pool to build temple	I Kings 5:13,14
P17– Mob of workers stoned Adoram to death early in Rehoboam's reign	I Kings 12:16-19

Chapter 7, Section 3 - The nation of Ammon foolishly offends David

P1– Hiram, King of Tyre, was a close ally of David	I Kings 5: 1
P1– King Saul had routed the Ammonite army led by Nahash	I Samuel 11: 1-11
P1– Nahash, King of Ammon, had showed kindness to David	I Chronicles 19: 2; II Samuel 10: 2
P2– Nahash died; David sent support; Hanun shamed David's envoy	I Chronicles 19: 1-4; II Samuel 10: 1-4
P3– Joab led successful attack against Ammon and the hired mercenaries	I Chronicles 19: 5-15; II Samuel 10: 5-14

P4– David & all Israel joined battle to defeat other armies aiding Ammon	I Chronicles 19:16-19; II Samuel 10:15-19
P5– Joab battled against Ammon while David stays home	I Chronicles 20: 1; II Samuel 11: 1; 12:26
P6– David tarried at Jerusalem while his army was on the battle-field	I Chronicles 20: 1; II Samuel 11: 1
P7– David sinned against Uriah the Hittite	II Samuel 11
P7– Nathan delivered a condemnation and curse for David's sins	II Samuel 12
P8– Ammon's capital city and king fall to Joab and David	I Chronicles 20: 2,3; II Samuel 12:27-31
P8– Nahash's son, Shobi, came to aid David when Absalom revolted	II Samuel 17:27

Chapter 7, Section 4 - Timeline and later encounters with Philistine giants

P1– David was a powerful king and Israel was secure in its land	
P2– There was more peace in Israel than in David's family	
P3– Timeline of Key events in David's life	

Below are 39 Timeline references. Passages in the books of Samuel indicating an age or time reference have been listed. Some of the details that follow are difficult to fit together.

P3– Eli's sons served as priests one year before Samuel is born	I Samuel 1: 3
P3– Eli the priest judged Israel forty years and died at 98 years old	I Samuel 4:15-18
P3– Eli the priest died when he heard the Philistines captured the Ark	I Samuel 4:15-18
P3– Ark remained at the house of Abinadab in Kirjathjearim 20 years	I Samuel 7: 2
P3– Abinadab's sons helped move Ark from Kirjathjearim to Jerusalem	II Samuel 6: 3
P3– Samuel judged Israel all his life. (How long concurrent with Eli?)	I Samuel 7:15-17
P3– Samuel made his two sons judges when he was old	I Samuel 8: 1,2
P3– Samuel's sons were corrupt and Israel asks for a king	I Samuel 8: 1,2
P3– Saul described as a choice young man before Samuel anointed him	I Samuel 9: 2
P3– Samuel anointed Saul & presented him to Israel - some doubted Saul	I Samuel 10: 1,24
P3– Nahash, king of Ammonites, was defeated at the start of Saul's reign	I Samuel 11: 1-11
P3– Nahash, king of Ammonites, died about 10 yrs into David's 's reign	II Samuel 10: 1,2
P3– Samuel is very old when all Israel accepted Saul at his coronation	I Samuel 11:14 – 12:25

P3– Some versions: Saul's age 30 or 40,but the age is in no Hebrew text	I Samuel 13: 1
P3– Some versions: Saul reigned 42 years but forty is in no Hebrew text	I Samuel 13: 1
P3– Saul organized 3000 soldiers in the second year of his reign	I Samuel 13: 1-3
P3– Ahiah, Eli's great-grandson, a priest in the 2nd year of Saul's reign	I Samuel 14: 3
P3– Saul's son Jonathan commanded 1000 and led raid on Philistines	I Samuel 13: 1-3
P3– Samuel died after David becomes a fugitive	I Samuel 25:1
P3– David stayed in asylum in Ziklag for more than one year	I Samuel 27: 7
P3– Saul's three oldest sons died with him in battle	I Samuel 31:2; I Chronicles 8:33
P3– Isbosheth Saul's youngest son was 40 when Saul died	II Samuel 2:10
P3– Isbosheth is not listed among Saul's sons early in Saul's reign	I Samuel 14:49
P3– Jonathan's son Mephibosheth was five years old when Saul died	II Samuel 4: 4; 9:12,13
P3– David's age was 30 when Saul died & he began to reign over Judah	II Samuel 5: 4
P3– David's first six sons born when he reigned over Judah in Hebron	II Samuel 3: 2-5
P3– David was 37 yrs old when he began a 33 year reign over all Israel	II Samuel 5: 5
P3– Amnon raped then hated Absalom's sister Tamar	II Samuel 13: 1-19
P3– Absalom has Amnon killed two years after the rape	II Samuel 13:20-33
P3– Absalom spent the next three years in exile	II Samuel 13:37-39
P3– Absalom returned to Jerusalem; did not see father David for two yrs	II Samuel 14:23-28
P3– Absalom planned coup after 40 years – 40 years after what is unclear	II Samuel 15: 7
P3– Some versions say after four years – Hebrew text has 40 years	II Samuel 15: 7
P3– David reigned over Judah and Israel a total of forty years	I Chronicles 29:27; I Kings 2:11
P4– Paul stated that God gave Saul (and Samuel) to Israel for 40 years	Acts 13:20,21
P4– Ark in Abinadab's house 20 years until ?Israel serves God?	I Samuel 7: 2-5
P5– Was Solomon the second son of Bathsheba born to David	II Samuel 12:24
P5– David's sons born in Jerusalem	II Samuel 5:14; I Chronicles 14: 4
P5– Solomon as the fourth son of Bathsheba born to David	I Chronicles 3: 5

Summary of David's troubles from II Samuel (not detailed in this book)	
David's sins against Uriah the Hittite:	II Samuel 11,12
When her husband Uriah was on the battlefield with Israel's armies, Bathsheba washed herself in view of the king's palace.	
When Israel's armies were on the battlefield, King David looked at a neighbor woman bathing on a roof.	
David asked about her, had her brought to him, and had an adulterous affair with the wife of Uriah the Hittite.	
Bathsheba informed David that she was pregnant.	
David sent for Uriah, seemingly to get a report from the battlefield.	
For two days, and even when David made him drink, Uriah refused to see his wife because the rest of Israel's soldiers were still fighting the King's battles.	
David sent Uriah back to battle, carrying orders for his own death – David commanded Joab to make sure Uriah died in battle.	
Joab obeyed and Uriah the Hittite died in battle.	
After her mourning period, David took Bathsheba to be his wife.	
God sent Nathan to confront David about his sins. Nathan delivered God's condemnation of David's actions and His curse upon David's family.	
The punishment was that the child born from his adulterous union with the wife of Uriah the Hittite must die and that David would have trouble in his family.	
David's troubles with his third son Absalom:	II Samuel 15-19
David had many wives.	
Amnon was David's firstborn son and his half-brother Absalom was David's third son	
Absalom had a sister named Tamar.	
Amnon loved Tamar, raped her, then hated her and sent her away from him.	
Two years later, Absalom had Amnon killed during a feast with all of King David's sons.	
After the murder, Absalom ran and found refuge for three years with a neighboring king.	
David wanted Absalom back and Joab convinced David to send for his estranged son.	
Absalom stayed in Jerusalem for two years before David met with his son face to face.	
Absalom exalted himself to the Israelites, heard their complaints, and sympathized with their needs.	
When he had the people's support, Absalom went to Hebron to proclaim himself king.	
David fled Jerusalem for his life, taking his guard and other friends and helpers with him.	
Absalom took over Jerusalem and then led Israel's army to find and kill David	
David's forces were victorious and Absalom died in battle.	

P6– An older David is in trouble during later battles with the Philistines	I Chronicles 20: 4, 5; II Samuel 21:15-19
P7– David's nephew defeated imposing son of Goliath who defied Israel	I Chronicles 20: 6-8; II Samuel 21:20-22
P7– David's brother Shimea in Saul's army when David fought Goliath	I Samuel 17:13

Chapter 7, Section 5 - Israel endures famine for an action of King Saul

P1– David asked God about the three-year famine in Israel	II Samuel 21: 1
P1– God had promised Israel early and late rains	Deuteronomy 11:14
P2– God said the famine was caused by Saul killing the Gibeonites	II Samuel 21: 1
P3– Fearing Israel, the Gibeonites had tricked Joshua into making a treaty	Joshua 9: 1-16,22-27
P3– Israel had come to aid Gibeon when other Canaanites attacked them	Joshua 10: 1-7
P3– Gibeonites helped Nehemiah repair the Jerusalem wall	Nehemiah 3: 7
P3– Gibeonites submitted to Israel	Joshua 9:17-21
P4– Why did Saul's zeal for Israel lead him to kill the Gibeonites?	II Samuel 21: 2, 5
P4– Israel had been responsible to wipe out Canaanites	Deuteronomy 12: 1-14,28-32
P4– Tribes responsible to expel remaining Canaanites from their lands	Joshua 23: 2-10
P4– Gibeon was located in the tribe of Benjamin	Joshua 18:11,25,28
P5– Saul acted to destroy all the Gibeonites in Israel	II Samuel 21: 5
P6– Saul's committed a national sin and all Israel was punished	
P7– King David must act to correct King Saul's national sin	II Samuel 21: 1,2
P7– King David asked the Gibeonites what they needed for an atonement	II Samuel 21: 2, 3
P8– Gibeonites asked to hang seven sons of Saul to the LORD in Gibeah	II Samuel 21: 3-6
P9– David chose the seven men who were to be hung	II Samuel 21: 7, 8
P9– Michal's sister Merab married Adriel, who fathered five of the men	I Samuel 18:19
P10– The Gibeonites hung the seven men before the LORD	II Samuel 21: 9
P11– David buried remains of the dead and God answered Israel's prayers	II Samuel 21:10-14

Chapter 8 - David Orders a Disastrous Census	
Chapter 8, Section 1 - God and Satan oppose Israel	
P1– Satan stood up against Israel	I Chronicles 21: 1
P1– God was angry with Israel	II Samuel 24: 1
P2– Satan opposed Israel's godly kingdom under David	I Chronicles 21: 1
P2– Satan always seeks the honor that belongs only to God	Isaiah 14:12-14; Matthew 4: 8-10
P2– Satan had rebelled and was cast out of heaven with his angels	Revelation 12: 7-9; Ezekiel 28:12-17
P2– Satan's purpose to cause Job to curse God	Job 1: 9-11; 2: 4,5
P2– Satan's purpose to cause Eve to rebel and disobey God	Genesis 3: 1-6
P3– Satan unable to act against Israel	I Chronicles 21:1
P3– Before God, Satan accuses God's people of wrong day & night	Revelation 12:9,10
P3– God shows Satan a way to torment Job	Job 1:12; 2:6
P3– There was nothing in Jesus that Satan could influence	John 14:30
P3– God had forsaken Jesus when he was crucified	Mark 15:34; Luke 22:37
P4– Something kindled God's anger against Israel	
P5– Why was the gracious God angry with Israel?	
P5– God's merciful and gracious character	Psalm 103:8; Jonah 4:2
P5– God desires His people to choose life & receive His great blessings	Deuteronomy 30:14-20
P5– God's promises to David and to Israel	I Chronicles 17:8-14
P5– Judgment and justice in Israel under David	I Chronicles 18:14
P6– To forget God and seek other gods could provoke God's anger	Deuteronomy 32:15-17; 31:20
P6– Israel had often provoked God to anger in the wilderness	Numbers 14:11,20-23; Deuteronomy 9:22-24; Hebrews 3:7-19
P6– Israel had provoked God to anger after possessing Canaan	Judges 2:8-12
P6– Israel's kings provoked God to anger	I Kings 14 9; 16: 2,26,33; 22:51-53; II Kings 17:11-17
P6– Example: Judah provoked God to anger before Babylonian captivity	Jeremiah 32:29-35
P7– David led Israel to honor God and live in His ways	
P7– Consequences of David's adultery were upon his family, not nation	II Samuel 12: 9-14
P7– David's sins had been dealt with by confession and repentance	Psalm 51

P8– Without a national sin God did not punish the nation of Israel	
P8– God gave humanity authority over the earth and everything on it	Genesis 9: 1,2; Psalm 8: 4-6; Hebrews 2: 6-9
P9– Satan is a condemned creature	Isaiah 14:12-20; Ezekiel 28:12-19; Romans 16:20
P9– Satan's activity is restricted	Job 1:6-12; Matthew 4: 1-11; Luke 10:18-20; 22:31,32
P10– Satan had an opening to tempt David to commit a national sin	
P10– God moved David against Israel to count the people	II Samuel 24:1
P11– Satan tempted David to take a national census in Israel	I Chronicles 21: 1
P11– At God's specific direction, Moses had counted the Israelites twice	Numbers 1: 1-4; 26: 1,2
P12– God's instructions about taking a census – plague if done wrong	Exodus 30:12-16
P13– David was the man to commit a national sin and order a census	
P14– Why did God side with Satan against Israel?	
P15– God did not give David or Israel a chance to avoid punishment	
P15– God's desire that the wicked turn from evil and not be punished	Ezekiel 18:30-32; Jeremiah 25: 4-6
P15– Repentant nations spared, even after God spoke to destroy them	Jeremiah 18: 5-10
P15– After Jonah pronounced destruction, repentant Nineveh was spared	Jonah 3
P16– What issue did Satan use to kindle God's anger?	
P17– Why did God not tell David or Israel why He was angry?	
P17– Humble prayer and repentance give God reason to heal a land	II Chronicles 7:14
P18– God was angry prior to David's decision to take the census	

Chapter 8, Section 2 - King David orders Joab to take a census

P1– What was the source of David's temptation	
P2– What was the nature of the temptation	
P3– David yielded to the temptation to take a census	
P3– David ordered Joab to count all the people of Israel	I Chronicles 21: 2; II Samuel 24: 2
P4– David's order for the census seemed to happen abruptly	
P4– Why did David not ask for advice prior to ordering the census?	

P7– Abiathar had helped David ask God for direction in difficult times	I Samuel 23: 9; 30: 7
P8– David never prayed with hypocrisy	
P8– David prayed for deliverance from the sin of presumption	Psalm 19:13
P8– David wrote about confessing secret sin and following God's way	Psalm 32: 1-9
P9– God made certain David could not claim ignorance	
P10– Joab strongly objected to David order to take the census	I Chronicles 21: 3; II Samuel 24: 3
P11– It would have been wise for David to heed Joab's counsel	Proverbs 19:20,21
P11– Joab killed Absalom against David's express orders	II Samuel 18: 5,14
P11– David appointed Amasa the new captain; Joab murdered Amasa	II Samuel 19:13,14; 20: 4-10
P11– Amasa was David's nephew and cousin to Joab, Abishai, and Asahel	I Chronicles 2:16,17; II Samuel 2:18; 17:25
P12– His census was willful disobedience after ignoring Joab's objection	
P12– The wise receive instruction and find God's counsel	Proverbs 19:20,21
P13– Possible consequences could have alerted David to abort the census	
P14– How would David learn that a problem in Israel had angered God?	
P15– David could then ask God to reveal problem and solution	
P16– How David could turn an impending judgment into a blessing	
P17– How David might have avoided sin with Uriah's wife, Bathsheba	

Chapter 8, Section 3 - Under protest, Joab obeys the King's order

P1– Under David's orders, Joab took a census in Israel	I Chronicles 21: 4,5; I Chronicles 27:23
P1– Joab and the captains resisted taking the census	II Samuel 24: 4-9
P2– Joab did not count tribes of Levi and Benjamin	I Chronicles 21: 6
P2– Tribe of Benjamin had been given land next to tribe of Judah	Joshua 18:11
P2– Tribe of Levi given 48 cities scattered among other tribes of Israel	Joshua 21:41
P2– Tribe of Levi set apart for God and not counted in military census	Numbers 1:45-53
P3– Joab did not complete census because he hated the assignment	I Chronicles 21: 6
P3– Joab did not complete the census because punishment began	I Chronicles 27:24

Chapter 8, Section 4 - God punishes Israel for David's census

P1– God sent a plague upon Israel because David ordered the census	I Chronicles 21:7; I Chronicles 27:24

P2– David was convicted and accepted responsibility	I Chronicles 21:8; II Samuel 24:10
P3– God gave David three options for Israel's punishment	I Chronicles 21: 9-12; II Samuel 24:11-13
P4– David chose a three-day plague to be Israel's punishment	I Chronicles 21:13; II Samuel 24:14
P5– God sent the prophet Gad to David simply to get David's choice	
P6– David accepted Gad but God's response was not pleasing	
P7– David did not relate well to God during the census-taking	
P8– God sent a 3-day plague; the destroying angel was above Jerusalem	I Chronicles 21:14,15; II Samuel 24:15,16

Chapter 8, Section 5 - David makes an offering to end the judgment

P1– David mourned as the one responsible for plague & deaths in Israel	I Chronicles 21:16,17; II Samuel 24:17
P2– David saw the destroying angel and prayed that the people be spared	I Chronicles 21:16,17; II Samuel 24:17
P3– David must build altar on threshing floor below the angel	I Chronicles 21:18; II Samuel 24:18
P4– David talked to Ornan about purchasing his threshing floor	I Chronicles 21:19-24; II Samuel 24:19-24
P5– David purchased Ornan's threshing floor & business implements	I Chronicles 21:25; II Samuel 24:24
P5– Ornan's threshing floor was located on top of Mount Moriah	II Chronicles 3: 1
P6– David built the altar on the newly purchased threshing floor	I Chronicles 21:23,26; II Samuel 24:25
P6– Altars must be built from uncut stone	Exodus 20:25; Deuteronomy 27: 5
P6– Abraham had built altars and called upon God	Genesis 12: 7,8; 13: 4,18
P6– Abraham had offered a ram instead of Isaac on Mt Moriah	Genesis 22: 1-18
P6– Isaac built an altar and called upon God	Genesis 26:25
P6– Jacob built altars and called upon God	Genesis 33:20; 35: 1-7
P6– Jacob's name had been changed to Israel	Genesis 32:24-28
P7– David offered sacrifices on the altar	I Chronicles 21:23,26; II Samuel 24:24,25
P8– God answered David by fire and told the angel to put his sword away	I Chronicles 21:26,27; II Samuel 24:25

Chapter 9 - David Receives Mercy ... and a Revelation

Chapter 9, Section 1 - David worships on the threshing floor

P1– God's answer by fire on David's altar meant the end of the plague	I Chronicles 21:26,27

P1– God rained fire & brimstone in judgment upon Sodom & Gomorrah	Genesis 19:24,25
P1– Sodom and Gomorrah located in a garden plain of the Jordan River	Genesis 13:10
P1– God had led Israel out of Egypt with pillars of cloud and fire	Exodus 13:21,22
P1– God upon Mt Sinai in fire, cloud, thunder, lightning, and trumpet	Exodus 19:18,19; Deuteronomy 4:11,12; 5:4,24
P1– Pillars of cloud and fire on the tabernacle in the wilderness	Numbers 9:15; Exodus 40:36-38
P2– David realized the fire was God's answer; God heard & accepted	I Chronicles 21:28
P3– God to send fire from heaven on the altar Solomon builds here	II Chronicles 7: 1-4
P3– God to send fire from heaven on the altar Elijah builds at Mt Carmel	I Kings 18:38, 39
P4– David in awe of God's answer	
P5– David sacrificed again after God answered him by fire	I Chronicles 21:28
P6– Why David sacrificed here instead of at the tabernacle in Gibeon	I Chronicles 21:29,30

Chapter 9, Section 2 - The temple location is revealed!

P1– God revealed the new location of His house and altar to David	I Chronicles 22:1
P2– David overwhelmed that the God's house was to be built here	I Chronicles 22:7,10
P3– God renewed and expanded David's desire to build God's house	
P4– The place of David's altar fulfilled of two significant promises	Deuteronomy 12:1-14
P5– David understood the significance of this threshing floor location	I Chronicles 22:1
P6– Moses had proclaimed God's purpose to choose a place for His name	Deuteronomy 12:1-14

Chapter 9, Section 3 - God reveals how He must worshipped

P1– Israel not allowed to worship God however or wherever they chose	Deuteronomy 12:13,14
P1– God has set a way of blessing or cursing before His people	Deuteronomy 11:26-28
P2– God created heaven, earth, and all life, ordered by physical laws	Genesis 1: 1,11,12,22, 24-26,28-30
P2– God in His wisdom and for His joy created the earth to be inhabited	Isaiah 45:18; Proverbs 8:23-31
P2– God created Adam with physical and spiritual life	Genesis 2: 7; Isaiah 42: 5
P2– Eve was made out of man and had the same physical & spiritual life	Genesis 2:20-23
P2– All humanity descends from Adam and Eve	Genesis 1:27,28; 5: 1,2

P2– Every human is born with a natural body and becomes a living soul	I Corinthians 15:44-48
P2– Examples of laws ordering spiritual life	Proverbs 15: 4,13; 17:22; 18:14; Psalm 34:18; Deuteronomy 12:13,14
P2– Adam lost his ability to be with God after he broke God's rules	Genesis 2:16,17; 3: 8,9
P3– Adam and Eve sinned in not obeying God and were corrupted	Genesis 3: 1-19
P3– Adam and Eve passed their corruption to every person born	I Corinthians 15:21,22; Romans 5:12-14
P3– No longer could anyone approach God as Adam did before his sin	Genesis 3: 8,22-24
P3– No one in the human race can live acceptably before God or anyone	Romans 3:10-12; Psalm 53: 1-3
P3– Permanent atonement impossible to Israel's priests, being corrupted	Hebrews 7:27,28
P4– God's common revelation in everyone's conscience and in creation	Romans 1:18-25; 2:14,15
P4– In a rare act, God proved Himself by sending fire on Elijah's altar	I Kings 18:21-40
P4– Glorious experiences of God's greatness degrade	Psalm 106: 9-25
P4– God does not coerce obedience to His ways, even from His people	Deuteronomy 30
P5– Adam's sin ruined God's direct access to His people	Genesis 3: 8-11,22-24
P5– Moses not able – no one able – to see God's face	Exodus 33:18-23
P6– From the beginning, God saw Jesus, the Lamb of God, sacrificed	Revelation 13: 8
P6– God ultimately finishes his plan to reconcile the world to Himself	II Corinthians 5:18-21; Ephesians 2:16,17; Colossians 1:20,21
P6– God can be approached & also live among His people made perfect	II Corinthians 5:21; Colossians 1:27,28, 2:10
P7– God gradually revealed how the human race must worship Him	
P7– God gracious to Noah when the human race deserved destruction	Genesis 6: 7,8; 7: 1,-5
P7– Noah obeyed God & built an ark to save his family from drowning	Hebrews 11: 7; Genesis 6:22; 7:5,9,16 (11-23)
P7– God maked covenant with Noah and the entire human race	Genesis 6:8,18; 9: 1-17
P8– God called Abraham to leave his home and family	Genesis 11:31-12:4; Acts 7: 2-5
P8– God made promises & covenants to give Abraham a land & a seed	Genesis 13:14-17; 15:18-21; 17 :1-10

P8– Abraham believed God against all hope for a very long time	Romans 4:17-22
P8– God honored his covenants and gave Abraham a land and a seed	Genesis 21: 1-5; Acts 7: 8; Romans 4:19
P9– God chose Israel to be His special people & showed them His ways	Deuteronomy 10:14-22
P9– God-promised Israel the same land He gave to Abraham & Isaac	Genesis 35:11, 12
P9– Canaanites lived in the land God promised to give Abraham's family	Genesis 15:16-21
P9– Canaanites descended from Noah's son Ham & grandson Canaan	Genesis 10: 1,6,15-19
P9– Abraham's family descended from Noah's son Shem	Genesis 10: 1; 11:10-26
P10– Israel was honored to receive a special revelation of God's laws	Deuteronomy 4: 5-8; Psalm 147:19,20
P10– Canaanite wickedness caused the land they lived in to reject them	Leviticus 18:24-28 (3-23); Deuteronomy 9:1-7
P10– Heathen god's are man-made and not a threat to the God of Israel	Psalm 135:15 (4-18)
P10– Israel must not ask about heathen gods or be distracted by them	Numbers 33:55; Deuteronomy 12:29-32; Joshua 23:12-16
P11– God is Jealous for the pure allegiance of His people	Exodus 34:12-16; Deuteronomy 32:21; Joel 2:18; Nahum 1:7
P11– God's commandments for the good of His people	Deuteronomy 6:14-25
P11– God created His people and all things for His glory and pleasure	Revelation 4:11; Isaiah 43: 7
P11– To worship and follow God is the most fulfilling way of life	Psalm 16:11; Jeremiah 29:11-13; Isaiah 65:18
P11– God's people move Him to jealousy	Psalm 78:55-62
P12– God's power over Egypt's gods and Pharoah's cavalry	Exodus 14:23-25; 15:11-19; Joshua 24: 6,7
P12– Moses spoke of Israel's tendency to rebel against their God	Deuteronomy 31:27
P12– On Mt. Sinai God wrote His law & gave it to Moses for Israel	Exodus 24:12-18
P12– With Moses on mount, Aaron sculpted a calf that Israel worshipped	Exodus 32: 1-8, 21-25; Deuteronomy 9: 8-17
P13– Urgent need! Israel be true to God after possessing promised land	Deuteronomy 11:16-25
P13– God's clear instructions to destroy the Canaanites and their gods	Deuteronomy 12: 1-3; 7: 1-6; Exodus 23:20-33
P13– Land to reject Israel if they followed depraved Canaanite behavior	Leviticus 18:24-30; 20:22; Deuteronomy 30:17-20; 8:19,20

P13– God would cast His own rebellious people out of their land	Deuteronomy 29:18-29
P13– God's clear instructions about where and how to worship Him	Deuteronomy 12: 5,6
P14– Israel's tabernacle was located at the high place in Gibeon	I Chronicles 21:29
P14– Israel, tricked into a treaty, spares Gibeon from being destroyed	Joshua 9: 3-20
P14– Totally destroy depraved Canaanite worship lest Israelites learn it	Deuteronomy 20:16-18; 7:23-26
P15– God did not choose Gibeon as a place for His house and name	
P16– Ornan's threshing floor was a key location	I Chronicles 21:18-22:2
P17– The prophecy to choose place for His name that God fulfilled	Deuteronomy 12:10,11
P17– God protected David, Israel is secure; His condition for place is met	I Chronicles 18:13,14; II Samuel 8:14,15
P17– God revealed to David where he would place His name	I Chronicles 22: 1

Chapter 9, Section 4 - The temple pattern is given!

P1– God gave David the blueprint for His house by the spirit	I Chronicles 28:19,12
P2– The pattern for physical temple	I Chronicles 28:12
P2– Dimensions of the new temple building and porch	I Kings 6: 2,3; II Chronicles 3: 3;4
P2– God had given Moses a pattern for the tabernacle in the wilderness	Exodus 25: 8,9; Hebrews 8: 5
P2– Tabernacle dimensions (uncertain width from 5-6 y/m)	Exodus 26:16,18,20,22-25
P2– Priests minister to God for the people in the holy place	Exodus 28:43; Leviticus 10:13,17; 7: 6; Numbers 18: 9,10
P2– The roof and its beams were made of cedar wood	I Kings 6: 9
P2– Costly, precious stones were used to build and adorn the temple	I Kings 5:17; 7: 9-12; I Chronicles 29: 2; II Chronicles 3: 6
P2– Details about the pillars at the entrance of the temple	I Kings 7:15-22; II Chronicles 3:15-17
P3– Division of tabernacle's holy places at 10 y/m, curtain mid-point	Exodus 26:33
P3– Cedar & fir wood used for the floors, walls, and ceiling inside temple	I Kings 6:15-20; II Chronicles 3: 5
P3– Ministry items inside the holy place for the priests' daily ministry	I Chronicles 28:14-17; II Chronicles 4: 7,8,19-22
P4– The entrance to the most holy place	I Kings 6:21,22,31,32; II Chronicles 3:14
P4– Chain partition in the most holy entrance replicated on pillars outside	II Chronicles 3:16; I Kings 7:17

P5– The grandeur of the most holy place of God's presence	I Kings 6:19-30; I Chronicles 28:18; II Chronicles 3: 8-13
P5– Dimensions of the most holy place in Ezekiel's vision	Ezekiel 41:4
P6– The sacrifice altar and wash basins in the priests' court of the temple	I Kings 7:38,39; II Chronicles 4: 1,2,6
P6– Dimensions of the altar of burnt offering built for the tabernacle	Exodus 21: 1
P6– Detailed design of the base under each of the 10 lavers	I Kings 7:27-37
P7– The detailed pattern for the large, bronze wash basin	I Kings 7:23-26; II Chronicles 4: 2-5
P8– The courtyard and storage chambers for the temple	II Chronicles 4: 9; I Chronicles 28:11,12; I Kings 6: 5-10
P8– Chambers in the rebuilt temple for storing supplies and valuables	Ezra 8:28-30; Nehemiah 10:34-39; 12: 4-14
P8– Gates allowed access into the temple complex	I Chronicles 26:12-18
P9– David received the pattern for the ministry of the priests	I Chronicles 28:13; II Chronicles 4:20
P9– The priests and their clothes anointed by Moses at Mt. Sinai	Exodus 40:12-15; Leviticus 8: 6-13,30
P9– The priests' daily service of God in the temple	Hebrews 9: 7
P9– Priests' specific services in the temple	Leviticus 24:2-8; Exodus 27:21
P10– David received the pattern for the Levites' service in God's house	I Chronicles 28:13
P10– Levites were given music ministry in new temple	I Chronicles 23:30
P10– Levites were in charge of maintenance in new temple	I Chronicles 23:32
P11– David worshipped on threshing floor after such mercy & revelation	

Chapter 9, Section 5 - Temple-building preparations begin

P1– David realized the immensity of the task to prepare for building	
P2– Workers and managers recruited	I Kings 5:15,16
P3– David hired many laborers for the various tasks	I Chronicles 22: 2,14,15; I Chronicles 2:17,18
P4– The temple site prepared for a massive construction project	
P5– David gathered the raw materials needed for building the temple	I Chronicles 22: 2,4,14,16
P5– David and Solomon contracted with Tyre for cedar wood	I Kings 5:1-12; I Chronicles 22: 4
P6– David made production facilities to prepare finished parts	I Chronicles 22: 3
P6– During temple construction, no hammer, axe, or iron tool was heard	I Kings 6: 7
P7– David gave reasons for his extensive building preparations	I Chronicles 22: 5

P8– David summarized his building preparations	I Chronicles 22:14-16
P8– Specific brass looted in early conquest used in pillars & wash basin	I Chronicles 18: 8
P9– David's extensive building preparations were not easy for him	I Chronicles 22:14

Chapter 10 - David Transfers Responsibility to Solomon

Chapter 10, Section 1 - Solomon is appointed to build God's house

P1– David put Solomon in charge of building the temple	I Chronicles 22: 6
P2– David told Solomon he still wanted to build the temple himself	I Chronicles 22: 7
P2–God's first response to David's desire to build His house	I Chronicles 17: 4-6,11,12
P3– God promised to choose a place for His name when Israel was secure	Deuteronomy 12: 9-11
P3– God promised Israel peace and David's enemies subdued	I Chronicles 17: 9,10
P4– In part, God anointed David to defeat Israel's enemies, bring peace	Psalm 89:19-28
P4– God's protection and blessing during David's military campaigns	I Chronicles 18:13,14
P5– David still wanted to build the temple himself	
P5– David prepared to build the temple himself	I Chronicles 28:2
P6– God again told David that he could not build the temple	I Chronicles 22: 8
P6– Due to wars & the blood he shed, David could not build God's house	I Kings 5: 3
P7– The same man could not bring peace and build God's house	
P8– God's son, Jesus, the Prince of Peace established peace forever	Isaiah 9: 6,7
P8– Jesus is reigning at God's side while God subdues all his enemies	Hebrews 1: 8-13; 10:12,13; I Corinthians 15:25
P8– Jesus is building a clean people to become God's temple	Ephesians 2:19-22; 5:25-27; Matthew 16:18
P9– God chose David's son Solomon, before his birth, to build temple	I Chronicles 22: 9,10
P10– God told David new promises for his son Solomon	I Chronicles 22: 9
P11– God applied previous prophecies to Solomon	I Chronicles 22:10
P12– David blessed & exhorted Solomon to build God's house	I Chronicles 22:11-13,16
P13– David did not warn Solomon since failure was not an option	I Chronicles 22:11-13,16

Chapter 10, Section 2 - David commands the support of Israel's leadership

P1– David commanded all the princes of Israel to help Solomon	I Chronicles 22:17
P2– David had consulted with Israel's leaders before moving the Ark	I Chronicles 13: 1
P3– David asked leadership two rhetorical questions	I Chronicles 22:18
P4– David reminded the leaders that this was a time of peace for Israel	I Chronicles 22:18

P5– David instructed the leadership to seek the LORD	I Chronicles 22:19
P6– How seeking the LORD would help the leadership in their duties	
P7– David commanded Israel's leadership to rise up and build the temple	I Chronicles 22:19

Chapter 10, Section 3 - Solomon is made king

P1– David was getting old and could not stay warm	I Kings 1: 1
P2– David had not clearly announced the successor to his throne as king	
P3– David's fourth son Adonijah acted on his desire to be king	I Kings 1: 5
P4– David did not oppose Adonijah's desire to be king	I Kings 1: 6
P5– Adonijah enlisted Joab & Abiathar & threw his own coronation feast	I Kings 1: 7-10
P5– Abiathar had joined David as a fugitive from King Saul	I Samuel 22:20-23; 23: 9; 30: 7
P6– Nathan & Bathsheba's plan to tell David about Adonijah's actions	I Kings 1:11-14
P7– David saw urgency & resolved to make Solomon king	I Kings 1:15-31
P8– David directed Solomon's immediate coronation	I Kings 1:32-37
P9– Solomon was made king and Adonijah's party scattered	I Kings 1:38-53
P9– Solomon has Joab executed	I Kings 2:28-34
P9– Solomon has Adonijah executed	I Kings 2:22-25
P9– Solomon removes Abiathar from his office as priest	I Kings 2:26,27
P10– Some of God's promises fulfilled in Solomon's being king	I Chronicles 17: 9-14; 22: 9,10

Chapter 11 - David Organizes Temple Worship

Chapter 11, Section 1 - God has another job for David

P1– Preparations for building God's house well underway	I Chronicles 22: 1-5
P2– The people's dreams for this temple vs. God's purposes	
P3– God's glorious house: not a museum to display its artistry	
P4– God's glorious house: not a theatre to entertain His people	
P5– God showed David the organization of ministry at His temple	I Chronicles 28:13
P6– David was God's man to organize the ministry of God's house	I Chronicles 23: 1,2

Chapter 11, Section 2 - The authority of David's reorganization of the Levites

P1– David's rules for temple worship hold same authority as Moses' rules	
P2– 5 temple worship installations using rules of both David & Moses	
P3– Solomon initially implemented David's & Moses' commandments	II Chronicles 8:12-15

P4– Jehoiada implemented David & Moses' commandments after Athalia	II Chronicles 23:18, 19
P5– Hezekiah implemented David & Moses' commandments after Ahaz	II Chronicles 29:25-27
P6– Josiah implemented David & Moses' commands after Manasseh	II Chronicles 35: 4-6,15
P7– Nehemiah implemented David's & Moses' commands after captivity	Nehemiah 12:24,25,44-47
P8– God's ongoing and eternal purposes for David & the Levites	Jeremiah 33:20-22

Chapter 11, Section 3 - David eliminates a major Levite duty

P1– Why were David's worship commandments necessary?	
P2– David declared the Levites will no longer carry the tabernacle	I Chronicles 23:26
P2– God by Moses had assigned the Levites to carry the tabernacle	Numbers 1:50,51; ch4
P2– Families of Levi's 3 sons had been given separate tabernacle duties	Numbers 3:11-38
P3– David declared his hope for God's permanent temple in Jerusalem	I Chronicles 23:25
P3– Moses had overseen building the tabernacle exactly to God's pattern	Exodus 39:32-43
P4– God had assigned the Levites to assist the priests	Numbers 8:19; 3: 5-10; I Chronicles 23:28-32

Chapter 11, Section 4 - Special Levite ministry is neglected prior to David

P1– Levi was one of the twelve sons of Israel	I Chronicles 2: 1,2
P1– God claimed Israel's firstborn after he 'passed over' them in Egypt	Exodus 12 – 13: 2
P1– Levi had stood with God and Moses against Israel's idolatry	Exodus 32:26-29
P1– God chose the Levites to serve priests & shield Israelites from wrath	Numbers 1:53; 3: 5-10; 8:18,19
P1– God had exchanged all firstborn for Levites, now His special servants	Numbers 3:11-13; 39-51
P1– The firstborn remained holy unto God and had to be redeemed	Numbers 18:15-17
P1– Special ceremony to set the Levites apart as God's special servants	Numbers 8: 5-26
P2– The tabernacle & Levites both camped & journeyed at Israel's center	Numbers 2:17; 1:51-53
P2– Israel's required ritual feasts and sacrifices	Numbers 28: 2; 29:39 (Chapters 28 & 29)
P2– Details about the sacrifices Israel were required to offer	Leviticus 1 - 6
P3– God had promised Canaan land to family of Abraham, Isaac, & Jacob	Genesis 17: 8; Exodus 6: 4-8; 13: 5,11

P3– Conquered Canaan in 7 years (45 from Kadesh rebellion - 38 wander)	Joshua 14: 7,10; Deuteronomy 2:14
P3– Sections of Canaan were assigned to the tribes of Israel	Joshua 18: 1-10
P4– Various judges had ruled in Israel after Joshua	Judges 1 – 13
P5– The tabernacle had been located in Shiloh, a city central in Israel	Joshua 18: 1; Judges 21:19
P5– God had commanded Israel to worship in His presence 3 times a year	Exodus 23:14-17; 34:22-24
P5– Samuel's parents attended a yearly sacrifice at Shiloh	I Samuel 1: 3,21-24
P6– Israelites did what was right in their own eyes	Judges 17: 6; 21:25
P6– Israelites had set up their own images(gods) and priests	Judges 17: 5-13; 18:14-24
P7– Israelite tithes offered to God must be used to support Levites	Numbers 18:20-24; Deuteronomy 26:12
P7– Example of a specific Levite needing work	Judges 17: 7-10
P7– Example of Levites doing secular work	Nehemiah 13:10-12
P8– Priest Eli's sons abused the priestly position & work they inherited	I Samuel 2:12-17
P9– Eli's death out of concern for the Ark of the Covenant	I Samuel 4:13-18
P9– Samuel was known in Israel to be a prophet of the LORD	I Samuel 3:19,20
P9– God twice sends thunderstorm after Samuel prays	I Samuel 7: 8-10; 12:17,18
P9– Samuel anointed Saul to be Israel's first king	I Samuel 9:25-10:1

Chapter 11, Section 5 - David expands the Levite duties

P1– After moving Ark, David gave the Levites honorable new ministries	I Chronicles 16:37-43
P2– God showed David how Levites were to serve in the new temple	I Chronicles 28:11-13
P2– The Levites were to assist the priests in the temple ministry	I Chronicles 23:28,29
P2– The priests placed bread on the golden tables every Sabbath day	Leviticus 24: 5-9
P2– The priests made atonement for the people before God	Leviticus 6: 7; 16:30-33
P2– The Levites were to thank and praise God at the new temple	I Chronicles 23:30
P2– The Levites were to take care of the house of God	I Chronicles 23:32
P2– The Levites were to assist the priests in offering ritual sacrifices	I Chronicles 23:31
P2– Many details about Israel's ritual sacrifices:	Leviticus 23; Numbers 28,29
P3– Step-by-step process of offering ritual sacrifices	
P3– A Levite offering a ritual sacrifice brought an animal as commanded	Leviticus 1: 2,3
P3– The Levite presented animal for approval as an acceptable sacrifice	Leviticus 1: 4
P3– The Levite killed the animal in the presence of the LORD	Leviticus 1: 5
P3– The priest sprinkled the blood on and around the altar	Leviticus 1: 5

P3– The life of the sacrificial animal was in the blood	Leviticus 17:11
P3– Priest put blood on right ear, thumb & big toe of cleansed leper	Leviticus 14:14
P3– Priest put blood on corners of altar; he poured out remaining blood	Leviticus 4:18,25
P3– The Levite cut up the sacrifice	Leviticus 1: 6
P3– The priests added wood to keep the fire burning on the altar	Leviticus 1: 7; 6:12,13
P3– The Levite presented necessary pieces of the sacrifice to the priests	Leviticus 1: 8
P3– Examples of different parts of the sacrifice burnt on the altar	Leviticus 1:13; 3:12-16
P3– The priests burned the required parts of the sacrifice on the altar	Leviticus 1: 8
P3– The priest must eat certain parts of some sacrifices	Leviticus 6:25-30; 7: 6-34
P3– Priests eat of sacrifices for atonement to be accepted	Exodus 29:33; Leviticus 10:17-19
P3– Neither the blood nor fat of the sacrifice could ever be eaten	Leviticus 3:17
P3– Drink & grain offerings accompany Israel's ritual feasts & sacrifices	Numbers 28 & 29
P3– Details on the grain offering	Leviticus 2; 7: 9-14
P4– Israel was allowed to offer sacrifices only in the place God chose	Deuteronomy 12: 5-12

Chapter 11, Section 6 - David organizes the priests and Levites for their work

P1– David assigned the Levites to specific tasks	I Chronicles 23 – 26
P2– David and the princes of Israel counted the Levites	I Chronicles 23: 1-3
P2– 70,000 men of Israel had died because of David's first census	I Chronicles 21: 7,14
P2– Moses had counted 8580 Levites male between 30 & 50 at Mt. Sinai	Numbers 4:46-49
P2– Moses had counted 22,000 Levites older than one month at Mt Sinai	Numbers 3:39-41
P3– David allocated the Levites into four job categories	I Chronicles 23: 4,5
P4– David separated the Levites into family groups	I Chronicles 23: 6-23
P4– God had chosen Aaron and his sons to minister as priests	Exodus 28: 1
P5– Aaron's sons Eleazar & Ithamar had overseen Levite wilderness tasks	Numbers 4:16,28,33
P5– 24 priests chosen to oversee the 24,000 Levites serving the priests	I Chronicles 24: 1-4
P6– Random lot determined the 24 Levite groups and ministry order	I Chronicles 24: 5-19
P7– 4000 Levites who praised & prophesied separated into 24 groups	I Chronicles 25
P8– Asaph, Heman & Jeduthun each from different son of Levi	I Chronicles 6:33-48
P9– Families of Levi's 3 sons had been given separate wilderness tasks	Numbers 3:25-37

P9– Details on distinct tabernacle-moving jobs given to Levi's 3 sons	Numbers 4: 1-33; 7:1-9
P9– Asaph, Heman, & Jeduthun families were given different ministries	I Chronicles 25: 1-6
P10– David organized the 4000 Levites allocated to be porters	I Chronicles 26:1-19
P10– Porters at the gates of temple kept anything unclean from entering	II Chronicles 23:19
P11– David organized the 4000 Levites allocated as officers & judges	I Chronicles 26:20-32
P12– David very old & finished organizing Levites in his last year	I Chronicles 26:31; 23:1,27
P12– God had descended upon Mt. Sinai in fire	Exodus 19:18

Chapter 12 - David Inspires Public Support for God's Temple

Chapter 12, Section 1 - David calls Israel's leadership to a national celebration

P1– Groups of leaders assembled in Jerusalem	I Chronicles 28: 1
P2– A frail but revered King David stood up	I Chronicles 28: 2
P3– A God's anointed king spoke with authority and asked a hearing	I Chronicles 28: 2
P4– God's successive choices resulted in David's being king	I Chronicles 28:4; Psalm 78:68-71

Chapter 12, Section 2 - King David: you have been the Man

P1– Nathan convicted David, declaring, 'Thou art the man!'	II Samuel 12:7
P1– David was the man specially chosen and graced by God'	
P2– From his youth to king David was the man who honored God	I Kings 15: 5
P3– David's priority to exalt God in moving the Ark of the Covenant	I Chronicles 13,15
P4– David was the man to appoint Levites to worship God with music	I Chronicles 16
P5– David was the man to desire to build God a house of worship	I Chronicles 28:2; I Chronicles 17:1,2
P6– David was not the man chosen to build God's house	I Chronicles 17:3-8; 28:3
P7– David was the man to whom God revealed awesome, eternal plans	I Chronicles 17: 9-27
P8– David was the man chosen to make war & to make to Israel secure	I Chronicles 28:3
P8– David was the man who did, in fact, make war & make Israel secure	I Chronicles 18:1-13
P9– David was the man who ruled Israel with judgment and justice	I Chronicles 18:14
P10– David was the man responsible for a deadly census in Israel	I Chronicles 21
P11– David was the man to whom God revealed temple location & plans	I Chronicles 21:26-22:1

P12– After second revelation, David completes several God-given tasks	I Chronicles 23-26
P13– David ended his life well	

Chapter 12, Section 3 - David informs and exhorts Israel's leadership

P1– David's final actions displayed his heart for God and Israel	I Chronicles 28 & 29
P2– God had chosen Solomon to succeed David as King of Israel	I Chronicles 28: 5
P2– God had chosen Solomon before by name he was born	I Chronicles 22: 9
P2– God chose Solomon to build His house	I Chronicles 28: 6
P2– God chose Solomon to be His son & establish kingdom for-ever	I Chronicles 28: 6,7
P3– God's great promises had stunned David 30 years ago	I Chronicles 17:16-18
P3– Why leaders should believe stunning promises for David's son	
P4– David appealed to the leaders to keep God's commandments	I Chronicles 28: 8
P5– Leaders must seek and obey God to continue in God's bless-ings	I Chronicles 28:8
P6– David encouraged the leaders to honor God and embrace future	I Chronicles 28: 1-8

Chapter 12, Section 4 - David commissions and exhorts Solomon publicly

P1– David instructed Solomon to serve God properly	I Chronicles 28: 9
P2– God sees into the heart and understands every thought	I Chronicles 28: 9
P3– The consequences of forsaking God would be severe	I Chronicles 28: 9
P4– God chose Solomon to build a sanctuary for God's presence	I Chronicles 28:10
P5– Solomon prepared to build God's house	
P6– David urged his son to be strong and build God's house	I Chronicles 28:10
P7– David gave the pattern for God's house to his son	I Chronicles 28:11-13
P8– David gave the pattern for the leadership	I Chronicles 28:11-18
P9– David had received pattern by the God's hand	I Chronicles 28:19
P9– God had written the law of Moses on tables of stone	Exodus 31:18; 32:16; Deuteronomy 9:10; 10: 1-4
P9– God had commanded Moses to follow the wilderness pattern exactly	Exodus 25: 9,40; Hebrews 8: 5
P10– David encouraged Solomon to be strong and courageous	I Chronicles 28:20
P11– David assured Solomon of God's presence and help	I Chronicles 28:20
P12– David's faithful, merciful, gracious, wise, and eternal God	
P13– Groups of Israelites ready to assist Solomon in building temple	I Chronicles 28:21

Chapter 12, Section 5 - David and leaders make offerings to build God's house

P1– David told leaders that Solomon is young & building God's house	I Chronicles 29: 1

P1– David had earlier talked of Solomon's youth & his preparation	I Chronicles 22: 5
P2– David listed the preparation he has now made	I Chronicles 29: 2
P3– David's affection for the house of God	I Chronicles 29: 3
P4– David itemized his gifts	I Chronicles 29: 4,5
P5– David offered willing leaders a chance to give toward the temple	I Chronicles 29: 5
P6– David did not in any way coerce the leaders to give	
P7– The leaders could direct their giving	
P8– Leaders gave an overabundance toward the temple	I Chronicles 29: 6-8
P9– Leaders gave overwhelmingly and willingly toward the temple	I Chronicles 29: 9

Chapter 12, Section 6 - David blesses God

P1– David blessed God before the assembly	I Chronicles 29:10
P2– David exalted God's greatness	I Chronicles 29:11
P3– David proclaimed God as over all and as the source of all	I Chronicles 29:11,12
P4– David thanked God, the Giver of all	I Chronicles 29:13-15
P5– David blessed God further	I Chronicles 29:16,17
P6– David prayed that God bless Solomon and the people of Israel	I Chronicles 29:17-19
P7– David exhorted the people to bless their God	I Chronicles 29:20
P8– The people worshipped and sacrificed to God	I Chronicles 29:20,21
P9– The Israelites do indeed need God	I Chronicles 29:21

Chapter 12, Section 7 - The coronation of Solomon

P1– Worship grew into coronation of Solomon	I Chronicles 29:22
P2– Solomon's coronation was the joyful desire of all in attendance	I Chronicles 29:22
P3– King Solomon began well; the nation submitted to him	I Chronicles 29:22-24
P4– David's final instructions for Solomon	I Kings 2: 1-3
P5– David shared conditional promise with Solomon	I Kings 2: 4
P5– Earlier, God had assured David of mercy for his royal family	I Chronicles 17:13; II Samuel 7:14,15
P6– David's final instructions for Solomon	I Kings 2: 5-9
P6– Barzillai blessed David when he fled from Absalom	II Samuel 19:31-40
P6– Shimei cursed David when he fled from Absalom	II Samuel 16: 5-13; 19:16-23
P7– God magnified Solomon and greatly established his kingdom	I Chronicles 29:25; I Kings 2:12

Chapter 12, Section 8 - The end is not the end ...

P1– David reigned over Israel forty years	I Chronicles 29:26,27; I Kings 2:10,11
P1– Introducing David's last words	II Samuel 23: 1

P2– David introduced his last words	II Samuel 23: 2,3
P3– David said that rulers must be just	II Samuel 23: 3
P4– Just rulers bring fresh life and light to their world	II Samuel 23: 4
P4– David was confident in God's covenant, not in his royal house	II Samuel 23: 5
P5– Obstinate rulers shall be removed	II Samuel 23: 6,7
P6– David's eulogy; several wrote of his life and deeds	I Chronicles 29:28-30
P7– God has future for David's family and all of his people	
P8– Psalmist recalled David's intense longing of for the house of God	Psalm 132: 1-5
P9– Psalmist expressed corporate desire to worship in God's presence	Psalm 132: 6-9
P10– God's promise to David and His choice to dwell in Zion	Psalm 132:10-14
P11– Enjoying God's presence results in abundant blessing	Psalm 132:15-18

Author's Epilogue

1 - Honesty about David's sins

P1– David's horrible sins against Uriah	II Samuel 11
P1– David was the man who deserved to die for his sins	II Samuel 12

2 - The reality of David's repentant heart

P2– The Bible chronicled David's disobedience regarding Uriah	I Kings 15: 5
P2– David's impressive early reputation	I Samuel 16:18
P2– David's heart remained perfect toward God until his death	I Kings 11: 4-6; 14: 8; 15: 3-5
P3– God told Samuel to look on the heart	I Samuel 16:7
P3– Stubborn Cain did not correct his evil actions	Genesis 4: 2-7; I John 3:12
P3– Cain despised God's way and killed Abel	Genesis 4: 8-10
P3– Esau despised his birthright	Genesis 25:29-34; Hebrews 12:16
P3– Balaam abandoned his commitment to God because of greed	II Peter 2:15; Jude 11; Revelation 2:14
P3– God's treatment of David demonstrates His sure mercies	Isaiah 55: 3,4; Psalm 89: 1-4, 33-36; 132:10,11

3 - The astonishing fact that David was so special to God

4 - Trust God: His choices and His purposes

P3– Creation as a revelation of God	Romans 1:20; Psalm 19: 1-4
P4– The knowledge of God in the human conscience	Romans 1:19; 2:14,15
P5– The human moral problem	Romans 3:10-19

5 - Trust the God Who has solved our moral problem

P2– The God of Love sent His Son Jesus to earth in the flesh	John 1:14; 3:16; I John 4: 2
P3– The Holy God was fully satisfied by the righteous obedience of Jesus	Hebrews 7:25-27; 9:14; I Peter 2:22,23
P4– The Merciful God laid the sin of the world on His Son Jesus	Isaiah 53: 5,6; I Peter 2:24

P5– The Just God made final judgment against the sin Jesus carried	Hebrews 10:12-14; Romans 8: 3
P6– The Gracious God was well-pleased with Jesus' willing sacrifice	Ephesians 5: 2
P7– The Righteous God was fully satisfied with the blood of Jesus	Hebrews 9:12-14, 23-28
P8– The Saving God makes believing sinners righteous in Christ	Romans 5: 1-11; 18,19
P9– The Almighty God raised Jesus from the dead	Romans 6: 1-6; 8:34
P9– God exalted Jesus and all will submit to Him	I Corinthians 15:24-28; Philippians 2:8-11

6 - Believing in this God of purpose and power

P1– Human need: Believe on Jesus; confess Jesus as Lord	Romans 10: 9,10; Galations 2:16

7 - Committing to this God of purpose and power

P1– God's ways are higher, yet we can trust Him and His word	Isaiah 55: 8-11
P1– Pouring out our heart to God; our expectations from Him	Psalm 62: 5-8
P1– Commitment to God's higher ways	Romans 11:33-36

Bg-1 Background - Overview of the development of the nation of Israel

Paragraph 1

P1– God chose the family of Jacob the seed of Abraham	Isaiah 41:8; Psalm 135:4
P1– God made a covenant with Abraham, Isaac and Jacob	Exodus 6:2-8
P1– Israel is God's special people	Deuteronomy 32:8,9
P1– Jacob's name changed to Israel	Genesis 32:28
P1– Israelites move from Canaan to Egypt	Genesis 46:1-3
P1– Israelites multiplied and became slaves	Exodus 1
P1– Israel cried to God for deliverance from slavery in Egypt	Exodus 2:23-25
P1– God heard Israel's cry	Exodus 3:7-10
P1– God plagued Egypt	Exodus 7 - 12
P1– Pharaoh sent Israel out of Egypt	Exodus 12:31-39
P1– Pharaoh pursued Israelites	Exodus 14:1-10
P1– Pharaoh's cavalry was destroyed	Exodus 14:27,28
P1– Israelites miraculously crossed the Red Sea	Exodus 14:11-31

Paragraph 2

P2– God redeemed and guided Israel	Exodus 15:12-19
P2– How God promised to bring Israel into Canaan	Exodus 23:27-31
P2– God's promise to bring Israel into Canaan	Exodus 3:14-17
P2– Israel arrived at Mt. Sinai	Exodus 19:1,2
P2– Israel left Mt. Sinai	Numbers 10:11,12
P2– God spoke to Israel from Mt. Sinai	Exodus 19
P2– God wrote His laws on stone tablets	Exodus 24:12; 31:18; 34:1
P2– It was a special honor for Israel to receive God and His laws	Deuteronomy 4:5-8

P2– Covenant relationship established with blood	Exodus 24:3-8
P2– Israel promised to obey God and be His people	Exodus 19:3-8
P2– Summary of God's covenant with Israel	Deuteronomy 29:12,13
P2– God gave Moses pattern for tabernacle	Exodus 25: 8,9
P2– Ttabernacle built as instructed	Exodus 39:32-43
P2– Priests ordained as instructed	Exodus 40:12-16
P2– God visibly present in cloud and fire	Exodus 40:36-38
P2– God personally led Israel in cloudy pillar	Numbers 9:15-23
P2– God led Israel through the wilderness	Deuteronomy 8:2-4
P2– God led Israel by the hand of Moses	Psalm 77:20
P2– Forty years wandering caused by Israel's rebellion	Numbers 14:32-35
P2– Moses commissioned Joshua	Deuteronomy 31:7-13
P2– Israel crosseed Jordan into Canaan	Joshua 3 & 4
P2– God commissions Joshua	Joshua 1:1-11
P2– Israel did not finish conquering Canaan	Judges 1:19-36; 2:1-23
Paragraph 3	
P3– Joshua led victories in Canaan	Joshua 12:1 (Chapters 6 - 12)
P3– Land distributed among twelve tribes	Joshua 14:1-3
P3– Israel possessed the land God promised them	Joshua 21:43-45
Paragraph 4	
P4– No national leader after Joshua	Judges 1:1
P4– Regional judges ruled in Israel	Judges 3 - 12
P4– Samuel's sons corrupt judges	I Samuel 8:1-3
P4– Israel demanded a king	I Samuel 8:4,5
P4– Samuel resisted people's request for a king	I Samuel 8:6,7
P4– God told Samuel to give them a king	I Samuel 8:8-10
P4– Samuel anointed Saul	I Samuel 9:26 - 10:1
P4– Saul called tribes together to fight	I Samuel 11:7
P4– Saul at war with Philistines	I Samuel 14:52
P4– Saul ruled from his home.	I Samuel 10:26; 11:4; 15:34; 23:19
Bg-2 Background - Contents of I Chronicles	
P1– I Chronicles' added details about the Ark of the Covenant move	I Chronicles 15, 16
P3– Nehemiah used book of the kings to confirm genealogies	I Chronicles 9: 1,22
P3– Chronicles and other records maintained to Nehemiah's day	Nehemiah 12:22, 23
P4– Chronicles of the kings of Persia	Esther 2:23; 6: 1: 10: 2
P3– David's worship instructions preserved for Nehemiah to use	Nehemiah 12:24, 45
P4– Books of prophets (examples)	II Chronicles 9:29; 20:34

P4– Prophets who recorded historical information on the life David	I Chronicles 29:29
P5– Chronicles of Israel and Judah (examples)	II Kings 14:15,18,28; II Chronicles 16:11; 20:34; 24:27; 32:32
P7– Books of prophets (further examples)	II Chronicles 16:11;:33:18; 32:32

Bg-3 Background - Brief chapter summaries of I Chronicles chapters 1 – 9

P4– Reuben's sexual misconduct	Genesis 35:22; 49: 3,4
P4– Father Israel gave Judah the authority to rule the nation	Genesis 49:8-10
P4– David and Jesus are descendants of Judah	Matthew 1
P4– Father Israel gave Joseph the blessing	Genesis 49:22-28
P4– Father Israel made each of Joseph's two sons a tribe in the nation	Genesis 48:5,6,22
P4– Two tribes for Joseph's family	Joshua 14: 4
P4– Levi inherited no territory in Canaan	Joshua 13:14,33
P4– Levite's special place of ministry	Numbers 4
P4– Aaron and his sons are the priests	Exodus 29: 9
P5– David appointed praise leaders after moving the Ark	I Chronicles 16:37-42
P5– David reappointed praise leaders for the new temple	I Chronicles 25
P8– Repopulating Jerusalem after Babylonian captivity	Nehemiah 11: 1,2
P8– Completion of the rebuilding of Jerusalem's wall	Nehemiah 6:15
P8– Completion of the rebuilding of the temple in Jerusalem	Ezra 6:15
P8– Israel's disgrace after returning to Jerusalem from Babylon	Nehemiah 1: 3
P9– Levites duties after Nehemiah reestablishes worship in Jerusalem	I Chronicles 9

Pronunciation Guide

Section paragraph location is given for names that do not appear in the Index.

Word	Accent Guide	Phonetic Guide
Aaron	er' ən	AIR-uhn
Abiathar	ə-bī' ə thär	uh-BI-uh-thahr
Abigail	ab'ə gāl I ab' i gāl	AB-uh-gayl I AB-ih-gayl
Abimelech (7-2:P9)	ə bim' ə lek	uh-BIM-uh-lek
Abinadab	ə bin' ə dab	uh-BIN-uh-dab
Abishai	ə bī'shī I ə bish' ī	uh-BI-shi / uh-BISH-i
Abner	ab' nər	AB-nuhr
Abram	ā' brəm	AY-bruhm
Abraham	ā' brə ham	AY-bruh-ham
Ab´salom	ab' sə ləm I ab' sə läm	AB-suh-luhm I AB-suh-lahm
Achish	ā' kish	AY-kish
Adam	ad' əm I a' dəm	AD-uhm I A-duhm
Adino (3-2:P1)	ə dī' nō	uh-DI-noh
Adonijah	ad' ə nī' jə I ad ō nī' jə	AD-uh-NI-juh I ad-oh-NI-juh
Adoniram (7-2:P17)	ad' ə nī' rəm I ad ō nī' ram	AD-uh-NI-ruhm I ad-oh-NI-ram
Adoram (7-2:P17)	ə dō' rəm I a dō' ram	uh-DOH-ruhm I a-DOH-ram
Adriel	ā' drē əl	AY-dree-uhl
Adullam	ə dəl' əm	uh-DUHL-uhm
Ahimelech	ə him' ə lek	uh-HIM-uh-lek
Ahio	ə hī' ō	uh-HI-oh
Ahithophel	ə hith' ə fel I ä hith' ə fel	uh-HITH-uh-fel I ah-HITH-uh-fel
Amalek	am' ə lek	AM-uh-lek
Amalekite	ə mal' ə kīt	uh-MAL-uh-kīt
Ammon	am' ən	AM-uhn (not AY-muhn)
Amnon	am' non I am' nən	AM-non I AM-nuhn
Araunah (8-5:P4)	ə rô' nə	uh-RAW-nuh
Asahel	as' ə hel	AS-uh-hel
Asaph	ā' saf	AY-saf
Athaliah (11-2:P3)	ath ə lī' ə	ath-uh-LI –uh
atonement	ə tōn' mənt	uh-TOHN-muhnt
Babylonian	bab i lō' nē ən	bab-ih-LOH-nee-uhn
	bab ə lō nē ən	bab-uh-LOH-nee-uhn
Bathsheba	bath shē' bə	bath-SHEE-buh
Benaiah	bi, bə nī' ə I bə nā' yə	bih-, buh-NI-uh / bih-NAY-yuh
Benjamin	ben' jə mən	BEN-juh-muhn
Bethlehem	beth' li hem I beth' lə hem	BETH-lih-hem I BETH-luh-hem

Word	Accent Guide	Phonetic Guide
Canaan	kā' nən	KAY-nuhn
Canaanites	kā' nə nīts	KAY-nuh-nīts
cherubim	châr' ə bim	CHAYR-uh-bim
circumcision	sur kum sizh' ən	sir-cuhm-SIZH-uhn
covenant	kuv' ə nənt	KUHV-uh-nuhnt
Dagon	dā' gon	DAY-gon
Damascus	də mas' kəs	duh-MAS-kuhs
Edom	ē' dum	EE-duhm
Eleazar	el ē ā' zär	el-ee-AY-zahr (not ee'lee-)
Eli	ē' lī	EE-l*i*
Eliab	i lī' əb l ē lī' ab	ih-L*I*-uhb l ee-L*I*-ab
Eliam	i lī' əm l ē lī' am	ih-L*I*-uhm l ee-L*I*-am
Elihu	i lī' hyū	ih-L*I*-hyoo
Elijah	i lī' jə	ih-L*I*-juh
Elisha	i lī' shə	ih-L*I*-shuh
Engedi	en ged' ē l en ged' ī	en-GED-ee l en-GED-*i*
Ephraim	ē' frē əm l ē' frā im	EE-free-uhm l EE-fray-im
Esau	ē' sô	EE-saw
Eshbaal (2-4:P2)	esh' bā əl l esh bā' əl	ESH-bay-uhl l esh-BAY-uhl
Ethan	ē' thən	EE-thuhn
Ezekiel	i zē' kē əl	ih-ZEE-kee-uhl
Gershom	gur' shəm	GUHR-shuhm
Gibeah	gib' ē ə	GIB-ee-uh
Gibeon	gib' ē ən	GIB-ee-uhn
Gibeonites	gib' ē ən īts l gib' ē ə nīts	GIB-ee-uhn-*i*ts l GIB-ee-uh-nīts
Goliath	gə lī' əth l gō lī' əth	guh-L*I*-uhth l goh-L*I*-uhth
Gomorrah	gə mōr' ə	guh-MOR-uh
Hadarezer	had är ē' zər l hā' dər ē' zər	had-ahr-EE-zuhr l HAY-duhr-EE-zuhr
Hanun	hā' nən	HAY-nuhn
Hebron	hē' brən l he' brän	HEE-bruhn l HE-brahn
Heman	hē' mən	HEE-muhn
Hezekiah (11-2:P4)	hez'- ə -kī' ə	HEZ-uh-K*I*-uh
Hiram	hī' rəm	H*I*-ruhm
Hushai	hū' shī l hūsh' ī	HOO-sh*i* l HOOSH-*i*
Isaac	ī' zik l ī' zək	*I*-zik l *I*-zuhk
Ishbosheth	ish bō' sheth l ish-bō' shith	ish-BOH-sheth l ish-BOH-shith
Ishmael (Bg-3:P2)	ish' mā-el	ISH-may-el
Issacar (2-6:P2)	is' ə kär	IS-uh-kahr
Jaasiel (7-2:P13)	jə ā' sē əl	juh-AY-see-uhl
Jashobeam	jə shō' bē əm	juh-SHOH-bee-uhm
Jebus	jē' bus	JEE-buhs
Jebusites	jeb' yū zīts, sīts	JEB-yoo-z*i*ts, s*i*ts
Jeduthun	ji dyū' thən	jih-DYOO-thuhn
Jehiel (7-2:P5)	jē hī' əl	jee-H*I*-uhl

Word	Accent Guide	Phonetic Guide
Jehoiada (7-2:P15) and (11-2:P3)	ji hoi' ə də	jih-HOI-uh-duh
Jehoshaphat (7-2:P11)	jə hosh' ə fat / ji hosh' ə fat	juh-HOSH-uh-fat / jih-HOSH-uh-fat
Jeremiah	jer ə mī' ə	jair-uh-MI-uh
Joab	jō' ab	JOH-ab
Job	jōb	JOHB (not JAHB)
Jonathan	jon' ə thən I jo' nə thən	JAHN-uh-thuhn I JAH-nuh-thuhn
Jordan	jōr' dən	JOR-duhn
Joshua	josh' yū ə	JOSH-yoo-uh
Judah	jū' də	JOO-duh
Kirjathjearim	kîr' ē ath jē' ə rim	KIHR-ee-ath-JEE-uh-rim
Kohath	kō' hath	KOH-hath
Levi	lē' vī	LEE-vi
Levites	lē' vīts	LEE-vits
Mahanaim	mā hə nā' im	may-huh-NAY-ihm
Manasseh	mə nas' ə I mə na' sə	muh-NAS-uh I muh-NA-suh
Merab	mē'rab	MEE-rab
Merari	mi rär' ī	mih-RAHR-i
Michal	mī' kəl	MI-kuhl
Moab	mō' ab	MOH-ab
Mt. Moriah	mə rī' ə	muh-RI-uh
Nabal	nā' bəl	NAY-buhl
Nahash	nā' hash	NAY-hash
Naphtali (2-6:P2)	naf' tə lī	NAF-tuh-li
Nathan	nā' thən	NAY-thuhn
Nehemiah	nē' he mī' ə I ne hem ī' ə	NEE-he-MI-uh I neh-hehm-I-uh
Nineveh	nin' ə və	NIN-uh-vuh
Noah	nō' ə	NOH-uh
Obededom	ō' bid ē' dəm lō' bed ē' dəm	OH-bid-EE-duhm I OH-bed-EE-duhm
Ornan	ôr' nan I ôr' nən	OR-nan I OR-nuhn
Philistines	fi lis' tēnz I fil' i stēnz	fih-LIS-teenz I FIL-ih-steenz
Rehoboam (7-2:P17)	rē' hə bō' əm	REE-huh-BOH-uhm
Reuben	rū' bən	ROO-buhn
Rizpah	riz' pə	RIZ-puh
Samuel	sam' yū əl I sam' yəl	SAM-yoo-uhl I SAM-yuhl
Shammah (3-2:P1)	sham' ə	SHAM-uh
Shavsha (7-2:P10)	shav' shə	SHAV-shuh
Shem	shem	SHEM
Shiloh	shī' lō	SHI-loh
Shobi	shō' bī	SHOH-bi
Simeon	sim' ē ən	SIM-ee-uhn
Sinai	sī' nī	SI-ni
Sodom	sod' əm	SOD-uhm

Word	Accent Guide	Phonetic Guide
Solomon	sol' ə mən I so' lə mən	SAHL-uh-muhn I SAH-luh-muhn
Syria	sîr' ē ə	SIHR-ee-uh
tabernacle	tab' ər nak əl	TAB-uhr-nak-uhl
Tamar	tā' mär	TAY-mahr
Tyre	tīr	T*I*R (rhymes with "fire")
Uriah	yū rī' ə	yoo-R*I*-uh
Uzza	uz' ə	UHZ-uh (not YOO-zuh)
Zadok	zā' dok	ZAY-dahk
Zebulun (2-6:P2)	zeb' yū lən I zeb' yə lən	ZEB-yoo-luhn I ZEB-yuh-luhn
Zeruiah	zə rū' yə	zuh-ROO-yuh
Ziklag	zik' lag	ZIK-lag
Ziphites	zif' īts	ZIF-*i*ts
Zobah	zō' bə	ZOH-buh

a	at, cat, mat, snap
ah	father, bother
ahr	lard, yard
ai	air, care, fair, prayer, there
aw	jaw, saw, all, caught
ay	[long "a"] day, obey, weigh
e, eh	bed, pet, peck
ee	[long "e"] beat, easy, seem
er	error
i (italicized)	[long "i"] tie, sky, buy, eye
i, ih	it, tip, active
ihr	ear, fear
o	cot, hot, not
oh	[long "o"] bone, know, toe
oi	boy, destroy
oo	boot, rule, youth
oor	poor
or	for, glory
ou	how, loud, now, out
u	book, foot, put, pull, wood
uh	ago, alone, banana, linen
uhr	bird, further, her
ə	item, edible (shwa)

Pronunciation Guide Sources

http://www.betterdaysarecoming.com/bible/pronunciation.html
Accent Guide:
    e-Sword – ISBE (International Standard Bible Encyclopedia)
Phonetic Guide:
    Harper's Bible Name Pronunciation Guide

Index

The location of indexed items are identified by chapter - section and paragraph numbers. Bolded words in the short descriptions of the indexed terms also have a listing in the index.

Appendix abbreviations in the Index listing:

Bg refers to the Background

Epi refers to the Epilogue

Ref refers to indexed items found in the Bible Reference table which are not found in the text of the book.

Four examples:

The third listing for Aaron is **9-3**:P12

    It refers to Chapter **9** Section **3** Paragraph 12.

The last listing for Aaron is **Bg-3**:P4,5.

    It refers to Section **3** Paragraphs 4 and 5 of the **Background** Information at the back of the book.

The first listing for Abigail is **1-7**:P9-13.

    It refers to Chapter **1** Section **7** Paragraphs 9, 10, 11, 12, and 13.

The third listing for Abner is **2-4:P***.

    The P* means that Abner is involved in most of section **2-4**.

circumcision (sign of **Abrahamic covenant**)
1-2:P7,9,10,12

City of David (fortress of **Jerusalem**)
3-1:P5; 3-3:P2,3; 4-4:P1,8; 4-5:P1,3; 4-6:P2,6; 5-1:P3,5; 5-2:P1,6; 10-2:P2

commander / captain (in the military: **Abner, Benaiah, Joab,** etc.)
1-1:P20; 1-2:P1; 1-3:P1; 1-4:P9; 1-5:P4; 1-6:P5,10; 2-2:P8; 2-4:P1,5,6,8,10,11;
2-5:P1-3; 2-6:P2,3; 3-1:P4; 3-2:P*; 5-2:P1; 7-1:P5; 7-2:P7,8,12,13; 7-3:P3-5,7,8;
8-2:P1,3,11; 8-3:P1,3; 10-3:P5; 11-6:P7; 12-1:P1; 12-7:P6; Bg-2:P13

covenant (bond / contract uniting two parties)
1-2:P10; 1-5:P10; 2-6:P4; 4-3:P1,15; 4-5:P2; 5-2:P8; 5-3:P9; 5-4:P1; 6-5:P15,17;
6-6:P7; 6-7:P9; 9-1:P1; 9-3:P6-10; 11-2:P8; 11-3:P3; 12-8:P4,8,10; Bg-1:P2

Dagon (name of **Philistine** god)
4-3:P8

Damascus (capitol of **Syria**)
7-1:P7; 7-2:P8

David's heart
1-1:P8,9; 1-2:P8,13; 1-4:P8; 1-5:P8; 1-6:P8-11,15,16; 1-7:P2,5,10,11; 2-3:P3;
2-5:P9; 4-1:P3; 4-4:P9; 4-6:P3; 5-1:P4,5; 5-2:P4,5; 6-1:P2,5; 6-2:P5; 6-3:P4;
6-5:P2; 6-6:P2,5,8; 6-7:P1,2,12; 6-8:P*; 7-1:P2,15; 7-2:P2; 8-1:P7,10;
8-2:P7,8; 8-4:P2; 8-5:P8; 9-1:P6; 9-2:p1,2; 9-4:P1,11; 12-2:P5-7; 12-3:P1;
12-5:P3; 12-6:P5; Epi-2; Epi-3; Epi-4

Dead Sea
1-7:P1; 7-1:P6

Edom (nation SE of Israel)
1-1:P20; 1-6:P3 (Edomite); 7-1:P9; 7-2:P8; 7-4:P1

Egypt (nation: SE shore of **Mediterranean Sea**)
1-1:P3,11; 1-2:P10; 1-3:P3; 4-3:P1,2,5; Ref 4-3:P3,6; 4-5:P3; 5-3:P5,8; 6-2:P2;
6-6:P7; 7-1:P12; 7-4:P1; 8-1:P6; 9-1:P1; 9-3:P10,12; 11-4:P1; Bg-1:P1

Eleazar (one of David's mighty men)
3-2:P1,2

Eleazar (son of **Abinadab**, cared for **Ark of the Covenant** 20 years)
4-3:P10

Eleazar (son of **Aaron**, a **priest**)
11-6:P5

Eli (priest & judge in Israel before **Samuel**)
4-2:P1; 4-3:P7,11; 7-4:P3,4; 11-4:P8,9

Eliab or Elihu (David's eldest brother)
1-2:P8; 1-4:P2; 7-2:P13;

Elijah (prophet in Israel)
9-1:P3; 9-3:P4

Elisha (prophet in Israel)
Ref 1-5:P3

harvests (protecting Israelite farms from **Philistine** raiders)
  1-6:P11; **2-5**:P7; **3-2**:P1-4; **3-4**:P1,3; **7-2**:P3

Hebron (city in **tribe** of **Judah**)
  2-3:P3,4; **2-4**:P4,7,8; **2-5**:P4; **2-6**:P2,3; **3-1**:P4,5; **3-2**:P3; **3-3**:P3; **Ref 7-4**:P3;
  12-8:P1

Heman (a **Levite music** leader)
  (see under **Levi**)

Hiram (King of **Tyre**)
  (see **Tyre**)

holiest place (of God's presence)
  4-3:P1-5,8-10,13-15; **4-4**:P1-3,7,10; **4-5**:P2,5; **4-6**:P4,5; **5-1**:P1,3,12,13;
  5-2:P4-8; **5-3**:P1,2,4,5,7; **6-2**:P3; **6-3**:P2; **6-5**:P9,13-16; **6-6**:P2; **6-8**:P2;
  7-1:P1,13; **8-1**:P2; **8-2**:P7; **9-1**:P1,3; **9-3**:P3,12,14,16; **9-4**:P2,4,5,11; **9-5**:P1;
  10-1:P8; **10-2**:P7; **11-1**:P1; **11-3**:P3,4; **11-4**:P1,5; **11-5**:P2,3; **12-2**:P3,5; **12-4**:P4;
  12-6:P7; **12-8**:P7-11; **Epi-3,5**; **Bg-1**:P3

holiest place (of Israel's **tabernacle**)
  4-3:P2,3,11,13,14; **4-4**:P1; **5-1**:P12,13; **9-4**:P2,4-6; **11-5**:P3

holy place (of Israel's **tabernacle**)
  4-3:P2,3; **6-2**:P3; **9-4**:P2-4,9; **11-2**:P6; **11-5**:P2,3

Hushai (David's friend and counselor)
  7-2:P16

Isaac (son of **Abraham,** father of Jacob / Israel)
  Ref 1-1:P3; **5-4**:P1; **8-5**:P6; **9-3**:P8,9; **Ref 11-4**:P3; **12-6**:P6; **Bg-1**:P1

Ishbosheth (son of **Saul,** king of northern Israel, also called Eshbaal)
  2-4:P1-3,6,11; **2-5**:P4; **7-4**:P3

Israel (Jacob's new name, or the nation of his descendants, or the land of the Israelites)

Ithamar (son of **Aaron** and priest)
  11-6:P5

Jabesh (Israelite city east of **Jordan River**)
  1-1:P6; **2-2**:P6; **7-2**:P2

Jacob (son of **Isaac** – name changed to Israel)

Jashobeam (David's foremost **captain**)
  3-1:P1; **7-2**:P12

Jebusites (the **Canaanite** clan which inhabited **Jerusalem**)
  3-1:P4,5; **3-4**:P2; **7-2**:P7; **8-4**:P8; **8-5**:P3

Jeduthun (a **Levite music** leader also called **Ethan**)(see under **Levi**)

Jericho (**Canaanite** city near **Jordan River**)
  4-3:P5; **5-3**:P5;

Jeremiah (prophet of God)
  4-3:P12; **6-5**:P17; **8-1**:P15; **11-2**:P8

Jerusalem
  1-1:P5; **3-1**:P4,5; **3-2**:P3; **3-3**:P1-3; **3-4**:P2,4; **4-1**:P1,3; **4-2**:P*; **4-3**:P6,10,11;
  4-4:P1,2,5,6,8; **4-5**:P1,4; **4-6**:P1,4,6; **5-1**:P8,12,13; **5-2**:P1,5; **6-1**:P1; **6-2**:P3;

law (established / given by God)
  4-3:P1,2,14,15; **4-4**:P10; **5-1**:P7,9,10; **5-2**:P8; **5-3**:P3,5,7; **5-4**:P1; **6-5**:P9,12;
  7-2:P10; **8-1**:P12; **8-2**:P6; **9-3**:P2-4,10,12; **9-4**:P9,10; **10-1**:P12; **11-1**:P5;
  11-2:P4,7; **11-3:P1**; **11-4**:P7,8; **11-5**:P2; **12-7**:P4; **Epi-5**; **Bg-1**:P2

leaders (Israel's official leadership)
  (see princes / leaders)

Levi (son of Israel and a **tribe** with 48 cities spread throughout Israel)
  2-6:P2; **8-3**:P2; **11-3**:P2; **11-4**:P1; **11-6**:P4,8,9; **Bg-3**:P4,5

— **Gershom** (son of **Levi**)
  11-3:P2; **11-6**:P4,8-11; **Bg-3**:P5

— **Kohath** (son of **Levi**)
  11-3:P2; **11-6**:P4,8,9,11; **Bg-3**:P5

— **Merari** (son of **Levi**)
  11-3:P2; **11-6**:P4,8-10; **Bg-3**:P5

Levites (those in **Levi**'s **tribe**: **priests** & ministers)
  4-3:P4,9,11; **4-4**:P6,10; **4-5**:P3,4; **5-1**:P6-11; **5-2**:P1-3,8; **5-3**:P1-5,7; **6-1**:P1;
  8-1:P7; **8-3**:P2; **9-2**:P6; **9-4**:P1,10; chapter **11**; **12-1**:P1; **12-2**:P4,12; **12-4**:P13;
  Epi-3; **Bg-2**:P2,3,12; **Bg-3**:P4,5,9

— **Asaph** (**music** leader from the family of **Gershom**)
  5-1:P11; **5-3**:P1; **5-4**:P1; **6-1**:P3; **11-2**:P6,7; **11-6**:P7-9; **Bg-3**:P5

— **Heman** (**music** leader from the family of **Kohath**)
  5-1:P11; **5-3**:P3; **11-2**:P6; **11-6**:P7-9; **Bg-3**:P5

— **Jeduthun** (**music** leader from the family of **Merari** also called **Ethan**)
  5-1:P11; **5-3**:P3; **11-2**:P6; **11-6**:P7-9; **Bg-3**:P5

Mahanaim (city east of the **Jordan River**)
  2-4:P3

Manasseh (son of **Joseph** and a **tribe** in Israel)
  2-2:P8; **2-6**:P2; **Bg-3**:P4,6

Manasseh (corrupt king of **Judah**)
  11-2:P6

Mary (mother of **Jesus**)
  6-5:P6,7

Mediterranean Sea
  1-1:P13; **4-3**:P3

Merab (older daughter of **Saul**)
  1-5:P5; **7-5**:P9

mercy seat (cover for the **Ark of the Covenant**)
  4-3:P1,14; **5-1**:P12; **9-4**:P5

Michal (young daughter of **Saul**, wife of David)
  1-5:P5,7; **1-7**:P12; **2-4**:P7; **5-2**:P5; **7-5**:P9

Moab (country east of the **Dead Sea**)
  1-1:P20; **1-6**:P5; **7-1**:P6

4-5:P4; 4-6:P6; 5-1:P2,13; 5-2:P1; 6-3:P2; 6-8:P1; 7-1:P3-5,12; 7-3:P1; 7-4:P2,6; Ref 7-4:P3; 10-1:P3; Bg-1:P4

plague / pestilence
4-2:P1; 4-3:P8,9; 5-3:P5; 8-1:P12,15; 8-2:P6; 8-4:P4; 8-5:P1,2,4,8; 9-1:P1,5; 9-2:P2,4; 9-4:P11; 11-4:P1; 11-6:P2; 12-2:P10; Epi-3; Bg-1:P1

porter (Levite ministry)
5-1:P11; 5-3:P2,3; 11-2:P3,4,6,7; 11-5:P1; 11-6:P3,10; Bg-3:P9

princes / leaders (administrative leadership – not king, **priest,** or **Levite**)
1-1:P3; 2-2:P3; 2-3:P4,5,9; 2-5:P1-3,5; 2-6:P2,5; 3-4:P5; 4-3:P5,7,11; 4-4:P4-6,8,10; 4-5:P3; 5-1:P4; 5-2:P1; 6-2:P4; 6-5:P10,11; 7-2:P*; 7-4:P3; 7-5:P3; 8-1:P16; 8-5:P1; 10-1:P5,12; 10-2:P*; 10-3:P2; 11-1:P1; 11-4:P3,4,9; 11-6:P2-4; 12-1:P*; 12-2:P5,6; 12-3:P*; 12-4:P1,3,7,9,13; 12-5:P1,5-8; 12-6:P1,4,7; 12-7:P3; Bg-1:P3,4; Bg-3:P8

priest (sons of **Aaron**)
1-1:P3; 1-6:P3,7,8,12; 2-2:P2; 4-2:P1; 4-3:P2,4,5,7,13; 4-4:P2,6,10; 4-5:P3; 4-6:P6; 5-1:P7,9-11; 5-2:P5; 5-3:P1,3,5; 6-2:P3; 6-5:P9; 7-2:P9; 7-4:P3; 8-2:P7; 8-3:P2; 9-3:P16; 9-4:P1-3,6,8-10; 10-3:P5,8,9; 11-1:P3-6; 11-2:P*; 11-3:P2,4; 11-4:P1,2,7,8; 11-5:P2-4; 11-6:P2-6; 12-4:P13; 12-7:P3; 12-8:P9,11; Bg-1:P2; Bg-3:P4,5,9

— **high priest**
4-3:P2,14,15; 4-6:P5; 5-1:P12; 5-2:P4; 11-5:P3; Bg-3:P5

Red Sea (narrow inlet between Arabia & Africa)
4-3:P1,5; 5-3:P8; 7-1:P10; Bg-1:P1

Reuben (son of Israel and a **tribe** located east of the Jordan River)
2-6:P2; Bg-3:P4

Rizpah (**Saul**'s concubine)
1-1:P5; 7-5:P9,11

sacrifices / offerings (of Israel)
1-1:P16; 1-3:P2,8-10; 1-4:P2; 4-3:P2,10,13-15; 5-1:P10; 5-2:P2,7,8; 5-3:P3; 5-4:P1; 6-2:P3; 6-5:P9,11-16; 7-2:P9; 8-5:P7; 9-1:P5,6; 9-2:P6; 9-3:P1,14-16; 9-4:P6,9; 11-2:P3-5,7; 11-4:P1,2,6; 11-5:P2-4; 12-2:P10; 12-6:P8,9; 12-7:P1; Epi-5; Bg-3:P9

— **blood of the sacrifice**
4-3:P2,14,15; 5-1:P12; 6-5:P9,13,14; 9-4:P9; 11-5:P3; Epi-5; Bg-1:P2

— **feast** (regular ceremonies special to Israel)
1-2:P5; 1-5:P9; 4-3:P13,14; 5-1:P10; 5-3:P3; 7-2:P9; 11-2:P3,6; 11-4:P1,2; 11-5:P2

— (See also **atonement - Day of Atonement**)

Samuel (prophet in Israel)
1-1:P1-4,10-17; 1-3:P*; 1-4:P1-3,5,9; 1-5:P1,7; 1-6:P5; 1-7:P5,6; 2-1:P5,6; 2-3:P1,8; 3-1:P1,3; 4-3:P7,12; 6-1:P5; 6-3:P3; 6-7:P12; 7-4:P3,4; 9-3:P17; 11-4:P6,9; 12-8:P6; Epi-2; Bg-1:P3,4

threshing floor (for processing harvested grain)
 4-6:P1,2; 8-4:P8; 8-5:P3-7; 9-1:P6; 9-2:P5; 9-3:P16,17; 9-4:P11; 9-5:P4,6

tribe (family divisions of the nation of Israel)
 1-1:P3,5,7; 1-6:P5,9; 2-1:P1,7; Ref_2-1:P3; 2-2:P3,8; 2-3:P3-6; 2-4:P1,4,7,11;
 2-5:P1-4,6; 2-6:P1,2,5; 3-1:P3,4; 4-3:P4,6,11; 5-1:P11; 5-2:P4; 7-2:P5,12,13;
 7-5:P4; 8-2:P3; 8-3:P2; 9-2:P6; 11-4:P1,3,4,6; 11-6:P4,6,11; 12-1:P1,4;
 Bg-1:P3,4; Bg-2:P10; Bg-3:P3-6

Tyre (nation NW of Israel ruled by King Hiram)
 3-3:P2,3; 3-4:P3; 7-1:P11,12; 7-3:P1; 9-5:P5

Uriah (a Hittite, **Bathsheba**'s husband, and a valiant, faithful **soldier**.)
 3-2:P7, 6-1:P4; 6-6:P3; 7-2:P6; 7-3:P7; 7-4:P3; 8-1:P7; 8-2:P5,17; 12-2:P1;
 Epi-3; Bg-2:P11,13

Uzza (son of **Abinidab**, drove cart carrying **Ark**)
 4-5:P4; 4-6:P*; 5-1:P2,5,6,9,13; 5-3:P4,5,7; 8-4:P8

wilderness
 1-6:P13; 2-1:P3,7; 4-2:P1; 4-3:P3,4; 5-1:P6; 8-1:P6,11; 9-1:P1; 9-4:P2; 10-1:P12;
 10-2:P7; 11-3:P2,4; 11-4:P2,4; 12-2:P5; 12-4:P9; Bg-1:P2

Zadok (**priest** during reigns David & **Solomon**)
 5-1:P9; 5-3:P3; 7-2:P9; 8-2:P7; 10-3:P5,8,9; 11-6:P5,6; 12-7:P3

Zeruiah (mother of **Joab**, **Abishai**, and **Asahel**)
 2-4:P9

Ziklag (city in southern Israel where David lived during his asylum)
 2-1:P3,7,12; 2-2:P1,4,8; 2-3:P3; 7-2:P3; 7-4:P3,4; Bg-3:P3

Ziph / Ziphites (a clan in the **tribe** of **Judah**; they helped **Saul** find David)
 1-6:P13,14; 1-7:P13; 2-1:P1

Zobah (powerful nation north of Israel.)
 1-1:P20; 7-1:P7; 7-3:P3 (see also **Hadarezer**)

CPSIA information can be obtained at www.ICGtesting.com
Printed in the USA
LVOW122218040412

276232LV00001B/8/P